IDENTITIES IN TRANSITION

IDENTITIES IN TRANSITION
The Growth and Development
of a Multicultural Therapist

Edited by
Monisha Nayar-Akhtar

KARNAC

First published in 2015 by
Karnac Books Ltd
118 Finchley Road
London NW3 5HT

British Library Cataloguing in Publication Data

A C.I.P. for this book is available from the British Library

ISBN-13: 978-1-78220-109-0

Typeset by V Publishing Solutions Pvt Ltd., Chennai, India

www.karnacbooks.com

This book is dedicated to my daughters
Yamini and Kavita
whose journey in self-discovery continues to inspire me

CONTENTS

ACKNOWLEDGEMENTS   ix

ABOUT THE EDITOR AND CONTRIBUTORS   xiii

FOREWORD   xix
by Stuart W. Twemlow

PREFACE   xxv

CHAPTER ONE
The confluence of cultures: an Iranian–American story   1
Kamelia Alavi

CHAPTER TWO
Lost luggage: analytic training as search for
    objects lost in migration   17
Salomon Bankier

CHAPTER THREE
A tale of two cities   29
Amar Ghorpade

CHAPTER FOUR
Navigating our cultural identifications: individual,
    social, and political struggle in the therapy room   45
Fatima El-Jamil

CHAPTER FIVE
De dónde eres? Finding a "from" in psychoanalysis   59
Norka T. Malberg

CHAPTER SIX
A wound of no return: in search of self, loss, and transformation   79
Monisha Nayar-Akhtar

CHAPTER SEVEN
A demand for training   97
Marco Posadas

CHAPTER EIGHT
Stolen freedom   111
Deborah A. Reeves

CHAPTER NINE
Crossing the border within: migration, transience,
    and analytic identity   125
Gabriel Ruiz

CHAPTER TEN
The unmatched twin: enactments of otherness and
    the autobiography of an immigrant clinician   137
Lara Sheehi

CHAPTER ELEVEN
Conclusion: change is us   155
M. Hossein Etezady

INDEX   177

ACKNOWLEDGEMENTS

According to Wilfred Bion, a prominent British psychoanalyst, ideas and thoughts are not the propriety of the thinker. They exist, so to speak, in space and wait (albeit in quiet motion) to find a suitable container or receptacle in which they can germinate and find expression. This can be said of this edited book, which has many origins, conscious and unconscious. A product of co-created inspirations and dialogues, my conscious thought for this book, appeared during the 2013 January meetings of the American Psychoanalytic Association, when I had the pleasure of having breakfast with a fellow analyst and colleague, Barbara Killian. Barbara and I had graduated from the same training program, the Michigan Psychoanalytic Institute and shared much in common, from our immigration roots, to histories of raising our children in a "foreign culture," to acculturating to a new culture, to assimilating values, social norms, and mores quite different from those we were familiar with. We spent much of that Friday comparing notes, laughing at our challenges and discussing the trials and tribulations of working with training analysts who did not share our cultural history. In the end, we concluded that as immigrant analysts we probably worked and conceptualized our analytic identity differently from our non-immigrant colleagues. Having been informed by a wide range of social, political, and cultural narratives, our analytic identities could be viewed as being a work in progress—in transition, so-to-speak. We noted that despite a growing awareness of cultural dimension in the psychoanalytic discourse there was no reference point to understand how our immigrant identities evolved and how therapists with widely varying cultural backgrounds came to understand their clinical practice.

This meeting was perhaps the first conscious impetus to this book though one might say its origins began many years ago, in a complex biographical and ancestral history of strife and struggle. I explore this history in my paper. Suffice to say, that this initial conversion sparked my interest, peaked my curiosity, and in the end was compelling enough for me to embark on a journey of editing a book that would draw upon the personal narratives of fellow immigrants who had obtained psychoanalytically oriented training in the United States and practiced as analysts or analytically oriented therapists. To my friend, Barbara, who served as the initial catalyst, I owe a deep gratitude. To my contributors who stuck with me through the end, my deepest thanks. Without them this book would not have been possible.

I have been very fortunate to have trained in Michigan where I benefited and continue to benefit from the wisdom, knowledge, and creativity of many of its members. I am deeply grateful to my analyst whose gentle humor, wisdom, and insight shaped much of my initial years of practice, to my supervisors who broadened my thinking and provided the essential components for my analytic identity to emerge, and finally to my cadre of friends and colleagues who over the years have shared personal clinical insights and experiences related to working with patients from different cultural backgrounds. Their professional growth and our ongoing personal affiliations provided me with essential sustenance and nurturance to embark on many a journey. I am fortunate to have ongoing relationships with Carol Levin, Marcy Broder, Sue Orbach, Diana Constance and Paula Kliger. Their faith and belief in what I do has provided the emotional scaffolding for many transitions in my life. I am very grateful for their ongoing love and support.

After practicing in Michigan for many years, I moved to Philadelphia and affiliated with the Psychoanalytic Center of Philadelphia. Since my move, I have found kindred souls in training and thinking. Philadelphia has a rich psychoanalytic heritage and I have benefited from understanding how this Center evolved over the course of many decades. Their organizational trajectory informed me in various ways and strengthened my ongoing practice as a middle career analyst. Philadelphia has among its many creative thinkers, Salman Akhtar whose seminal contribution on the topic of immigration and identity fuelled my initial interest in 1996, shaped my thinking, and in the end propelled me to go beyond. I am also grateful to Henri Parens for his gift of friendship and for the warmth he has shown towards me in my personal and professional endeavours. My move to Philadelphia stirred profound feelings of loss for my training institute, but it also opened the door to new beginnings and friendships. During the course of the last several years, I have benefited from the wisdom of my Philadelphia colleagues. Many have gone on to become good friends. I am very grateful for the laughter that I have shared with Susan Levine, Dick Cornfield, Mike Kowitt, June Greenspan Margolis, Diana Rosenstein, and Jed Yalof. I have been fortunate to also been embraced by several study groups that now provide me with the professional anchoring necessary for the development of my ongoing 'analytic identity.' I am very grateful to Harold Kolansky, Naomi Rosenberg and Dewitt Montgomery and Gerry Margolis for their encouragement of my professional growth and their willingness to embrace me as a colleague.

My professional trajectory has taken me beyond the boundaries of my training institute and adopted land. In 2011 I affiliated with an orphanage in New Delhi and initiated a professional goal of exporting psychoanalytic ideas to the mental health practitioners associated with this institution and beyond. I am deeply indebted to Dr. Kiran Modi, the managing trustee of the orphanage who believed in me and gave me an opportunity to develop ongoing training workshops for her staff. Later, in 2012, I established the Indian Institute of Psychotherapy Training in New Delhi, India with the help of a local child psychiatrist, Dr. Deepak Gupta, whose support for my clinical knowledge, interest and enthusiasm in psychoanalytic ideas and a willingness to grow as a clinician, sustains me in my bi-yearly journey to India. I am very grateful to him and Dr. Modi for giving me an opportunity to reconnect with my country of origin, and helping me to further incorporate cultural nuances and variations into my theory and practice.

No book can be completed without the assistance of someone who gives countless hours perusing and editing papers, and reminding me of a concrete deadline with which I needed to work. I am very grateful to Ksera Dyette, my assistant who formatted and edited the book, provided critical input and advised me on the selection of epigraphs that were poignant and right on the mark. Were it not for her, this book would have been further delayed. Her diligence and keen eye for detail and superb editing skills served to strengthen the papers and added clarity and precision to many of the papers. Her sense of commitment to this project was also informed by her own personal history of migration (having immigrated to this country from Trinidad). Ksera is a fourth year graduate student at Widener University, in Chester, Pennsylvania and is pursuing a PsyD degree in clinical psychology, and is partial to psychodynamic thinking and technique. Like me, Ksera's personal and professional identity has been informed by a rich array of life experiences. Participating in pulling this book together has, as she puts it, inspired her further to actively pursue analytic training in the future. In perusing the different papers, she has found kindred souls and identified with how immigrants differ from each other and their struggle in attempting to synthesize and integrate various aspects of their multifaceted configured and diverse identities. It has given her hope and a belief that she can be understood and can find within the field likeminded souls who will enhance her personal and professional life. She has been and continues to be a valuable resource and I look forward to one day welcoming her to the psychoanalytic community!

I would also like to thank my daughters Yamini and Kavita Nayar who have in their own way, given powerful expression to their voices in their chosen field of study. Their individual journeys to live their diversified, culturally determined and subtly nuanced identities, with freedom and clarity, has been filled with transitions of their own. Their ongoing faith and belief in me provides me with the essential ingredients for emotional nurturance and sustains me in many of my personal and professional endeavors. Raising them has been the most satisfying part of my identity and I cherish the moments when we share and come together in matters of the heart and the mind.

Finally, I am deeply indebted to my constant four-legged companion, Majnun whose devotion to me is unquestionable. Sustaining me through my journey in life, his needs and pleas for engagement provide me with much needed (though not always timely) breaks and distractions. While I am sure that without him I would have finished the book much sooner, his absence would have also left me wanting in many ways.

Kamelia Alavi, PhD, MFT, obtained her master's in economics at Tufts University followed by a PhD in managerial economics at Rensselaer Polytechnic Institute in Troy, New York. Later in her career, Dr. Alavi obtained her MFT at the Family Institute of Philadelphia. Over the past fifteen years, Dr. Alavi has applied her expertise as a mental health specialist both in the academic and business sectors. She has utilized her knowledge not only to better understand her students and employees, but to enrich students' coursework with discussions of relationships, self-improvement, cultural competency, ethics, boundary issues, group dynamics, personal emotions and experiences, and how they affect the productivity of the work environment. Dr. Alavi also provides business consultation during all life cycle stages, particularly for family businesses. Furthermore, she offers professional coaching for CEOs, managers, and employees.

Salomon Bankier, PhD, is a clinical psychologist and psychoanalyst with a clinical practice for adults, adolescents, and children. He is on the faculty at the Institute for Psychoanalytic Education and the Department of Psychiatry at the NYU Langone School of Medicine. He is also an adjunct faculty member at the Long Island University Doctoral Program in Clinical Psychology and the City University Doctoral Program in Clinical Psychology where he provides clinical supervision to doctoral candidates.

Fatima El-Jamil, PhD, is a clinical assistant professor in the department of psychology at the American University of Beirut, and the founder and director of the Graduate Clinical Program. She earned her PhD in clinical psychology from St. John's University in New York, in 2003 and has been teaching, practicing, and supervising clinical cases in Beirut, Lebanon since 2005. Her writing interests include addressing the relevance and challenges of a western-based psychotherapy in the Arab region, examining the legal, religious, and sociocultural factors affecting domestic violence, and understanding the ways in which autonomous, dependent and interdependent living are felt and practiced in Lebanon.

M. Hossein Etezady, MD, is a board certified child and adult psychiatrist and psychoanalyst in private practice. He has worked in multiple settings of in-patient, outpatient, and consultation services in child and adolescent, as well as adult psychiatry. For over thirty years he has served as the moderator, coordinator, contributor, and is currently serving as the senior co-chair of the Vulnerable Child Discussion Group of the American Psychoanalytic Association and The Association for Child Psychoanalysis. Dr. Etezady has written numerous articles on clinical, theoretical, and research work in child and adult psychoanalysis. His recent writings include updated psychoanalytic perspectives on topics such as development of the self, narcissism in pathology and normality, faith and transformation, creativity and play. In addition he has edited several books, including *The Neurotic Child and Adolescent* (1990), *Psychoanalytic Treatment of the Young* (1993), *The Vulnerable Child, volume I* (1993), *The Vulnerable Child, volume II* (1995), *The Vulnerable Child, volume III* (1996), and *Clinical Perspectives on Reflective Parenting* (2012). He is the co-editor of three additional volumes of The Vulnerable Child series including, *Disordered Thought and Development* (2014). Since 2007, Dr. Etezady has served as the head of the faculty and the chair of the Education Committee of the newly established Tehran Psychoanalytic Institute where he has been actively involved in construction and implementation of the training program in psychoanalytic psychotherapy. Dr. Etezady is a board member of Margaret Mahler Psychiatric Research Foundation and a faculty member of the Psychoanalytic Center of Philadelphia.

Amar Ghorpade, MD, completed medical school and residency training in psychiatry, prior to immigrating to the United States. He completed a Master's degree in Neurobiology from Louisiana State University, Baton Rouge, Louisiana. He then completed his residency in psychiatry from Cornell University and psychoanalytic training from Columbia University. He is currently in private practice in Long Island New York and also a lecturer at Columbia University Center for Psychoanalytic Training and Research and a lecturer at Advanced Center for Psychotherapy in New York.

Norka T. Malberg, PsyD, is a child and adolescent psychoanalyst in private practice in New Haven, Connecticut. She is an assistant clinical professor at Yale's Child Study Center and a member of the Contemporary Freudian Society and special member of the Western New England Psychoanalytic Society and Institute. She is co-editor of the *Lines of Development* book series by Karnac Books. Additionally, she is the editorial board member of the Psychoanalytic Study of the Child and *The Journal for Infant, Child, and Adolescent Psychotherapy.*

Monisha Nayar-Akhtar, PhD, obtained her masters and PhD in clinical psychology from Wayne State University in Detroit, Michigan. Later, she trained at the Michigan Psychoanalytic Institute in adult and child/adolescent analysis. Since 2007, she has been practicing in Philadelphia, Pennsylvania as an adult and child/adolescent psychoanalyst. She is on the faculty of the Psychoanalytic Center of Philadelphia. Dr. Nayar-Akhtar has a keen interest in applying psychoanalytic principles to community issues and promoting psychoanalytic thinking in India, her country of origin. Dr. Nayar-Akhtar has presented and published widely in the area of trauma, cultural issues, attachment, and impact of the Internet on adolescent development. She has also edited a book titled *Play and Playfulness: Developmental, Cultural and Clinical Aspects*, and is the guest editor for an issue of the *Psychoanalytic Inquiry* titled "Working with children in alternative care settings." Dr. Nayar-Akhtar is a training and supervising analyst and lives in Wynnewood, Pennsylvania with her dog, Majnun.

Marco Posadas, MSW, RSW, is a PhD candidate at Smith College School for Social Work. He was the Bathhouse counsellor and program coordinator at the AIDS Committee of Toronto and currently operates a private psychotherapy and psychoanalysis practice. He trained at the Toronto Institute of Psychoanalysis, and his focus is in long-term intensive psychoanalytic psychotherapy and psychoanalysis with Lesbian, Gay, Bisexual, Transsexual, Transgender, and Queer (LGBTTQ) populations and other marginalized communities. He is the vice president for North America of the International Psychoanalytical Studies Organization and works in several committees with the International Psychoanalytic Association. He served on the board of directors of the Ontario Association of Social Workers (OASW) Central Ontario Branch where he was recipient of the 2013 OASW Inspirational Leader Award for his work with underserved populations. He currently serves in the executive committee of the Advanced Training in Psychoanalytic Psychotherapy Program at the Toronto Psychoanalytic Society and Institute.

Deborah Reeves MGPGP, BCLP, DAPA, CGP, is a board certified professional counselor and certified group psychotherapist. She maintains an independent private practice in Philadelphia specializing in trauma spectrum disorders and women diagnosed with anorexia bulimia nervosa. Ms. Reeves is an adjunct faculty member at Drexel University in Philadelphia where she teaches individual and group psychodynamic theory. Ms. Reeves is the spokesperson for the American Association for Anorexia Nervosa/Bulimia Nervosa and other related eating disorders and is affiliated with APSSA and IPA.

Gabriel Ruiz, MA, is on the faculty of the Chicago Institute for Psychoanalysis and the Institute for Clinical Social Work. He maintains a private practice in psychoanalysis and psychotherapy with children, adolescents, and adults in Chicago. Mr. Ruiz supervises and consults with graduate students, therapists, and educators. His professional affiliations include the American Psychoanalytic Association, the Association for Child Psychoanalysis, and the National Board for Certified Counselors.

Lara Sheehi, PsyD, is a policy analyst in behavioral health at the South Carolina Department of Health and Human Services. She maintains a psychoanalytically oriented private practice in Columbia, SC. Lara has worked at the University of South Carolina's Counseling and Human Development Center and was part of the training faculty for the APA internship at the site. In her role there, she taught the diversity and assessment seminar, as well as seminars in psychodynamic therapy, technique, and practice. Lara is a member of the American Psychoanalytic Association's 2014 Teacher's Academy and is an award recipient of the 2014 APA Division 39 Minority Scholar's Program. She received her BA from the American University of Beirut in Lebanon, and her doctorate in clinical psychology from the George Washington University Professional Psychology Program.

Stuart Twemlow, MD, is a visiting professor at University College, London (health sciences), editor-in-chief of the *International Journal of Applied Psychoanalytic Studies*, retired professor of psychiatry at the Menninger department of Psychiatry and Baylor College of Medicine, Houston, Texas.

FOREWORD

There is great value in this book contributed to by experienced immigrant psychoanalysts who have particularly, the power to listen and to closely observe themselves regarding the influence of their country of origin and country of adoption on their personal growth and development as analysts. For twelve years I worked in charge of a psychodynamic psychiatry curriculum in a medical school setting where the vast majority of residents in psychiatry—some would have had trouble ordering in a restaurant. Our country has a very high percentage of international medical graduates and the complexities of their capacity to function in the "talking professions" with a limited grasp of English, let alone colloquial English is extraordinary. Unfortunately psychiatry is the least popular choice for medical specialization, and often has very unsuitable applicants. If I had my way I would ask all contributors to this volume to conduct cultural adjustment seminars in medical schools.

As a Psychiatry Board part II examiner for years, I would listen to bad jokes about the difficulties our students had in understanding basic colloquial English. For example a resident thought that when a patient spoke about getting the monkey off of his back that he was psychotic, not simply wishing to divorce his wife. So the prescription for that man included antipsychotic drugs which was completely inappropriate. Dozens if not hundreds of such examples of the inability to understand colloquial English let alone basic English is rampant throughout the international medical graduates who often teach and treat in low income settings and mental hospitals.

A group of psychiatrists (Rao, Kramer, Saunders, Twemlow *et al.*, 2007) have done a great deal of work trying to create a system of training and board examination appropriate for such difficulties. This group is in the main heavily influenced by psychodynamic thinking. In my university position I worked in special seminars held for high caste male Indian graduates who were unwittingly abusive to female nurses who were American and also for Indian female residents who were unconsciously submissive to the opinions of Indian male residents when in the same class. Such cultural seminars were essential for basic psychiatric functioning. Yet in contrast, a hard working Russian who was a major figure in the old Soviet Union mental health system started in the US as a nursing assistant and ended his residency with a prize for being the most popular and articulate resident. These highly resilient people of whatever basic training, benefit greatly from reading collections such as this one whether or not they have a psychoanalytic background. They are often very good at reading English. The majority of the papers in this collection are free from unnecessary jargon, so could be read by intelligent immigrants with great value. I myself came from New Zealand and although there were not many gross habitual differences, there were certainly colloquialisms that got me into all sorts of embarrassing situations including the quite frequent number of times I referred to a friend as a "trick" not realizing that in the United States it refers to some sort of prostitution where as in New Zealand it simply refers to a cute and funny person. So even the subtleties of language coming from a country which is entirely English speaking and very similar in many respects to America require some sort of way in which the process of being American requires the identity to develop both as a US person and specifically as a psychoanalyst and healer.

As Erik Erikson would see it, the main perspective he had on identity was to look at the place of psychosocial identity within the developmental logic of the human life cycle. Being very well-known for his stages of life and even his stages of the type of houses people would want to live in as they got older and as their ego identities began to shift. Although trained as a child analyst and occasionally practicing as a very popular adult analyst at the Austen Riggs Center, Erikson was primarily a teacher and most famously a teacher at Harvard in one of the most popular of all Harvard courses, Childhood and Society. This gave him a chance to see the children of the 1960s in all of their complexities with what he called "identity diffusion" with a need for that identity to have a social moratorium in early adult life so that identities could be shifted, houses occupied and reoccupied, colleges joined and left, courses taken and dropped out of, until finally maturity would have occurred at around age twenty-five. If we combine the normal eight-stage life cycle of identity a so-called psychosocial identity compared to the analytic identity with its focus on listening and close observation, certain similarities become obvious.

Analysts who come from very different countries especially those with different languages and different roles for religion, gender and dress, have an immense hurdle in front of them in the United States of America. The editor's primary goal in this book is to look at how a history of immigration and exposure to analytic training began to influence clinicians as they evolved as analytic therapists and analysts. What she calls a clinical working identity is the confluence of many different threads of development. The richness of these papers illustrates that almost each identity is cobbled together from uniquely different early experiences. So as one reads these papers and looks at Monisha Nayar-Akhtar's goals, one can begin to wonder what consensus one would come to about the role of these features in the development of an analytic identity. So much of such an identity depends to a great deal on the quality of teaching and especially of the quality of supervision and many unpredictable aspects of life including work, marriage, etc. Since most, if not all of these analysts would be what Erikson would have called fully grown adults, that model of Erikson's would be interesting to look at with each analyst and how they managed, for example, the development of a separate identity from parents and from parent's goals over time before they entered the working environment of the adult. One of his comments on adult life versus his fascination with the development of the young ego, Erikson notes:

> identity, in outbalancing at the conclusion of childhood, the potentially malignant dominance of the infantile superego permits the individual to forgo excessive repudiation and the diffused repudiation of others. Such freedom provides a necessary condition for the

> egos powers to integrate mature sexuality, ripened capacities, and
> adult commitments. (Erikson, 1959, p. 175)

Surely, these would be part of an analytic identity integrated thoroughly with a personal identity and made especially difficult in analysts from cultures as described where male and female dominance is often rigidly maintained yet is transported into a culture of "liberation" of sexual identity as in the United States. The matter of the absolute belief in the religion and various forms of prophets and gods must be extremely difficult for analysts to modify. They may likely need to resolve issues like the poisoning of nostalgia (Volkan, 1999), in which food and furnishings and religious rituals may conform absolutely to the culture of origin of the individual, yet home is very far away.

This rich, intelligently written, and extremely important book for us analyst's, has broader appeal in the psychodynamically sympathetic, but not analytically trained community of mental health professionals, who have tussled with similar issues. I am going to try to say what I think must be common challenges to most analysts immigrant or not, as a mindset. A non-exhaustive list might include the following:

1. **The capacity for self-determination**: I mean this in the very broad sense. The individual has to shift away from the idea that the analyst knows (religion knows, parents know, dictators know) to a position that only they and the patient know, and the regular consistent, non-judgmental quality of the analyst brings to their attention their own powers to change themselves in what ultimately seems to make the difference. These would be issues looked at from the patient's point of view that the clinician as they develop their identity may also think about for themselves.

2. **The ability to see life clearly**: to see it as it is now rather than as they wish it to be or was. In cultures where a primary part of a child's identity is as an individual owned and controlled by parents often with male dominance of the family in ways would be quite difficult to manage in certain cultures like the United States.

3. **The essential value of tolerance, altruism and seeing the enemy's viewpoint**: So many times this is very difficult to manage for all individuals. I remember on one occasion at a major analytic meeting an old analyst attacked me for suggesting that Osama Bin Laden had parents and may be a human being that one could possibly talk to.

He felt that by saying that in the comfort of the Waldorf Astoria, at a private meeting, I would be supporting the enemies of our troops, and thus be unpatriotic.

4. **The role of children**: People who seek analysis often become immensely narcissistic preoccupied as the process requires. On the other hand, the role of children in the life of an immigrant may have been very different than the role of children in the life of a United States born individual. The realization that children have rights and values and are not owned by parents and that parental role models have a lasting effect on the security and stability of children throughout their lives is difficult to balance out. We all may have found it quite difficult. I certainly was late to realize that as my children grew up into their forties and fifties, they still needed their dad from time to time and that my role in that process was an essential one, but that I had no other real control over their lives.

5. **Children need their parents** especially in the first two or three years of their lives, nannies and educational programs are not sufficient. Healthy professionals who have seen and learned from their own backgrounds and been taught by the analytic process in the role of patient see that these essential and unique parts of analytic training can work very well even if both have jobs, if their priorities are child focused. The joys as well as the wounds of life must be discussed and taken care of, whatever part of the world you come from. Read on. It's a great read.

—*Stuart W. Twemlow, MD*

References

Erikson, E. (1959). *Identity and the Life Cycle*. London: International Universities Press.

Rao, N. R., Kramer, M., Saunders, R., Twemlow, S. W., Lomax, J. W., Dewan, M. J., Myers, M. F., Goldberg, J., Cassimir, G., Kring, B. & Alami, O. (2007). An annotated bibliography of professional literature on international medical graduates. *Academic Psychiatry, 31* (1): 68–83.

Volkan, V. (1999). Nostalgia as a linking phenomenon. *Journal of Applied Psychoanalytic Studies, 1* (2): 169–179.

PREFACE

> "The real voyage of discovery consists not in seeking new landscapes, but in having new eyes."
>
> —*Marcel Proust*

Psychoanalytic identity—or the way we consciously and unconsciously think of ourselves as analysts or analytically oriented therapists, is a central concept in psychoanalysis (Wille, 2008). It is a developmental process that occurs during the course of one's training and beyond. It has been suggested that it often takes years to consolidate. Wille, in a 2008 paper titled "Psychoanalytic Identity," provides an extensive review of the relevant literature that is recent and rather sparse. He traces the earliest discussion on this subject to an International Psychoanalytic Association symposia held in 1976 with Joseph, Widlocher, and Grinberg as the main contributors. These analysts emphasize the power of self-reflection and the capacity to observe on another person's psychic functioning and the feeling of belonging to a psychoanalytic community as important components of the analytic identity. Grinberg (1990, as quoted by Wille, 2008) elaborates on a number of characteristics that together form what he calls the "psychoanalytic function of the personality" (as quoted by Wille, 2008, p. 1195). These range from being curious about another person's functioning, to a capacity for introspection and self-analysis, to a capacity for containing powerful affects to providing a holding environment, to a capacity to tolerate frustration and conducting oneself in an ethical manner, to a capacity to listen peacefully with sustained attention without judgment, and to tolerate uncertainties and doubt while remaining the same analyst as the analytic process unfolds.

To this, Kernberg adds three important superego contributions: These are:

> a degree of adulthood in the level of identification with social, political, or religious ideologies; the capacity to resist regression when the analyst is exposed to group processes; and the capacity to remain faithful to one's own system of values, as opposed to submitting to convention. (Kernberg, 1987, as quoted by Wille, 2008, p. 1196)

According to Wille, the developmental trajectory whereby many important aspects of psychoanalysis are internalized involves a complex process of introjections and identifications. This leads to an internal structure that is more than an amalgamation of ego and superego functions. In privileging the individual analysts trust in the potential of psychoanalytic method and in themselves as the analyzing instrument, Wille (2008) also draws attention to the differences among analysts in how they practice, the way they conceptualize analytic material, how they maintain the external frame and how they work with regard to termination. According to Wille, psychoanalysis becomes "an internal companion in our lives, with which we have a relationship that, like all relationships, assumes a large number of emotional colors and is constantly in motion. Psychoanalysis becomes an internal object whose quality, together with relationship we have with it, forms the nucleus of analytic identity" (Wille, 2008, pp. 1196–1197); Wille (2008) accounts for the differences among analysts as resulting partly from the inner world of each analyst.

The formation of psychoanalysis as an internal object begins long before one's formal training. Wille (2008) identifies three main stages of development. These are:

1. **Pre-analytic identity** during which the child develops curiosity, an eagerness and capacity to learn, to emotional sensitivity. Identification with parental figures, older siblings are key components of this stage. Very little has been written on this part of one's analytic identity though as Wille notes "long before the commencement of analytic training, an affinity with psychoanalysis grows, and the vision of becoming an analyst becomes part of the ego ideal. All-important figures of identification—such as parents, siblings, teachers, and possibly therapists—contribute to the ongoing formation of a pre-analytic identity" (Wille, 2008, p. 1199).
2. **Psychoanalytic identity during training** by which significant and enduring identifications with the collective ego-ideal ensues. Training analysts, supervisors, lecturers, and prominent analysts at home and abroad as well as one's colleagues furnish the building blocks for identifications.
3. **Psychoanalytic identity after training** draws attention to the constantly evolving process of developing one's identity. Klauber's (1986) commentary on this subject underscores the importance of years of non-supervised intensive analytic work that eventually allows for the emergence of an authentic analytic identity.

Analytic identity, however, has become more complex since its original conceptualization and subsequent literary explorations. Several factors have contributed to this. Of these numerous factors, the growing demand for training from individuals, many of them immigrants, who flocked to this country to obtain professional training, is striking. Arriving in this country as either children or as adults, many of these individuals have enrolled in graduate training programs in clinical psychology or social work, while others have come as psychiatrists and later pursued analytic training at various institutes. This of course is secondary to the expanding group of immigrants and others with diverse cultural backgrounds who seek treatment. Consequently, this necessitates knowledge in multicultural counseling and diversity training. Finally, many analysts have ventured beyond the boundaries of their own institutions and country to export psychoanalytic principles regarding theory and technique to countries all around the world, further stretching our borders and parameters of how we think and work. The Chinese American Psychoanalytic Alliance (CAPA) established by Elise Snyder (an analyst who resides in New York), speaks to this ever-growing enterprise. Finally, psychoanalysis today faces challenges in training, which are new, challenging, and need further exploration. The economics of training (which can be exorbitant) to the disturbing realization that most analysts are unable to practice psychoanalysis upon graduation, is contributing to shrinking candidate pools. The focus of training appears to be shifting to providing adequate psycho-analytic psychotherapy training programs instead. All of these factors challenge more contemporary notions of "analytic identity," forcing us to think outside the box, incorporate new ideas, and find innovative ways of understanding ourselves and others.

Responding to the challenges and demands of changing demograph-ics, the American Psychological Association mandated a course on mul-ticultural and diversity training for their graduate programs. Having taught one of these courses, I can attest to the depth and breadth of information that the students receive. While one course by itself may not entirely address the complexity of working with culturally differ-ent groups, it is a step in the right direction. While attending a recent Division 39 meeting, held in New York, I was struck by the number of papers that addressed multicultural perspectives and its presence/absence in our programs. The candor and honesty reflected in the dialogues that ensued illustrated both timeliness and relevance of this topic.

In contrast, the American psychoanalytical training programs, while drawing more candidates from diverse cultural backgrounds, has remained surprisingly silent on this topic. Despite significant con-tributions from prominent analysts on the subject of culture shock (Ainslie, Harlem, Tummala-Narra, Barbanel & Ruth, 2013; Akhtar, 1995; Antokoletz, 1993; Lobban, 2006) and the role of mourning in immigration, and the technical modifications when working with immigrant populations (Akhtar, 1995) most psychoanalytic institutes do not provide courses on this topic at all! This book is an attempt to partially fill that gap and provide an impetus for training programs to consider the world of the "other" in constructing their curriculum. The commitment and support of the President of the American Psychoana-lytic Association, Mark Smaller (personal communication, January and June 2014), to sponsor the task exploring nationally cultural diversity in our institutes, is encouraging and heralds a new era for psychoanalytic education in the twenty-first century.

Despite the silence in the local institutes on the subject of training culturally diverse candidates or informing others on multicultural issues, the psychoanalytic literature itself gives evidence of individuals who focus on issues of immigration, on the dialectic tensions inherent in working with culturally different groups and on the trajectories that perhaps define and shape different ethnic groups. Beginning with Salman Akhtar's (1995) seminal paper on the subject of immigration, to his more recently edited books on the emergence and practice of psychoanalysis in India (2005), the Far East (2011), cross currents between psychoanalysis and Islam (2008) and more recently looking at the African American experience (2012), Akhtar's contributions are noteworthy and significant in the relative literary bareness that plagues the cultural dialogue. While the dearth of literature is astonishingly surprising in teaching diversity in our institutions (Ciclitira & Foster, 2012; Tummala-Nara, 2009) it is encouraging to see growing contributions on the technical challenges faced by immigrant analysts (Agarwal, 2011; Akhtar, 2006; Gowrisunkur, Burman & Walker, 2002).

Nevertheless, how the immigrants "analytic identity" evolves and what structures are at play has remained elusive. Immigrants represent an increasingly growing percentage of our patient population. Furthermore, there is an increasing representation of immigrant psychoanalysts and analytically oriented therapists at our national meetings. Both underscore the need to understand how these analysts develop working identities, how they integrate various aspects of theory and technique into their practice and how they establish identities that integrate (or do they?) various dimensions of their internal selves shaped as it were by external realities. Are there various aspects of training (personal analyses, didactics, and supervision) that impede the development of an identity or does it facilitate the emergence of a more coherent and identifiable sense of self?

These and other related matters to the development of an "analytic identity" are the central theme of this edited book. There are eleven contributors to this book and they all have two characteristics in common. They all (at one time) arrived as immigrants to the United States and went on to pursue psychodynamically oriented training in their academic institutions. Some went on to pursue psychoanalytic training while others acquired psychoanalytic psychotherapy training. They are at different levels in their professional development, from some who are just beginning, to others who have years under their belt. All maintain clinical practices and adhere to the principle tenets of psychoanalytic practice in theory and technique. Some established practices within the United States and maintain various affiliations around the world that dovetail with what they do and who they are. Others returned to their countries of origin to pursue a practice in psychoanalytic psychotherapy. Each story is unique, compelling, and informative and I believe highlights the imperative need for the inclusion of multicultural competency training in our analytic programs. I will now expand on each paper which I hope will invite the reader to engage in a dialogue with the writer. I hope that this will stimulate further discussion on this subject and lead to more creative solutions to our institutional dilemmas and resistances.

Stuart Twemlow and Hossein Etezady are senior analysts who have written the foreword and concluding chapters of this edited book. They, in my mind, serve as stalwart bastions of psychoanalytic theory and technique and as anchoring pillars for a dialogue that I hope will continue beyond this contribution. Both travel to and fro from their country of origin to impart knowledge and wisdom to their native countrymen. Stuart Twemlow is an immigrant from New Zealand whose poignant biographical account of his personal and professional journey (Akhtar & Hooke (Eds.) 2007) elucidates the synthesis of various aspects of oneself in how one thinks and practices as an analyst. Stuart's ongoing clinical interests lie in the area of applied community based psychoanalytic thinking and practice and his extensive contributions (2000, 2003, 2013) gives evidence of years of thinking and practice in this field. Stuart's various community-based projects have taken him all around the globe in addition to his frequent and yearly visits to New Zealand. Nothing and no one could be more culturally informed and diverse as he is, in the depth and breadth of his practice! (see the foreword).

I had the pleasure of meeting Hossein Etezady several years ago when I moved to Philadelphia. Hossein is an immigrant from Iran and is a scholarly and prolific writer. As a child analyst, his immersion in the field is reflected in his several literary contributions on subject matter (especially on vulnerable children, see Etezady, 2008, 2010) relating to the development of children. Hossein also travels yearly to Iran to teach at the Tehran Psychoanalytic Institute. I have had the pleasure of also teaching courses on adolescent development to this group via Skype. This has further informed me on how various psychoanalytic groups training around the world integrate cultural elements into their practice and analytic identities. Hossein's depth of knowledge and ability and capacity to synthesize various aspects of child development and the emergence of the self and identity is reflected in his rich and highly informative paper.

The remaining papers come from therapists at various stages of identity development and clinical practice. I begin with Salomon Bankier's paper. The title of Sol's (as he likes to be called) paper captures the essence of what many immigrants struggle with in their daily life. Sol is an immigrant from Argentina and in using the metaphor of "lost luggage," to elicit the image of transformations that occur during the process of mourning and integrating disavowed aspects of ourselves. Sol's paper is a commentary on how a good analysis upon further reflection may find itself lacking. This is not necessarily a function of an inadequate analyst or a failure on the part of the analytic dyad to find the potential space to communicate and connect. Instead, it is a function of time, of thoughts and feelings that cannot be expressed in the language that one now finds oneself using and the limitations of time and structure that create illusions of intimacy and ruptures at the same time. This dialectic tension is inherent in the history of migration and Sol's paper testifies the lingering thoughts that surround the process of self-reflection.

Kamelia Alavi, migrated to this country from Iran. Her forced migration served as the impetus for personal growth and self-realizations but it had also led to ongoing struggles and battles. Her description of her personal challenges in raising her family, interacting within the social setting and finding ways to define herself illustrates the ongoing dialectic tensions within an immigrant. The significant losses spur thought and action and Kamelia's challenges and course of action echo with many of us who live with these internal dialogues. Her chapter highlights the growing understanding of immigration and its impact on individuals by highlighting examples from her life. This reinforces the need to expand our knowledge in this field as well provides encouragement to many who seek to work with culturally diverse populations.

Amar Ghorpade, is a native of India and in his paper, he explores how early attachment styles and patterns, are quite diverse and are informed by social and cultural contexts. Amar references his years in India as a young adult to explore the variances that emerge between patients (and therapists) who are culturally diverse and different from the treating therapist. Drawing upon the rich attachment literature and exploring the complexity of neurological underpinnings that define emotions, patterns of relating and eventually shaping our adult interactions, Amar reminds us that people all around the world relate to each other in different ways and that attachment patterns are not universal. In questioning Western notions of attachment styles as being universal and exemplifies his point by using several case examples, Amar establishes the imperative need for us to consider the cultural, social, and familial context of an individual's early childhood. Contextualized within this space, individual behaviors assume different meanings and outcomes.

Deborah Reeves, a native of England examines the dialectic tensions that emerge when one migrates as a young teenager. Reeves examines the undulating tensions that existed in her move to this country, from her sensitive delineating of tensions, which exist between cultures, from the minor internal schisms that emerge when one struggles to find meaning through language that while similar is yet so different. Deborah's paper highlights the homo ethnic identifications that color interactions between two people who on the surface appear to be the same. When subtleties of language, the various meanings assigned to different words, and when words themselves are different appear in the verbal and non-verbal discourse, tensions arise. Immigrants, like Deborah, retreat to the comfort of familiar objects and internal structures, guided by compelling internal forces to regain a suitable footing in their new found land. For Deborah, her refuge in music also underscores the soothing function of the universal language of music and its association with early attachment objects.

Lara Sheehi, a native of Lebanon underscores the critical role of how internal objects are co-constructed in a complex social, cultural, and political milieu. Her paper expands on how the "other" assumes a poignant role in the construction of an immigrant's identity. Lara's forced immigration from her native country to Canada and her attempts to assimilate into a new and "foreign environment," is beautifully elucidated in her paper. Capturing the subtleties of forced displacement for a teenager, Lara explores how her social and political history shaped her internal world. Later, pursuing her graduate training in the United States, Lara provides a sensitive account of how the socialcultural milieu of a training environment impacts her professional and personal journey. The theme of Lara's paper is similar to many contemporary psychoanalysts who examine the role of race, ethnicity, socioeconomic status, and political affiliations on the unfolding psychoanalytic process. Questioning and expanding on these, Lara highlights how the internal world of a therapist is co-constructed with the sociocultural and political milieu and is worth considering when conducting any analytically informed clinical treatment.

Fatima Jamil, also from Lebanon, is a psychotherapist who trained in New York and returned to her native country, to open a clinical practice. Fatima's sensitive portrayal of her training and the political Zeitgeist that surrounded the early part of this century marks the extraneous political and sociocultural influences that become part of one's inner world during psychoanalytic training. The intrapsychic is never too far from external realities that impinge, shape, and mold the practice of one's profession. Fatima's paper highlights the inevitable struggle of transforming what one has learned to work with the population one currently encounters. Psychoanalytic orthodoxy, appealing as it may be to some in its pristine presentation of beliefs, ideas, and values undergoes mutative changes in settings.

Gabriel Ruiz and Marco Posadas are both natives of Mexico. Though they trained in two different, but closely aligned neighboring countries. Marco describes the challenges he encountered as he struggled to enter a program of study in his country, one that would not accept homosexuals in to their training programs. In his quest to obtain psychoanalytic training, Marco made his way to Canada to enroll in their psychoanalytic training program. Marco's journey of immigration (one might even say it was forced!) parallels the course taken by any immigrant who chose to leave their country of origin. Loss and sorrow accompany such journeys as one now speaks in a different language, hears unfamiliar sounds, and eventually comes to terms with his training. Marco's journey, informed by his struggle to live his personal and professional life as a gay therapist, is a reminder of the limitations and prejudices that exist within the psychoanalytic community, internationally and in his own backyard. His personal and professional narrative voices the growing concern of many in our larger international community to broaden and deepen our perspectives on training.

Gabriel Ruiz recounts his poignant journey as a young child of transient migrant workers who migrated repeatedly between Mexico and the United States. Gabriel's sensitive account of this repetitive transition was internalized and possibly lay dormant till he entered psychoanalytic training. Upon self-reflection, Gabriel identified a familiar pattern in how he listened to his patients. This "to and fro" movement became a central internal construct/process, deeply embedded in the way he listened and understood his patients. An analytic stance and moments of reverie based on an internalization of an early childhood association and lived reality underscores the critical power of implicit memory in our intrapsychic space.

Norka Malberg provides a powerful and moving account of her family's migration from Puerto Rico to England. Her history of several migrations parallels that of other contributors, though her journey is unique to her. Moved by her history of migration, Norka remains attuned to the significance of the role of the caregiver in ameliorating the painful and traumatizing experience of migration especially for a child. Norka's training in child analysis informs her of the role of early attachment figures, the co-construction of early personal narratives and the gradual unfolding of this during the analytic process. Norka is a gifted clinician whose work informs her in her continual transition from one identity to another, as she playfully finds innovative ways to discover and rediscover herself. Her case vignettes illustrates how she draws deeply from within herself and her own experiences to understand sensitively the patients that she works with. Her story of repeated migrations within the family and how trauma is transmitted between generations is a reminder that migration is not only the trauma that accompanies an immigrant soul. Instead, a history of migration, unique to the family and identified by the prevalent social, economic, and political context informs the individual.

My paper on the confluence of identities examines the powerful internal forces at play as we transition from one life phase to another, developmentally, temporally, and spatially. My journey begins not with my migration from India but with the migration of my father to India, from what is now known as Bangladesh. His forced migration, during the partition of India and Pakistan, became central to my personal narrative and took on many meanings later in my development. My maternal family also fled to India during the time when India and her neighboring country Pakistan were embroiled in a fierce battle for land and religious parity. My mother's history was therefore more colored by the political movement of her adopted land and her political voice had a profound impact on my life. As for my father, his political and later professional struggles to become a psychiatrist, (the fledging field of psychiatry in India in the early 1950's when he began his training, led to a temporary move to England where he finished his psychiatric training and later became immersed in the emerging field of psychoanalysis) is echoed in my personal and professional journey, bearing witness to the enduring impact of early identifications. The immigrants neverending quest to find a homeostatic balance is reflected in the frequent visits to my homeland and the transformation of what was once lost to what is now more palpable and attainable in new found experiences and dreams. In the process my analytic identity has formed, undergone transformations, and continues to redefine, emerges as it incorporates and transitions in and out of various influences. These can run side by side like the Rio Negro and or blend in like the Beas and Parvati rivers in the Kulu valley region in India. Regardless, the influences are powerful, visually compelling and transformative in nature.

These eleven papers are a preliminary attempt to shed light on an issue that is center stage of our analytic discussions. The imperative need to broaden our training programs, to attract candidates, (especially those who are ethnically and culturally diverse), to deepen our understanding of issues related to how identities (of various kinds) develop and are sustained, is immediately gleaned from perusing these papers. While issues of immigration bind all of these contributors, their stories of how they are trained, how they evolved, and their conceptualizations of their internal dynamics and external realities are unique. The topic and subtitle for this book immediately suggests the inevitability of self disclosures. Pain and disappointments ride side by side with the joys of learning and growing in a profession that would otherwise have remained inaccessible to most. The contributions of the various training analyses and the deep sensitivity of those who supervised is implicit in such a venture. The courage to share and explore the intricacies of one's training, to draw attention to aspects of one's growth is an exercise in courage and self-discovery. There have been numerous times when one or more contributors have contacted me with a confession that despite the fact that writing their paper was at times profoundly painful, it also helped them to integrate, grow, and eventually find their own voice. I know that it did that for me as well and for that I am very grateful.

In conclusion, I would like to draw attention to the role of writing as a form of self-analysis, to telling one's biographical story as therapists, to the uncovering of unconscious dimensions that remain hidden until one undertakes the ongoing journey of self-analysis. As Fred Griffin, (2004) a gifted writer/analyst writes "it was in the very act of writing that (these) unanticipated words generate(d) a *new form* of experience (a more integrated experience of previously disconnected aspects of myself)" (p. 697, italics in original). Griffin (2004) expands on the role of the analyst as reader and reader as analyst, and writes that during this process we create self-analytic fiction. The process of mobilizing and transforming internal constructs and objects, while receiving impetus from many early identifications and ongoing sources during adulthood, is ongoing.

According to Griffin (2004), the power of transforming one's personal journey through the act of writing is immense and the self-revelatory process that ensues is informative and transformative in its own right. I quote Griffin when he says:

> I discovered a particular shape of experience—the oscillating states with which I am quite familiar. In turn, I was unable to discern a rhythm that is familiar to me, of experiences of hopefulness/aliveness and of barrenness/feeling deadened. The shape of which I speak not only contains a set of feeling states—of a sense of aliveness/spark and of deadness/inhibition—that I found to be truly familiar to me … My experiences of myself had never been (re) presented in quite this way. It was an experience in which the familiar became unfamiliar, and the unfamiliar became familiar. (Griffin, 2004, p. 700)

References

Agarwal, N. K. (2011). Intersubjectivity, transference, and the cultural third. *Contemporary Psychoanalysis, 47*: 204–223.

Akhtar, S. (1995). A third individuation: immigration, identity, and the psychoanalytic process. *Journal of the American Psychoanalytic Association, 43*: 1051–1084.

Akhtar, S. (Ed). (2005). *Freud Along the Ganges: Psychoanalytic Reflections on the People and Culture of India*. New York, NY: Jason Aronson.

Akhtar, S. (2006). Technical challenges faced by the immigrant analyst. *Psychoanalytic Quarterly, 75*: 21–43.

Akhtar, S. (Ed). (2008). *The Crescent and the Couch: Cross-Currents between Islam and Psychoanalysis*. New York, NY: Jason Aronson.

Akhtar, S. (Ed). (2011). *Freud and the Far East: Psychoanalytic Perspectives on the People and Culture of China, Japan and Korea*. New York, NY. Jason Aronson.

Akhtar, S. (2012). *The African American Experience: Psychoanalytic Perspectives*. New York, NY: Jason Aronson.

Ainslie, R. C., Harlem, A., Tummala-Narra, P., Barbanel, L., & Ruth, R. (2013). Contemporary psychoanalytic views on the experience of immigration. *Psychoanalytic Psychology, 30*: 663–679.

Antokoletz, J. C. (1993). A psychoanalytic view of cross-cultural passages. *American Journal of Psychoanalysis, 53*: 35–54.

Ciclitira, K. & Foster, N. (2012). Attention to culture and diversity in psychoanalytic trainings. *British Journal of Psychotherapy, 28*: 353–373.

Etezady, M. H. (2008). Faith and the couch: a psychoanalytic perspective on transformation. *Psychoanalytic Inquiry, 28*: 560–569.

Etezady, M. H. (2010). Psychoanalysis in a "shame culture": Japanese psychoanalytic insights. *International Journal of Psychoanalysis, 91*: 1242–1245.

Gowrisunkur, J., Burman, E., & Walker, K. (2002). Working in the mother-tongue: first language provision and cultural matching in the intercultural therapy. *British Journal of Psychotherapy, 19*: 45–58.

Griffin, F. L. (2004). One form of self-analysis. *The Psychoanalytic Quarterly, 73*: 683–715.

Klauber, J. (1986). *Difficulties in the Analytic Encounter*. London, UK: Free Association Books.

Lobban, G. (2006). Immigration and Dissociation. *Psychoanalytic Perspectives, 3*: 73–92.

Tummala-Nara, P. (2009). Teaching on diversity. *Psychoanalytic Psychology, 26*: 322–334.

Twemlow, S. W. (2000). The roots of violence: converging psychoanalytic explanatory models for power struggles and violence in schools. *Psychoanalytic Quarterly, 69*: 741–785.

Twemlow, S. W. (2003). A crucible for murder: the social context of violent children and adolescents. *Psychoanalytic Quarterly, 72*: 659–698.

Twemlow, S. W. (2013). Broadening the vision: a case for community-based psychoanalysis in the context of usual practice. *Journal of the American Psychoanalytic Association, 61*: 663–690.

Twemlow, S. W. & Twemlow, N. A. (2007). Creating mental space: assimilating recovered Maori self-representations. In: S. Akhtar & M. T. S. Hooke (Eds.), *The Geography of Meanings* (pp. 141–164). United Kingdom: International Psychoanalysis Library.

Wille, R. S. (2008). Psychoanalytic identity: Psychoanalysis as an internal object. *Psychoanalytic Quarterly, 77*: 1193–1229.

CHAPTER ONE

The confluence of cultures: an Iranian–American story

Kamelia Alavi

Brilliant-hued,
Deeply scarred,
Skeins of gold
Air,
breathe in—
Soul, unknown
to the Western World

—Ksera Dyette, *Confluence*

Exploring the development of one's identity as a therapist is a journey one takes with some trepidation. It forces one to reveal aspects of themselves that they would not otherwise reveal. It also pushes them to integrate and assimilate historical and cultural contexts that have shaped them over the years. I hope to illustrate some of the factors that contributed to my identity as a therapist. So, let me begin with my life as an adult in this country.

Immigration

Reflections and recollections

I came to this country in August 1973, to attend graduate school at Tufts University. They had awarded me a full scholarship, so financially I was in fairly good shape. Graduate school was an intense experience. The classes were small and the courses challenging. Furthermore, I had to become more comfortable speaking the English language (though I had grown up surrounded by several Americans and the British, who had settled in Iran), as well as adjust to many cultural aspects of living in a foreign environment. Initially, my goal was to finish my education and go back to Iran to become a college professor. At the time that I left Iran to attend graduate school, the two countries, Iran and USA, enjoyed a comfortable relationship. My country was also beginning to enjoy the benefits that come with economic gains and we were experiencing that specifically with the oil price hikes. Procuring a visa for travel was also quite easy for both countries. Travel between the two countries had increased and at that time I had no intention of immigrating permanently to the United States.

Several years went by and I did not consider myself an immigrant; just someone who had come to study and would return to her country of origin. However, during the course of my study, certain world events changed the trajectory of my life. Iran had a revolution, there were hostage crises, and eight years of war with Iraq. These events changed the lives of many people and impacted my future decision-making. Meanwhile, I married, started a family, finished my education, and began working. My husband and I socialized with families coming from other multicultural backgrounds. Many were highly educated and were our colleagues who had also immigrated to the United States. They came from countries such as Nigeria, Iran, Turkey, India, Pakistan, Jamaica, Japan, China, Israel, Jordan, Kuwait, and more.

In addition to these world and personal events, I was also impacted by the treatment I received from my host country. My recollections of this treatment are extremely positive especially as it concerns my relationship with my university and professors. During a dire time when I was not receiving any monetary funds from Iran, my university allowed me to stay in their campus housing without paying rent and my professors where very supportive.

Over the years, several factors have influenced and informed my developing identity as a therapist, including my decision to immigrate permanently and raising my children in the United States. In the beginning, my immigration was a voluntary and temporary decision. Yet, certain realities forced me to make the decision to stay permanently and largely out of necessity. Gradually, I realized that my life had more roots in the United States than in my country of origin. My children were being raised in the US, attending school, and making friends. I became increasingly aware that uprooting them would be detrimental. As such, the decision to return to Iran became even more distant. Not surprisingly, for years I remained in denial, not recognizing that my children were actually children of immigrants. They were exposed to an entirely different cultural environment than I was when I was their age. Their daily life was markedly different from that of mine. Even as an adult, what I was exposed to was quite different than what they faced in their natural school environment. I expected them to understand and follow my culture of origin, not recognizing that their external culture was quite different. As would be expected, conflicts eventually arose. It was only slowly that I could begin to understand their experience including the fact that they felt differently about certain things, especially cultural values. They were largely different from their peers, a painful reality that forced them at times to exist in two different worlds. In a way they lived with a double identity, sometimes referred to as a bicultural identity.

Emotional refueling

I did not go back home for thirty-eight years. I think my emotional refueling (Akhtar, 1999) was provided within the community of Iranians I hung out in and the fact that my siblings and parents immigrated too. Additionally, my in-laws came to visit very frequently. I missed my country, but having loved ones close eased mourning my homeland. My tight connection to my family and friends was an important factor for my adjustment to my host country. Keeping up traditions was also helpful.

My friend who worked in a retail store had a lot of interactions with people from all walks of life. One day she told me:

> "You have no idea how our children are treated or feel outside our homes. You are hanging out with more educated people, mostly

college professors from around the world so you fit in and feel comfortable. You are one of them. But our children are not in the same diversified environment and they are more like a sore thumb among all American kids in the school. Especially that in our school district there are no second generation immigrants other than our kids. Even teachers do not see them the same and may treat them differently. They are foreigners after all. So we have to be careful in our expectations from them and understand their bicultural selves. We cannot expect them to feel and behave like us."

It took me many years to understand what she said. Over the years when I noticed the conflict between my culture and my children's external environmental culture, I tried to find ways to understand them better. So I started a new journey. I became a mental health professional and attended many lectures and seminars related to immigrants and the impact of immigration on their psychology. At one of these meetings I realized that yes indeed I am an immigrant and my children are the second generation immigrants. I tried to become more culturally competent. Over the course of treating others I became more aware of my own shortcomings and strengths and started to understand myself, my family, but also my patients and students.

The sooner the immigrant accepts that his culture is different than the host country, the best thing is to assimilate and for the better.

The immigrant has few choices; to observe and act rigidly in his culture and defy the host country's culture, to adopt the culture of the host country fully and make obsolete his own culture, or to assimilate and use both cultures in an effort to mix and match. In each case the emotional, socioeconomic, and relational outcomes will be different. Especially when we consider that as children of immigrants we would clearly notice that the effect of these decisions would be different on our kids. With the first choice of keeping the original culture rigidly, we take a risk of creating a lot of conflict for our children inside and outside the home. With the second choice we lose our own self and create a sense of loss for ourselves. The choice of assimilation may be the best one. There are many ways to combine the two cultures and make everyone more comfortable.

Throughout my work, I have utilized the cultural knowledge and competency that I have gained in therapy. I treat Chinese patients online through ooVoo and Skype. It is interesting to see that in therapy with

Chinese patients, some of my immigration and bicultural experiences become useful. Many of my Chinese patients have migrated from their hometown to other cities, living far from their families and dealing with the separation. They have to raise their children by themselves and do not have their parents support since they live in another city. Sometimes one of the parents may come and live with them to take care of the child. This may create conflict about housework, child rearing, and so on, which in a way is very similar to some of the families I have seen whose grandparents will come to live with their children and take care of their grandchildren since the parents go to school or work.

Age at immigration

Adjustment and assimilation depends on many things. Age is one of them. The age of an immigrant at the time of immigration is very important. I immigrated when I was a young adult. At that age my culture was embedded in my psychology. Most of my peers had also immigrated between the ages of twenty to twenty-two. So we all had similar memories of our childhood and early adulthood.

Many years later after the revolution in Iran and during the Iran-Iraq war, some families with children who immigrated had very different experiences. They were mostly in their thirties or early forties. They had young children who had to adjust to a new environment and language. A psychiatrist told me that a couple brought their school age child to him and believed that the child was possessed by some spirits and did not talk at all in school. The psychiatrist went to school and after some research found out that the child could not speak English well. The kids in his class made fun of him so he decided to pretend he was mute. The proposed intervention was effective. The teachers and some friends in school made the child comfortable and slowly he talked again.

Immigration has its toll on younger children who do not have the option to go back home. They may feel angry with their parents that they uprooted them and brought them to a foreign environment. They may also miss their friends and relatives and feel a lack of support. The immigrants who have left a secure job back home and have to build up a new career in a foreign environment, while at the same time taking care of a family, may have a hard time. Another problem is that the home environment will change too. Parents have to deal with new problems and their frustration, homesickness, job difficulties, and financial hardships will affect the home environment. Younger children are more vulnerable and will panic faster. Especially when and if they adjust to the environment and they hear their parents' doubts and wonderings about their immigration status. They may feel that if the parents go back they will lose what they gained after some struggle. This may destabilize the psyche of the child.

Adolescent age immigration may also be a difficult process. This is the age at which things are hard on the child even in a stable well-known environment. In case of Mary (mentioned in a section to follow) she struggled more than her American peers with the issues of adolescence. On one hand she had conflicts at home with her mother, and on the other she had to handle the school culture, which she was not familiar with. Friendship is also challenging during this period. To be accepted is a big traumatic issue for adolescents to begin with. For second generation immigrants they constantly find themselves trying to justify the culture of their parents or become disloyal to parents and join their peers in defying their culture of origin.

Zero generation immigrants

Another age group of immigrants is the parents of the immigrants who join their children in the host country. I call them "Zero generation immigrants." They immigrate at an older age and sometimes when they are professionally and in other respects, well settled in their own country. Some of them may already be retired. In other countries, retirement is based on years of work and not age. Many of the parents of my friends who immigrated and joined their children were in their late fifties. They moved because their adult children had immigrated and their lives became empty without their children and their grandchildren. This move results in a big toll on them. They become dependent on their grown children for various purposes such as housing, language, healthcare, entertainment, legal matters, travel, food, and so on. They may feel they have become "Zero" because their position has changed from being a capable person in their home country to a needy and incompetent person in the host country. They may become bored since they remain stuck at home more often. My Indian friend one day called me and said "I have good news, my mother got a job at TJ Maxx and I don't have to entertain her all day."

Maggie a young woman from China with depression complained that her parents expected too much from her. She emigrated from China with her adoptive parents when she was twelve years old.

> "My parents expected me to translate and take care of documents such as the lease, insurance, and other legal and financial matters just because I could read and write and they could not. They thought since I can speak, read, and write English I could also understand the legal issues and would take care of them."

Zero generations also have conflicts with the upbringing of their grandchildren. They often complain and pressure their adult children about the way they are raising their children. They also complain about how they are treated by their grandchildren. They expect the same customs and traditions, which they were raised and brought up their children with, for their grandchildren.

> "We used to jump and say hello to our elderly when they entered the room. These kids here don't pay attention to us. They don't treat us with respect."

The healthcare of this group is very problematic for them and their adult children. For every appointment someone has to take them and speak for them. They may not be familiar with the rules and regulations and their expectations of health care professionals may also be a problem. This generation of immigrants may also go through another phase of separation individuation. They may feel anxious when their children leave home or they do not hear from them for a while. They may feel abandoned. They expect to be nurtured by their children and many of their needs to be taken care of as soon as they arise. Zero generation immigrants may become a big burden on the first generation immigrants. Even a ride may become a burden if the parents do not have a license and or do not drive. Another issue is the unequal responsibility on the adult children.

A friend of mine once said:

> "I have been taking care of my parents for month after month when they are here. Take care their health care and other needs and even modified my house to accommodate their disabilities. I did not

burden my sibling with the responsibilities. Once I asked my sister that I wanted to travel with my husband and if she could take care of our parents for few weeks. Her response was, no. She wondered why I wanted to travel and leave my parents to her care."

The care-taking child is often burned out and blamed too. If only one adult child takes care of the parents, she or he may be blamed by the siblings and even sometimes by the parent.

"Why you did this, why you did help them this way, why you did not do that?"

The children who do not take care of their parents are only blamed for not taking care of their parents. But the one who does everything can be blamed constantly for his/her decision-making.

"I wished my parents would have called all of us and divided the responsibilities from the beginning rather than waiting till I am burned out and exhausted. After all these years of service if I complain everyone accuses me of changing and being a complainer."
"My siblings even blame me for getting a loan for my parents so they could buy a house and now they cannot take care of it because they are too old and too stubborn to sell it," a patient of mine complained.

Another issue that this group is faced with is the issue of death. Where to be buried? Some may wish to be taken back home to be buried near their loved ones and in their home soil. This is not an easy task.

Tabout mara jaieh bolandi begozarid. Taa booye vatan beshna-vam as rekhneyeh tabout Taa baad barad booye mara bar vataneh man.
[Put my casket on a high place so I can smell the aroma of my countries soil from the cracks of the casket. Or wind takes my aroma to my home (country).]

Some nationalities over the years have purchased graves to make their own national cemetery. This has helped the process of mourning. They even go to the cemetery at the special days and visit other friends there and soothe each other.

Consolidation

Psyche consolidation at the age of immigration is important factor in adjusting to the immigration. As mentioned, each age group is faced with different challenges, especially for children whom their immigration is involuntary. Infants and children may be affected indirectly by their parents' psyche due to the immigration. If they are school age then the external environment can affect them directly too. The general effects of immigration could be analyzed as a SWOT analysis. In SWOT, S stands for strengths of the immigrant; a strong psyche, his resources, finances, etc. W stands for weaknesses. Again he could be weak and vulnerable, lack strong finances, etc. O stands for opportunities, such as a job, environmental support, family supports, etc. T stands for threats, such as hostility of the environment, political bitterness between the two countries, lack of environmental resources, and lack of family and community support. SWOT analyses can to some degree predict the outcome of the immigration on the immigrant.

Custom and traditions

Some immigrants try to keep their country of origins' customs. This may be a burden on their children since their friends do not observe the same customs. It may also strain their relationship with their children. Sleepovers were an issue for us. It took me some years to give in and let my children sleep over at their friend's house. I always suggested that they could have their sleepover in our house. Many of our immigrant friends had the same issue in their homes. It usually takes some negotiation to convince parents to allow their kids to stay at their friend's house.

> Often parents would say, "We Iranians/Indians/Pakistanis/ Africans/Egyptians and so on do not have sleepovers, or Prom."

A young woman told me that she still feels sad when she remembers that she was not allowed to go to prom, instead her dad took the family to a restaurant on prom night. She felt so sad and the next day at school she felt out of place.

The second generation immigrants often feel embarrassed of their parents' behavior and observing their customs and may become angry with them.

"Why can't my parents behave normally?"

Once the second generation passes, the years of anger towards the forced culture of their parents' home country, may move to embrace and start to try it. I have seen many young generations who start to pay attention to the music, poetry, language, and traditions of their parents and they begin to appreciate it. Often I have seen my adult children listen to Persian music and ask for Persian food and they are proud of their heritage, while they were resentful of these parts of their culture as a teen.

Holidays

Holidays are also an issue in the life of immigrants. Should we celebrate our own holidays and special days or the host countries? I adopted my host country's holidays as well as my country of origin. I celebrated Christmas, decorated the tree, bought gifts. My argument was that the children go to school after holiday and should not feel different and alienated. Like every other child they had their pictures, stories, and gifts to talk about with their friends. On my country of origin's holidays I again observed them, and for the Persian New Year I told the school that the children will observe the holiday and had permission for them to have the day off. Many immigrants observe their country of origin's customs and holidays. Especially if they have a large community they may even throw big parties and ceremonies. A few friends of mine, who are Jewish, would celebrate both Christmas and Hanukkah along with my children.

A patient was complaining that on New Year or any other national holiday of her country of origin she feels depressed. She said:

"I leave home and I do not see the same excitement as others. It is like an ordinary day. Back home I felt so excited and happy because everyone was celebrating."

Couples therapy for immigrants

Couples therapy with immigrants has its own uniqueness. The couple may be bi-racial or each comes from a different culture which may be strange to one another. Even couples from the same culture may find a strain in their relationship if one of them has assimilated more to the culture of the host country.

One of my patients in couple's therapy turned to me and said:

> "Don't you understand? He is from North Philadelphia and I am from West Philadelphia. We are very different. Our culture is different."

I have had many couples who at the time of immigration they felt compatible and in harmony. After some years one of them changed and they felt different from each other. One of my patients told me that she felt that she had changed:

> "My values, wishes, demands have changed. He is not the same in my eyes. I grew and adjusted to the environment well and I am more American. But he has not changed. He has stagnated. He did not even learn English well in these two years."

Some immigrants may insist that their children should marry a person from their culture and country of origin. This may be difficult especially if the family is not in connection with a large community of their own culture. Bicultural marriage may be more successful if both spouses tried to learn and respect the other's culture and customs.

Race and color of skin

Mary a young woman who at the age of twelve immigrated to USA from a Caribbean country had a difficult time in high school.

> "I was not white enough to fit in amongst the white kids and not black enough to fit in amongst the black kids. I was an ugly duckling and out of place."

Color of skin is an issue for immigrants. Feeling separate from the mainstream can create inner conflicts, anger, depression, hostility and in extreme, isolation. Mary's skin color created psychological conflicts. On one hand she tried hard to fit in by being a good student, while on the other hand she was not accepted easily in white or black groups. During political upheavals such as hostage crises, terrorist attacks, wars, and the like, a lot of foreigners may be profiled and suffer because of their physical appearances such as skin color. Businesses have been attacked just because of the owner's nationality, name, or skin color. After 9/11 many adults who suffered as a child during the hostage crises got sick and were referred to hospitals or were afraid to go out. Many small kids were traumatized because of their names, skin color, or even language.

Empathy

One of the important skills of the therapy is empathy. Without empathy, therapy at times may not be as effective. The ongoing question has been, where do we learn empathy? Is it embedded in our psyche when we are born or it is learned?

When I started my courses at Tufts University I had to struggle with the English language and sometimes it distracted me from what was going in the class. One day I went to class and noticed that the other students were preparing themselves to take the midterm exam. In the last class I did not notice that the exam was scheduled for the following class. I was distressed because I was not prepared for the exam. When the professor came to class he noticed that I was upset. He asked me what was wrong and I explained to him that I had not realized that we had the exam.

He turned to other students and asked them if it was okay to postpone the exam. His empathy affected me a lot. Some years later one of my students and later one of my patients asked me why I can empathize with them and recognize their stress. I automatically remembered that day and realized that my professor's recognition of the confusion in his foreign student impacted me in a positive way and helped me to be a more empathetic person. When it comes to my foreign students or patients, I try to understand their feelings and situations brought up because of their differences.

Religion

Jim an African immigrant came with his wife to therapy. He claimed that his wife could not have a child naturally, and in his religion the other ways of having a child were not accepted. It was obvious that his wife was not knowledgeable about her husband's religious rules. I realized that I had to challenge him to find out why he wanted to divorce his wife and discover if the issue of pregnancy and natural child bearing was only an excuse. I had to find a way. I had some knowledge of his religion and I knew that artificial pregnancy was not viewed in his religion the way he explained it. However, he could simply claim that where he comes from in his religious practice artificial pregnancy was forbidden. I asked him if he believed in miracles.

> He said: "yes in my religion we believe in miracles."
> I told him: "Suppose a miracle happens and you now have a child with your wife in the natural way. Would you then be satisfied and not want to leave your wife?"
> Suddenly he said: "I would still divorce her. I am now a more educated and successful man and I am not proud of her and I want to move on."

The issue of religion and a child became irrelevant. In my experience religion and culture can get so intertwined that it may become difficult to distinguish if a practice or behavior is purely coming from the religion or culture. I often try to ask and learn from my clients about their religion. Not every Moslem has the same religious practice. The same is true with other religious practices and beliefs. People from different parts of the world interpret and practice the same religion differently. It is a mistake if the therapist assumes that every Christian client thinks the same way and understands or practices Christianity the same way.

Nationality

When I moved to the USA I believed that all Iranians were the same. To me they ate, acted, behaved, and believed the same things. Maybe it was because back home your choice of friends was unlimited and you could choose friends similar to you. Abroad your choices are limited. You become friends with people mostly because they are from your home country, and that is when you realize that even the people from your country of origin are different.

> "I don't say Indians do this or that anymore. I learned that Indians are not all the same and behave the same. It is stereotyped to think

people who come from the same country are all the same." This is what one of my patients said after months of struggling with the issues of friendship.

"We and they," "ours and theirs," are often used by immigrants who have not assimilated well and they still constantly look for the differences between themselves and the host country people.

Passage of time

When we move to a different country, our memories of how things are in our country of origin freezes. I used to believe that people from my country lived the same way they used to at the time of my move to the United States. The reality is that specifically due to the broadening information highway, people all over the world are more informed about other countries culture, custom, fashions, and the like. As a result, people around the world change over time by learning from other cultures through the media. During the time of the immigrant's absence from his/her country of origin, things change. However, the immigrant still assumes that things have not changed and the conditions froze at the time of their immigration.

Someone told me:

> "I can't believe how much people back home have changed. I always blamed my children that back home kids are not so entitled, they are more polite. After years that I traveled back home I was shocked. Kids are more entitled, demanding, rude, etc. people have become more selfish."
>
> I asked her: "Do you think that people have changed or your fantasies were that people back home are better and you forgot about your past disappointment?"
>
> She thought a little and with a smile said, "I think both. I always had the fantasy that people back home treated me better especially when I was disappointed with how people treated me here. But things have changed there too. All these foreign satellite programs have influenced people."

The world has become smaller. News, fashion, TV sitcoms, music, art, and more travel instantly. Young people learn about things happening in other parts of the world and they want to imitate them immediately. The children of immigrants are being blamed for being different from kids at the time of their parent's immigration. Those families who travel often to their home countries may become more realistic about the changes in their country of origin, social, cultural, political, and economic factors included.

Reference

Akhtar, S. (1999). *Immigration and Identity: Turmoil, Treatment, and Transformation*. Lanham, MD: Jason Aronson.

CHAPTER TWO

Lost luggage: analytic training as search for objects lost in migration

Salomon Bankier

We do not receive wisdom, we must discover it for ourselves, after a journey through the wilderness which no one else can make for us, which no one can spare us.

—Marcel Proust, *Remembrance of Things Past*

The topic of migration has been the subject of psychoanalytic investigation and discussion for some time. Notably, in recent decades, the immigrant experience has received extensive attention of noted psychoanalysts whose scholarly work was informed by their own personal experience of migration (Grinberg & Grinberg, 1989; Akhtar, 1999). Their contributions have widened in great measure the scope of our knowledge about the psychological elements that derive from the migration experience. For their part, Gabbard and Ogden (2009) made a valuable contribution by discussing some of the important personal experiences that played a role in their maturation as psychoanalysts. Specifically, they point to the development of a voice of their own, drawing on their capacity to use what is unique to each of them as instrumental in their development of a psychoanalytic identity. In contrast, the role of migration and immigration in the formation of a psychoanalytic identity has received scant coverage in the psychoanalytic literature.

In this essay, I wish to contribute some of the salient elements of my own experience of migration and their role in my development as a psychoanalyst. I will attempt to do so all the while limiting my focus to autobiographical elements that my analysis has demonstrated to be relevant to this discussion. In using the term migration, I refer to the act of moving from one's country of origin to another. That may be the result of the individual's initiative, as in immigration, and it may not, as in the case of children who are brought over by their parents and are not involved in the decision-making process. In using both terms, I mean to highlight the nuances of agency in the individual's act of relocating.

Luggage

At thirty-one my soul was in an unhappy place. Two years before, I had ended psychotherapy sessions that had come to feel like their potential had been exhausted. I had started therapy in the context of an important life transition, and the support it provided had helped me cross chasms in my journey of self-development. However, more chasms lay ahead, and, to me, the therapeutic relationship never quite ceased to feel like a mismatch. Facing considerable internal obstacles, my anxieties and sense of vulnerability made it difficult to reach the next level. It did not help that my guide's demeanor in the room still left me with the sense, after several years of working together, that I was too much for him.

In the transference, that was a painfully familiar experience for me. I had often felt that way, albeit subconsciously, with my father when I was growing up; though his dangerous short temper made him a fearsome oedipal object, I was cunning in my efforts to rebel in order to preserve the little autonomy I had. My parents' overly anxious, authoritarian approach to parenting, combined with my guilt-ridden need to give them the ever-elusive experience of happiness, made it difficult for me to know who I was and what I wanted to be. My existence was defined by competing wishes to please, and oppose, the object.

However, by the age of thirty-one, I knew enough to recognize that my feeling that the treatment had reached its limit should get external confirmation. Having consulted with another professional as well as confidantes, I resolved with a heavy heart to end the treatment, complete with a proper termination phase. The satisfaction I felt in the knowledge that I had done what seemed best for me, did not, however, diminish my disappointment, and I despaired of finding the help I wanted. I continued on my journey, finding solace in the excitement I was feeling while pursuing a doctorate in clinical psychology. But in other ways, I still felt I was plodding along, weighed down by internal conflict. As I became better informed in psychodynamic theory, I began to envision the possibility of relief in the horizon. I concluded that my cure required psychoanalysis, which *had* to be conducted in Yiddish, because my problems were rooted in experiences that had been encoded in my mother tongue. (It is relevant to note, that Yiddish is *not* the language of my country of origin, but it is the language in which I communicated with my parents.) Also it had to be a seasoned individual, someone whom I could not outsmart. At a conscious level I was approaching my problem from a seemingly scientific perspective; I was less aware of the wish to find someone who would fill a certain role in my inner world.

From a different angle, at the threshold of my consciousness grew the recognition that the English language and my adopted American identity were possibly standing in the way of my continuing emotional integration. That process had formally begun two weeks after my sixteenth birthday, when I arrived in New York City with my family with little more than suitcases and the hope for a new beginning. I spoke no English, which only exacerbated my experience of being an alien in an unfamiliar culture. Emotionally unprepared for the transition, I found myself in a discomfiting personal space. I was an adolescent treading water, and the need to survive obviated fully dealing with the losses I had incurred, that is, the terra firma that friends and culture can provide. For my parents, on the other hand, the move was only the latest of a series of dislocations they had endured since their childhoods. They were inveterate survivors in many ways by then. Nonetheless, my mother was fully in touch with her emotions, especially her fears and the sadness of loss. The actual move and her experience during the months leading up to it, had caused her great distress, and she did not hide it. My father, who was the primary force behind the relocation, neither showed nor admitted any regrets. His stoic façade in the current situation was subsumed in his broader, complicated response to earlier trauma and ensuing unresolved bereavement. Yet, undoubtedly, this latest migration had taken its psychological toll on him, making him less emotionally available and rendering his defenses more brittle than ever.

For me, migration complicated the already considerable turmoil of my adolescence, as real losses compounded the normative intrapsychic object losses of this period. In the home front, I experienced my mother's unrelenting emotional distress as a threatening reminder of my own feelings of bereavement. Her effect on me was such that, as I tried to separate from my mother I also disowned the sadness in myself. On the other front, as my attempts at emancipation continued, my open conflict with my father expanded. As a result, the hostility between us effectively overshadowed my yearning for a warm paternal figure, and those feelings receded to the far reaches of my psyche. In the midst of this rather precarious emotional balance, I relied increasingly on the single resource that remained intact. Thus, my intellect, a precious source of self-esteem since earlier childhood, served me well. I took to learning English and losing my foreign accent with a vengeance. I absorbed language and culture by every means possible, all the while consciously distancing myself from my country of origin and its associations. The incorporation of the new language and culture, along with other intellectual activities, helped dilute the strength of loss and other troublesome emotions (Greenson, 1950).

However, to my unpleasant surprise, my parents soon came to see my incorporation of American culture as a threat. Unbeknownst to me, but like many immigrant parents, as I later learned, they had harbored all along fears of the very country to which they had opted to immigrate. On the surface, my parents reacted to my adolescent efforts to choose my own hairstyle and mode of dress. But on a deeper level, my assimilation to the American way of life concretized my parents' deeper conflicts around separation and loss stemming from their own traumatized beginnings in Eastern Europe. Now their message to me was confusing: I was to build a successful life here but without integrating into the surrounding culture, that is, remain an outsider, as they had been most of their lives. It felt like a double-bind: loyalty to them meant betraying myself, while to be true to my needs amounted to hurting my parents.

Individual truth vs. filial needs and duty

As a young adult, my deepening immersion in the field of psychology, although exciting to me and valued (at least in theory) by my family, became an additional source of intrapsychic conflict. My continuing efforts to understand my parents required closer scrutiny of family history and lore. I had to contend with issues that threatened to further disrupt the equilibrium of my family system. There were beliefs and attitudes that could not be challenged, and purported facts the veracity of which could not be questioned, let alone ascertained. I began to recognize that my family's attitudes *vis-à-vis* my interest in psychology were similar to their attitudes about American society: In theory it was an appealing and worthy endeavor, but in practice it posed dangers. The more I thought about things psychological, the more I saw that no one else in my family dared to go there. I found myself in familiar intrapsychic territory: questioning and exploration were to be undertaken cautiously, and kept strictly outside the family boundary.

I marched on, though as I worked toward completing my doctorate, I felt increasingly alienated from my family. By now, important aspects of my ethno-cultural identity seemed to be in flux, and I could not look to my family for guidance or understanding. Moreover, it seemed as though our paths had become inexorably divergent. As my existential angst grew, I began to contemplate again the need for help. I was aware that there were important issues that needed untangling, and recognized that nothing short of psychoanalysis would help. I also had the sense that the analytic method per se would be insufficient. I felt that the practitioner needed to possess knowledge that would make it possible to understand my psyche in the context of my particular ethnocultural background. Specifically, in what I believed at the time to be my scientific opinion, I needed someone who was fluent in my mother tongue. However, realistically I knew that it would not be easy to find someone fluent in Yiddish. By then the language had become largely a remnant of the past, known mostly by Eastern European immigrants of my parents' generation, and certain religious groups who were underrepresented in the psychoanalytic field. This and other reality based considerations conspired with my ambivalence and kept me from actively searching for the analyst I needed.

As fate would have it, I attended a talk given by a noted analyst. In itself this was not unusual; it was just one in the variety of scientific talks I attended with some regularity. I knew next to nothing about the man, his ideas or his work, yet there was something about his delivery that caught my attention. He struck me as a warm, engaging individual, and at a particular juncture, emphasizing a point he was making, he used a word in my mother tongue! I was flabbergasted; I felt as if I was in the presence of the disembodied analyst I had fantasied about. My visceral response was powerful enough that afterward the two close friends I had come with noticed it and honed in on it almost immediately. Without me saying much at all, they both exclaimed that the speaker was the analyst I needed. I felt vulnerable, almost embarrassed, feeling as though a private yearning had been exposed for all, including myself, to see. My friends told me about his psychoanalytic orientation and work, and reiterated their belief that it was worth pursuing. Soon after, though not without trepidation, I resolved to find out if I could make my fantasy a reality. Fortunately, I was eventually able to embark on my dream journey. Notably, though, I did not begin my formal analytic training until several years later, a fact that I believe worked in my favor. By that I mean that my immersion in the analytic process began free of institutional influences inherent in training that sometimes can detract from the personal analytic experience.

The analyst as "landsman"

Ripe as I was for analysis, it did not take long for a process to develop. Paternal transference themes unfolded, predictably negative initially, and followed their course. Although unconscious positive elements emerged only later in the analysis, I was conscious from the very beginning of a particular set of positive feelings about my analyst. In my case, the "unobjectionable positive transference" (Freud, 1912) included assumptions and attitudes deriving from my fantasies about my analyst's ethnic background.

In effect, his use of that word in my mother tongue during the lecture was enough to imbue my analyst with plentiful goodness. Through his use of a single Yiddish word my analyst came to embody the immigrant who embraces America and goes on to succeed without abandoning his parental Judaeo-European culture. I related to him much as my parents did to their contemporaries as I was growing up. That is, my parents tended to identify (and sometimes define) others according to their geographic origins, accents, and other ethnic criteria. Thus, the neighbors, for example, were "Varshever" (from Warsaw), others were "Galitzianer" (from the Polish Galicia region), and so on. My parents asserted, only half-seriously, I think, that each group had its own distinctive personality traits and the latter tended to influence at first blush my parents' attitudes toward these individuals. From earliest childhood I had been steeped in this familial and cultural milieu, a mentality and a way of life that was somehow lost—at least consciously—through migration and my own adolescent efforts to separate and individuate.

As a young adult in analysis, my conflicting and confusing fantasies notwithstanding, I did not need or want to discard my background in order to acculturate. But remnants of my unresolved adolescent opposition to overbearing parental demands made it seem as the only solution. This made it all the more difficult to acknowledge my own reservations about the new culture, and my fears of losing important aspects of myself in the process of acculturating.

It is worth noting that I found out much later in my treatment that in reality my analyst was not as fluent in Yiddish as my fantasy had conjured him up to be. By that point, however, I had changed in ways that no longer required him to be that object.

Only in retrospect did that phenomenon, and the question it raises, occur to me. That is, how did it turn out that, having found an analyst who fit my ideal, I did not then proceed to have the analysis in Yiddish? Clearly, had I attempted to do so I would have had to confront immediately the reality of my analyst's limited fluency. Instead, it would appear that the act of finding him satisfied an unconscious wish, and then I comfortably settled into an analysis in English. Any attempt to answer this question must of course include a focus on the unconscious determinants in my quest.

By the time I was considering analysis for myself, the role of language in the analysis of bilingual and multilingual individuals had already been the subject of discussion in the analytic community. At the conscious level, the idea that earliest experiences are inevitably encoded in the mother tongue and can best be accessed through it made sense to the scientist in me. I also knew, at a more affective level, that I saw a distinct beauty in the Yiddish language, especially in the realm of humor, and I delighted in the opportunities, scarce as they were, to share my appreciation for it with those who knew the language. Notably my mother was the more humorous and whimsical of my parents, and Yiddish embodied pleasurable and playful elements of my connection with her. These personal experiences coincided with the concept that "the mother tongue seems to represent the place where fantasy of complete mutuality resides" (Homayounpour & Movahedi, 2012, p. 124).

Thus, these two elements, the cognitive/scientific and the affective, represented my transferential wish to be *understood* by the maternal object. However, as Homayounpour and Movahedi point out, "paradise seems to be paved with anxiety" (ibid., p. 125) In their study, these authors found that bilingual and multilingual analysands reported feeling that analysis in their mother tongue would be more anxiety provoking. For the bliss of complete mutuality carries the danger of intrusion, punishment and shame in relation to the internal object. Their study also revealed that along with the desperate wish to be understood, there was a strong wish to hide through the use of the foreign language. In part, the need to hide may represent unconscious fantasies involving a wish to avoid narcissistic injury resulting from exposure of vulnerability in relation to the object (Rizzuto, 1991). It can also be seen as establishing a boundary between the weak self and the overwhelming maternal object. My own handling of the analytic experience can be understood as a compromise formation involving the wish for complete mutuality with, and the fear of, the omnipotent maternal object.

Learning psychoanalysis and joining the training institute

The buoyant feelings that accompanied me following the termination of my treatment began to fade after the initial years. Gradually I became aware of feelings of disappointment and disillusionment in the analytic method. During this period of time, the cumulative effect of significant personal losses had taken its toll, leaving me feeling battered and vulnerable. That time was also marked by professional growth, and greater involvement with other, more senior analysts, on a personal level. Ironically, this set of experiences slowly gave rise to other discomfiting feelings in me. These feelings were characterized by a heightened awareness that professionally esteemed figures could also be considerably flawed as individuals. For a while, it seemed as though everywhere I turned I was struck by evidence that shook my confidence in what psychoanalysis, as a therapy, actually accomplishes. My disappointment in my own inability to overcome certain obstacles, and a similar focus on others' personal struggles, gave rise to a deep sense of hopelessness in the therapeutic power of the analytic method. I began to feel that psychoanalysis was the source of much that was positive and pleasurable, but in the end its value as a healing experience was questionable. As I wrestled with these troubling feelings and doubts, I dared to share them only with those to whom I felt closest. Though I knew I was not alone, it was unclear to me to what extent others shared these concerns. I wondered if, as in religious practice, a substantial gap could exist between what one does in a house of worship and how one behaves in one's private life.

Frustratingly unaware of, and unable to articulate the deeper nature of my conflictual feelings, my mind kept returning to a theme that emerged in my consciousness early in my analytic training: the concern that more than anything else psychoanalysis is a cult. At those early stages of my analytic education, I had the sense that some faculty at my institute perceived me as capable enough, but also a bit of a skeptic. Naturally, that sense only reinforced in me the need to question, even as I was progressing in my training. I was comfortable in my effort to be intellectually honest, satisfied that I was motivated by a scientific ideal. As I mused about those early years, I recalled that at the time, my zeal to question seemed to neutralize my own analyst's attempts to bring to light my unacknowledged wish to idealize psychoanalysis and to regard it as the key to deciphering life's riddles and dilemmas.

So it was with a great deal of effort that I began to unearth elements of my youth that had remained hidden from my own view but very much alive in my struggles. As I grew more capable of fully integrating disowned identifications with aspects of my father, I began to recall facts about his life. As a youth growing up in Eastern Europe around the time of the Russian Revolution, my father had rebelled against his religious upbringing through his active membership in the Communist party. Like many in his time, he felt drawn to utopian Communist ideals as answers and solutions to life's misfortunes and pain. Years later, as a young adult, he became bitterly disappointed when the realities of life in the Soviet Union betrayed the ideals he had embraced. Later still, in midlife, my father returned to religion and became a rather rigid, if not strict, follower of religious ritual. But again, ideology did not work for him, as his intrapsychic conflicts repeatedly led him to become embroiled in synagogue politics, which he solved by repeatedly switching congregations. Witnessing my father's behavior vis-à-vis religion through the prism of my early adolescence, I felt embarrassment, if not contempt. These feelings effectively obscured my earlier childhood identifications with him and his reliance on ideological solutions to life's challenges and uncertainties. Later, my response to migration conspired in its own way against the integration of these experiences.

Recognition of these dynamics helped me better understand my varied reactions to the psychoanalytic institute where I trained. On a larger level, problematic elements in institutional dynamics have been identified and expertly explicated elsewhere (Kirsner, 2009; Kernberg, 2000). At a personal level, it was helpful to realize how my identification with my father's attitudes and ways of being in these contexts contributed to my own, over-determined dissatisfaction with institute politics.

Concluding thoughts

My effort to understand continues, as it must. The ideal of searching for truth through psychoanalysis comes face to face first with one's family of origin and later one's family of psychoanalytic supervisors, teachers, and colleagues. The wish to strive towards the above ideal inevitably forces us as clinicians to confront the hard questions: what *is* psychoanalysis? As an instrument of healing, what does it really do? Does it live up to its reputed potential?

How can we define psychoanalytic training? Is it like formal religious training? Must one have faith in psychoanalysis in order to successfully learn and practice it? Can a psychoanalyst-in-training openly question its value, or the opinion of elders, without incurring criticism? As is the case with religious practice, the public persona of papers, presentations, and teaching is sometimes at odds with one's private existence. Save for the unethical, does that discrepancy compromise the method?

I have tried to illustrate how my individual version of that effort is best seen in the light of intrapsychic conflict embedded in a background of ethnicity and migration. How does a multi-ethnic background influence my definition of psychoanalysis, and the definition of how it works and doesn't work? Why was the phenomenon of ethnicity and culture as shaping the individual's worldview hardly mentioned in the curriculum of my training?

I conclude with the thought that my training was but a beginning foray into the field, a necessary introduction to a methodology currently available and how to use it. Does methodology define reality, or is it merely a vehicle to help us explore it? As in other endeavors, it is human to want to believe that we know. But knowledge includes the recognition of what we don't know. The mark of progress is finding that the instrumentation we initially utilized was rudimentary, and in need of continuing refinement. Thus what I have come to value most about psychoanalysis is its inherent mandate to keep an open mind, and to question, to be ever mindful of the difference between two forms of the wish to know. One is driven by the recognition that we don't know enough; the other is fueled by the wish to feel that one knows and to experience the sense of security it generates. It is the second form that all too often misleads us to believe that phenomena observed at the individual level are also universal truths.

References

Akhtar, S. (1999). *Immigration and Identity*. Northvale, NJ: Jason Aronson.

Freud, S. (1912). *The Dynamics of Transference. S. E., 12*: 97–108.

Gabbard, G. O. & Ogden, T. H. (2009). On becoming a psychoanalyst. *The International Journal of Psychoanalysis, 90*: 311–327.

Greenson, R. (1950). The mother tongue and the mother. *The International Journal of Psychoanalysis, 31*: 18–23.

Grinberg, L. & Grinberg, R. (1989). *Psychoanalytic perspectives on migration and exile*. New Haven, CT: Yale University Press.

Homayounpour, G. & Movahedi, S. (2012). Transferential discourse in the language of the (m)other. *Canadian Journal of Psychoanalysis, 20*: 114–143.

Kernberg, O. (2000). A concerned critique of psychoanalytic education. *The International Journal of Psychoanalysis, 81*: 97–120.

Kirsner, D. (2009). *Unfree Associations: Inside Psychoanalytic Institutes*. Lanham, MD: Jason Aronson.

Rizzuto, A. (1991). Shame in psychoanalysis: The function of unconscious fantasies. *The International Journal of Psychoanalysis, 72*: 297–312.

CHAPTER THREE

A tale of two cities

Amar Ghorpade

… his sky seems to ache with the pain of countless meetings and partings, and a longing pervades this spring breeze, the longing that is full of the whisper of ages without beginning.

—Rabindranath Tagore,
Lover's Gifts XXXIX: There Is a Looker-On

India

The first tale is from Pune, a city near Bombay, in India. I was sixteen years old, and I shared a room with my cousin in his house. We went to the same college and would often commute on bicycles. The dating scenes in those days were prototypes of scenes from Bollywood movies, where the hero pursues the heroine and the heroine plays hard to get. My cousin developed an affliction for a girl he did not know and it was unclear what sparked the interest. It could have been something as trivial as an unintended glance by the girl. Regardless, the pursuit began. I was drafted to find out details such as her name, where she lived, her family background, and so on. I did my due diligence in the hope that one day I would be paid back in kind. Once we had her demographic data, our next mission was to follow her and her friends on a bicycle, even though it meant travelling an additional five miles from home to college. She would be riding her bicycle with her group of friends and we would be following them with our group of friends. This scenario was least likely to raise suspicion, as it was not clear if anybody was being followed. Thanks, to the extra ten miles of biking every day, my mother complained that I had started eating more, while my cricket coach was happy that my legs were getting stronger. After several weeks of such pursuit, the emotions intensified, unfortunately only on my cousin's part as the girl was totally unaware that she had a Romeo.

Such unilateral love affairs are not uncommon in Bollywood movies even to this day. Soon I had a room-mate who was growing a beard and writing poetry and singing romantic Bollywood movie songs. One fine day he asked me to approach her to ask if she would be interested in going out with him. I gladly obliged as I was getting tired of listening to the same songs over and over. The next day in college, I approached her and introduced myself to her and asked her if she would be interested in going out with my cousin. Not surprisingly she looked at me confused and asked me, which one of the boys standing in the hallway was my cousin. I pointed to a tall, lanky boy with a beard. She glanced at him and said to me that she did not even know him. How could she go out with a stranger? Her logic made sense to me and I conveyed the message to my cousin. This probably threw him into a depression, yet intensified his feelings more. He could not stop thinking about her and we watched the same romantic movie over several times. I knew every dialogue in the movie, every scene, and where it was shot. Our bicycle pursuits continued and the difference this time around was that she was aware! However since it was a group of boys following a group of girls on a bicycle on their way to college, it hardly raised suspicion. After several weeks I obliged my cousin by approaching her again and this time it was a flat "No, I don't want to go out with your cousin." I hoped that this would end the saga and I would go back to my regular route to college. To my dismay, the bicycle pursuit continued and so did the poetry and romantic songs. At no point was there a direct conversation between the girl and my cousin.

Eventually we both graduated college and much to my relief, I was accepted into a medical school and had to move to live on the medical school premises. Several months in to medical school, I had forgotten the whole saga until one day my cousin showed up at my hostel. I was delighted to see him, but his grown beard still irked me and brought back memories of those bicycle pursuits. Over dinner my cousin said to me that he had found out that the girl's older sister was in medical school with me. He asked me if I could speak to her and tell her to put in a good word for him and convince her sister to go out with him. As awkward as it sounded, I agreed to do it to get him off my back and once again found myself making introductions to a total stranger with a proposition for her sister. She seemed bewildered, but with a bit of convincing agreed. The answer was a resounding "No." I hoped that this would put an end to it. Unfortunately, a few months later, my cousin paid me another visit, this time with an even more absurd proposition. He asked to meet her parents and convince them that he was a good guy. He also argued that since I was a doctor in the making, I had some credibility and would not be thrown out of their house. I obliged and a week later was ringing the doorbell of a total stranger. I introduced myself and fortunately, her father recognized me since I was in medical school with his other daughter. I presented my case and he burst into laughter and said that the matter was entirely up to his daughter.

Since then, thirty years have passed. Today my cousin is married to that girl and they have two beautiful children.

New York, New York

The second tale is from New York City, United States. One of my colleagues at Columbia University referred to me a patient he had seen a few times. The patient was a physician in residency training and was from Pakistan. He was born into a wealthy family in Pakistan and both his parents were physicians who had started a hospital in Pakistan. Their dream was to have their son train in the United States and return to Pakistan to enrich their practice. The patient was tall, lanky, and reminded me of my cousin and his tale. He took the subway to work every day and as many passengers do, would carry a novel with him to read. One day, he was reading a novel that was on the *New York Times* bestseller list and caught the attention of a Caucasian woman. She approached him and asked him if he liked the novel and what it was about. This led to a small talk and exchange of minor personal details, which again is not an uncommon occurrence for people who travel on the subway in New York City. A few days later, the same woman accosted him and asked him if he had finished the novel. A brief conversation followed after which they exchanged more personal details.

This triggered off the "unilateral Romeo" in my patient. He started writing poetry and listening to romantic songs. The days that he did not see her on the subway, he would long and pine for her and on the days that he met her he would be joyous and animated. This continued for a few weeks and by this time they knew where each other lived. He would get on to the downtown subway at Seventy-Second Street and she would get on to the subway at Ninety-Sixth Street. After not seeing her for a few days he decided to take the uptown subway to Ninety-Sixth Street and travel downtown with her. He was excited to see her at the Ninety-Sixth Street station and he approached her as soon as he got on the train. They had another conversation and towards the end of the conversation the woman realized that he had gotten on to the subway at Ninety-Sixth Street instead of his usual Seventy-Second Street. She asked him about it and he replied that he had not seen her for a few days and wanted to spend more time with her. This alarmed the woman and she showed her displeasure by not talking to him the next day they met on the subway. He made several attempts to initiate a conversation or broker a meeting with her and she declined his offer. One day he met her at a supermarket on Ninety-Sixth Street and it was unclear if he had deliberately travelled uptown, when in fact, it was a specialty supermarket that was not available in his neighborhood. Following that incident the woman warned him and threatened to inform the police if he continued to follow her. A few days later, police arrived at his apartment and served him an order of protection. At this point my patient became depressed and was seen by a psychiatrist. The psychiatrist, after listening to the story and his obsessive preoccupation with the woman suggested a trial of a small dose of Zyprexa. This infuriated my patient and he sought consultation with my colleague who then referred him to me. I saw him for several months essentially helping him mourn the loss and he eventually finished his fellowship and moved back to Pakistan.

I also briefly treated a Japanese woman, who was a veterinarian by profession. She got romantically involved with her Caucasian colleague and the relationship lasted several months. Eventually her colleague decided to end the relationship and my patient became depressed. She struggled with the depression for several months before she saw me. By the time I saw her, her colleague had warned her that she would get an order of protection against her if she did not stop contacting her. Her romantic story also suggested a unilateral love story that progressed rapidly for my patient, but not so for her partner. This lack of synchronicity led her partner to be turned off and she saw my patient as needy and clingy. After a few months of mourning my patient returned to her usual self and was able to move on.

A few more tales

I had a similar experience with a Spanish artist, who after briefly dating a Caucasian woman got enamored by her and began writing poetry and making paintings of her. Under different circumstances, this gesture could have been perceived as very romantic, but in his case was perceived as a clingy, needy, and not so desirable a quality. The relationship ended thereafter, and he pursued the woman relentlessly and eventually gave up when she threatened to inform the police.

I also happened to treat a Middle Eastern physician who became romantically involved with a colleague who was Middle Eastern as well, but was born in the United States. He was referred to me by his program director because his partner complained about his "stalking" behavior (sending frequent text messages, staying in the hospital while she was on call, changing his rotations to match hers etc.). He became depressed and could not stop thinking about her. He struggled with his urges to text her and at times threw his phone out of his apartment window into the courtyard only to retrieve it later when his urge to text her had passed. His depression worsened and I had to put him on antidepressants. He responded well and graduated from his program and moved to another hospital for a fellowship. I met him at a conference a few years later and to my surprise he informed me that he had married the same woman who had accused him of stalking and they had a child together.

What I find interesting in these tales is that the same behavior in one culture is considered romantic, yet in another culture, considered stalking. Stalking is defined by the United States Department of Justice as a "pattern of repeated and unwanted attention, harassment, contact, or any other course of conduct directed at a specific person that would cause a reasonable person to feel fear" (Stalking Resource Center, January 2014). For example, sending flowers, writing love notes, and waiting for someone outside her place of work are actions that, on their own, are not criminal. When these actions are coupled with intent to instill fear or injury, however, they may constitute a pattern of behavior that is illegal. A very important aspect of the definition is the "intent to instill fear or injury." In none of the cases described above was there that intent, and whenever the Romeo's described above became aware that the person they loved was afraid of them, they stopped the pursuit. Even though they were not stalkers, they were perceived as such because of the fear it caused.

I will describe a couple of other cases that will help illustrate the difference. I practiced as a psychiatrist in India prior to my arrival in the United States. I was treating a male patient who was referred to me for depressive symptoms and also had borderline personality features. He was dysthymic for the most part and would engage various friends during times of crisis as the Indian social structure provided him with an abundance of social contact. Therefore, he always had a listening ear. Despite his struggles with depression and his reluctance to take medications, he managed to do well on the GRE (Graduate Record Exam) and was accepted with a fellowship into a university in the United States. I came to the United States shortly after him to pursue my PhD in Psychobiology. One evening I had a message on my answering machine accusing me of having an affair with his girlfriend who was in India and I met only once. The message went on and after several profanities it said, "I am going to put a bullet through your head." I did not recognize the voice and dismissed the message as a prank. A few days later there was another message in the same voice saying I know where you live and I am going to get you. I ignored that message as well, but it got me thinking, and to humor myself I went through a list of my enemies that would want to see me dead. Several weeks passed and one evening my phone rang and I picked it up. There was a long pause at the other end and it was followed by a series of accusations and profanities in Hindi and ended in, "I am going to put a bullet through your head." After the initial shock, I was able to compose myself and recognized his voice. The phone calls continued and I eventually got in touch with his graduate studies advisor who informed me that he had been placed on probation because he had been stalking a woman on campus and the police were involved on several occasions. A few months later he was deported back to India. Several years later I found out from a colleague in India that he had completed his graduate studies in India and had gotten married.

Gostin (2002) summarized another case that made history in the United States, the Tarasoff case. Prosenjit Poddar was a student from India who came to the University of California at Berkeley as a graduate student in the fall of 1968. He met Tatiana Tarasoff at a dancing class. They saw each other weekly and on New Year's Eve she kissed Poddar. He interpreted the act to be recognition of the existence of a serious relationship. Tarasoff, who upon learning of his feelings, told him that she was involved with other men and otherwise indicated that she was not interested in entering into an intimate relationship with him. After this rebuff, Poddar became depressed and neglected his appearance, his studies, and his health. He remained by himself, speaking disjointedly and often weeping. This condition persisted with steady deterioration. Poddar had occasional meetings with Tarasoff during this period and tape-recorded their various conversations to try to find out why she did not love him. Later, Tarasoff went to South America and after her departure Poddar began to improve and at the suggestion of a friend sought psychological help.

Dr. Lawrence Moore, a psychologist at UC Berkeley's Cowell Memorial Hospital, treated him. Poddar confided his intent to kill Tarasoff and Dr. Moore requested that the campus police detain Poddar, writing that, in his opinion, Poddar was suffering from acute paranoid schizophrenia. The psychologist recommended that the defendant be civilly committed as a dangerous person. Poddar was detained, but shortly thereafter released, as he appeared rational. Poddar then befriended Tarasoff's brother, even moving in with him. Several months later, on 27 October 1969, Poddar carried out the plan he had confided to his psychologist, stabbing and killing Tarasoff. Tarasoff's parents then sued Moore and various other employees of the University. Poddar was subsequently convicted of second degree murder, but the conviction was later appealed and overturned on the grounds that the jury was inadequately instructed. A second trial was not held, and Poddar was released on the condition that he would return to India. He agreed to leave the country in order to avoid being retried. He returned to India, where he is rumored to be married. What makes the above two cases, true cases of stalking, is that Prosenjit Poddar and my former patient, continued to pursue the women despite the awareness that the women were scared, and they exhibited obvious psychopathology which was probably unearthed by the stress of immigration and other aggravating factors. It is worth noting that the patients from Eastern cultures eventually married and in the case of my cousin and the Middle Eastern physician, they were married to the women they were stalking. If we exclude the latter two cases with obvious psychopathology, how can one understand the former patients that I described? Namely, how can one understand the difference in the style of romance between Western and Eastern culture? And does this style of romance ever acculturate? How does one romantically be Roman when in Rome? Having been trained in neuroscience, I looked for answers in neurobiology.

Neurobiology of stalking

The literature on stalking and its neurobiological underpinnings is exhaustive. For the purpose of the present discussion, I will summarize the relevant findings. There are several phenomena that are common to stalking and romantic love, for example, obsessively thinking about the person, wanting to be with the person at all times, repeatedly texting or calling the person, and so on. Romantic love is one of the three primary brain systems that evolved in avian and mammalian species to direct reproduction. The sex drive (testosterone) evolved to motivate individuals to seek a range of mating partners; attraction (dopamine) evolved to motivate individuals to prefer and pursue specific partners; and attachment (oxytocin) evolved to motivate individuals to remain together long enough to complete species-specific parenting duties (Fisher, Aron & Brown, 2006). These three behavioral repertoires appear to be based on brain systems that are largely distinct yet interrelated, and they interact in specific ways to orchestrate reproduction, using both hormones and monoamines. Romantic attraction in humans and its antecedent in other mammalian species play a primary role: this neural mechanism motivates individuals to focus their courtship energy on specific others, thereby conserving valuable time and metabolic energy, and facilitating mate choice. Meloy and Fisher (2005) discuss data from functional magnetic resonance imaging (fMRI) studies of romantic love which suggest that these forms of stalking may be associated with heightened activity of sub cortical dopaminergic pathways of the "Reward System" of the brain, perhaps in combination with low activity of central serotonin. The authors propose that this set of neural correlates may contribute to the stalker's focused attention, increased energy, following behaviors, obsessive thinking about and impulsivity directed toward the victim. The heightened activity of sub cortical dopaminergic pathways of the "Reward System" of the brain seems to be common to stalkers and people in love. Hence, it would be difficult to distinguish between a stalker and a person in love based on fMRI studies alone.

However, Meloy and Fisher (2005) also provide empirical support for an insecure form of attachment during childhood for stalkers. In this vein, attachment is believed to be driven by the hormone oxytocin, also known as the cuddle hormone. The role of oxytocin in attachment has been studied extensively. Infant cues, such as smiling or crying facial expressions, are powerful motivators of human maternal behavior, activating dopamine-associated brain reward circuits. Strathearn, Fonagy, Amico, and Montague (2009), examined thirty first-time mothers to test whether differences in attachment, based on the Adult Attachment Interview (AAI), were related to brain-reward and peripheral oxytocin response to infant cues (abstract). On viewing their own infant's smiling and crying faces during functional MRI scanning, mothers with secure attachment showed greater activation of brain reward regions, including the ventral striatum, and the oxytocin-associated hypothalamic/pituitary region (Strathearn, Fonagy, Amico & Montague, 2009). Peripheral oxytocin response to infant contact at seven months was also significantly higher in secure mothers, and was positively correlated with brain activation in both regions. Insecure/dismissing mothers, which may be associated with emotional neglect, showed reduced activation of the mesocorticolimbic dopamine reward system in response to infant face cues, as well as decreased peripheral oxytocin response to mother–infant contact (Strathearn, 2011). "Administration of intranasal oxytocin … may reverse some of these neurological differences, and potentially augment psychosocial and behavioral interventions for maternal neglect" (Strathearn, 2011, p. 1054). These results suggest that individual differences in maternal attachment may be linked with development of the dopaminergic and oxytocinergic neuroendocrine systems (Strathearn, 2011). Since, attachment style may help differentiate a stalker from a person in love, I will briefly review the literature on attachment theory.

Attachment theory

First described by John Bowlby during World War Two, attachment theory has received enormous amount of research attention. Bowlby saw attachment as being crucial to a child's personality development and to the development of healthy ways of relating to others. In addition, the research suggests that attachment security predicts other aspects of a child's development such as social competence, or problem solving (Sroufe, Egeland, Kreutzer, 1990). Mary Ainsworth's work is seminal in understanding the currently accepted distinctive patterns of different attachment relationships. Her use of the so-called "strange situation" experiments allowed classification of observable attachment patterns (Ainsworth & Wittig, 1969; Ainsworth, Bell & Stayton, 1971). The procedure, known as the "Strange Situation" was conducted by observing the behavior of the infant in a series of seven three-minute episodes, as follows:

1. Parent and infant alone
2. Stranger joins parent and infant
3. Parent leaves infant and stranger alone
4. Parent returns and stranger leaves
5. Parent leaves; infant left completely alone
6. Stranger returns
7. Parent returns and stranger leaves.

Four categories of behaviors are measured and observed: (1) separation anxiety: the unease the infant shows when left by the caregiver, (2) the infant's willingness to explore, (3) stranger anxiety: the infant's response to the presence of a stranger, and (4) reunion behavior: the way the caregiver was greeted on return (Ainsworth & Bell, 1970). The observer notes the behavior displayed and scores the behavior for intensity on a scale from one to seven. The measures emphasized the child's autonomy, individuation, and exploration that in turn depended on the mother's sensitivity. Ainsworth (1970) identified three main attachment styles: secure, insecure avoidant, and insecure ambivalent. She concluded that these attachment styles were the result of early interactions with the mother. A fourth attachment style known as disorganized was later identified (Main & Solomon, 1990). Since this landmark formulation by Ainsworth, many authors have questioned the applicability of the strange situation experiment and the classification of attachment styles, across cultures. Heidi Keller (2013) has done extensive work and proposed to reconceptualize attachment theory as a culture-sensitive framework. She argues that attachment theory has "expanded the framework with respect to the intergenerational transmission and the organizational nature of attachment, relations with psychopathology and clinical applications, and its psychophysiological foundation" (Keller, 2013, p. 175). She also argues that:

> assumptions of monotropy, the conception of stranger anxiety, as well as the definition of attachment in mainstream attachment research are in line with the conception of psychological autonomy, adaptive for Western middle-class, but deviate from the cultural values of many non-Western and mainly rural ecosocial environments. (Keller, 2013, p. 175).

In 2000, Rothbaum, Pott, Azuma, Miyake, and Weisz conducted studies to examine the universal qualities (or lack thereof) of attachment theory (Keller, 2013, p. 179). They used the nation of Japan as their study base to contrast the Western cultural values that are often used to understand the premise of attachment theory (Keller, 2013, p. 181). Rothbaum found significant cultural differences between the Japanese and Western caregiver/child relationships. Generally, a tension was maintained between a Japanese mother trying to maintain a secure environment for their child, while Western mother's tended to facilitate exploration (Akiyama, Antonucci & Campbell, 2008). This is why the concept of the "secure base" is fundamentally Western in nature. A base that one has in order to achieve that independence and exploration espoused in Western families. Therefore, it is important to realize cultural differences regarding attachment and upbringing. This particular point elucidates the themes found throughout many of my case illustrations and a few more to follow.

Clinicians treating patients from various cultures have described the differences in the inner workings of the mind of patients from non-western cultures. Salman Akhtar (1999) in his book, *Immigration and Identity* has described Indian patients with multiple transferences which included feelings towards uncles, aunts, teachers, and other caregivers and the challenge for the analyst is to be comfortable with the multiple roles assigned to him in contrast to the mother and father transferences which are characteristic of nuclear, western families. He also emphasized the concept of Indian Standard Time, where time was more fluid. This is in striking contrast to the Western concept of time and punctuality. Irregularities around time and, particularly lateness, are the bread and butter of psychoanalysis today. Lateness, with disregard for the analysts' time, is often seen as a resistance and a narcissistic defense, and it very well might be. However, interpreting it in a cultural context one might not see as a resistance, but a longing on part of the patient for the analyst to co-identify with the patients culture. I have often not commented on lateness with Indian patients and they have, on more occasions than not, accused me of being non-analytic. That, then, has become all grist for the mill.

The clinician's attachment style

Does the clinician's attachment style impact his or her clinical work? I will elaborate on this topic by beginning with two case presentations.

During my residency in psychiatry in India, I treated a patient with bipolar disorder. He was a bus driver by profession and his family treated his previous episodes by moving him to the farm that was several miles from any paved roads. However, during his current manic episodes he managed to walk several miles and hitch hike, travelling to several towns. Eventually, he was located by the family and brought to the hospital. He was floridly manic when he was hospitalized.

In India it is common practice for a family member to stay with the patient while the patient is in the hospital. This particular family had limited resources and the patient's wife had informed me that she could not stay beyond five days. With the most aggressive psychopharmacology, I knew the patient would not be stable enough for discharge in five days. I decided to use ECT (electroconvulsive therapy) and the patient received three consecutive ECT treatments. Some of his manic symptoms were controlled and I started him on Lithium. I was reluctant to discharge him, but his family had no more resources left. I shared my room with a friend who was doing his residency in orthopedic surgery and I shared this dilemma with him. After listening to the story he suggested that we put the patient in hard casts below the knee (as he was an orthopedic surgeon). The idea being that, it would not let him wander far enough to reach a paved road and hitch hike. I presented this option to the family, not as a psychiatric treatment, but as a practical intervention that might work. The family agreed and despite the patient's protests we put him in below the knee casts and he was discharged to his farm. The family would give him his morning medications and leave for work and when they returned in the evening they would find him within a half mile radius from the farm. They would bring him back home and give him the evening medications. Several months later, the patient came with his wife for a follow-up visit. He was euthymic and had started working again. I would not dare make such an intervention in the United States, but back in India I did not have any second thoughts. In this example there was no conflict between what the family wanted and what I wanted to achieve. The boundary between us was fluid and I felt a part of the family. That aspect of me as a clinician has not changed.

The second patient is a physician that I am treating in the United States. He has been married for the past thirty years and has two adult children. His wife is a physician of Indian origin as well. Per current presentation, they have not had sex for the last seven years of their marriage. My patient admitted to an ongoing sexual relationship with a Caucasian colleague during this period. Rather than the obvious split between the sex object and the love object, I instead will focus on his ambivalently held maternal image. For several weeks I had not said much and had listened to him. In one session I felt particularly distracted and started scribbling down what he was saying and reading it over as he continued. In most of these sessions he described two entirely different views of his wife in the same breath. My patient and I both had been unaware of this contradiction. The contradiction did not arouse anxiety or awareness until I read it on a piece of paper. I seemed quite comfortable with his ambivalent description of his wife and, when I reviewed my notes, this included descriptions of his mother. When I pointed it out to him, he said, "What are you going to do, women have many faces and you have to accept them all." There was no conflict, but I felt like I was on a witch hunt. I also realized, in hindsight, that he had picked me as an analyst because I was Indian and in the first session was pleasantly surprised that my office looked anything but Indian. However, later in the same session he jokingly said that I could have afforded better furniture (indicating his belief that Indians are cheap). I was an ambivalently held figure from the first session or probably from the time he picked me as an analyst. I have found that dyadic conflicts the core conflicts in Indian patients in contrast to their Western counterparts.

Since the time that Bose wrote to Freud stating that castration anxiety in Indian men is replaced by a desire to be a woman, several Indian analysts have described mainly dyadic conflicts in Indian patients. Could this be the result of a prolonged exposure to the mother and the peripheral presence of the father in Indian culture as Stanley Kurtz (1992) suggests? Or could it be a manifestation of the attachment style in Indians. My patients often comment that I treat them like family. It is true that as a psychiatrist and a psychoanalyst, I know more about their life than many of their family members. Is this countertransference, over-identification with the patient or me being true to my "self"? All my patients have my cell phone number and I rarely get calls. Patients find it very endearing. The calls I get do not last longer than thirty to forty-five seconds if that, and ten to fifteen of those seconds are spent by the patient apologizing for making the call. I have found that because of my "perceived availability," many estranged families have come together. Taking phone calls on my cell phone from patients is not unique to me. It is one of the main tenants of dialectical behavior therapy for borderline patients (Linehan & Heard, 1992). Not surprisingly, one of the main pillars of dialectical behavior therapy is the Eastern concept of mindfulness and connectedness. In my practice, the phone call becomes, again, grist for the mill. Throughout residency training and psychoanalytic training in the United States I learned and read about the perils of not maintaining boundaries. But I never questioned the notion of boundaries and the cultural variations within boundaries. The Western concept of boundaries, to me, is very clearly defined and somewhat rigid. For a self that is defined by its relationship to the other it is impossible to disregard the other.

> A human being is a part of the whole called by us "Universe," a part limited in time and space. He experiences himself, his thoughts and feelings as something separated from the rest—a kind of optical delusion of his consciousness. The striving to free oneself from this delusion is in the one issue of true religion. Not to nourish the delusion but to try to overcome it is the way to reach the attainable measure of peace of mind. (Einstein, 1950, Letter of Condolence to Dr. Robert Marcus, World Jewish Congress)

References

Akhtar, S. (1999). *Immigration and Identity: Turmoil, Treatment, and Transformation*. New York, NY: Jason Aronson.

Akiyama, H., Antonucci, T. C. & Campbell, R. (2008). Exchange and reciprocity among two generations of Japanese and American women. In: J. Sokolovsky (Ed.), *The Cultural Context of Aging: Worldwide Perspectives, Third Edition*. Westport, CT: Greenwood Publishing Group.

Ainsworth, M. D. & Bell, S. M. (1970). Attachment, exploration, and separation: illustrated by the behavior of one-year-olds in a strange situation. *Child Development, 41*: 49–67.

Ainsworth, M. D., Bell, S. M. & Stayton, D. J. (1971). Individual differences in strange-situation behaviour of one-year-olds. In: H. R. Schaffer (Ed.), *The Origins of Human Social Relations* (pp. 17–58). London and New York: Academic Press.

Ainsworth, M. D. S. & Wittig, B. A. (1969). Attachment and exploratory behavior of one-year-olds in a strange situation. In: B. M. Foss (Ed.), *Determinants of Infant Behavior* (Volume 4, pp. 111–136). London: Methuen.

Fisher, H. E., Aron, A. & Brown, L. L. (2006). Philosophical transactions of the Royal Society of London. *Series B, Biological Sciences, 361* (1476): 2173–2186.

Gostin, L. O. (2002). Tarasoff v. Regents of the University of California. In: *Surveillance and Public Health Research: Privacy and the "Right to Know" (Chapter Ten)*. Retrieved from https://owl.english.purdue.edu/owl/resource/560/10/ last accessed 16 November 2014.

Keller, H. (2013). Attachment and culture. *Journal of Cross-Cultural Psychology, 44* (2): 175–194.

Kurtz, S. N. (1992). *All Mothers are One: Hindu India and the Cultural Reshaping of Psychoanalysis*. New York, NY: Columbia University Press.

Linehan, M. & Heard, H. L. (1992). Dialectical behavior therapy for borderline personality disorder. In: J. F. Clarkin, E. Marziali & H. Munroe-Blum (Eds.), *Borderline Personality Disorder: Clinical and Empirical Perspectives*. The Guilford Personality Disorders Series (pp. 248–267). New York, NY: Guilford Press.

Main, M. & Solomon, J. (1990). Procedures for identifying infants as disorganized/disoriented during the Ainsworth Strange Situation. In: M. T. Greenberg, D. Cicchetti & E. M. Cummings (Eds.), *Attachment in the Preschool Years* (pp. 121–160). Chicago, IL: University of Chicago Press.

Meloy J. M. & Fisher, H. (2005). Some thoughts on the neurobiology of stalking. *Journal of Forensic Science, 50* (6): 1–9. Paper ID: JFS2004508.

Sroufe, L. A., Egeland, B. & Kreutzer, T. (1990). The fate of early experience following developmental change: Longitudinal approaches to individual adaptation in childhood. *Child Development, 61*: 1363–1373.

Stalking Resource Center. (2014). *National Center For Victims of Crime.* www.victimsofcrime.org/our-programs/stalking-resource-center (Last accessed January 2014).

Strathearn, L. (2011). The parental brain. *Journal of Neuroendocrinology, 23* (11): 1054–1065.

Strathearn, L., Fonagy, P., Amico, J. & Montague, P. R. (2009). Adult attachment predicts maternal brain and oxytocin response to infant cues. *Neuropsychopharmacology, 34* (13): 2655–2666.

CHAPTER FOUR

Navigating our cultural identifications: individual, social, and political struggle in the therapy room

Fatima El-Jamil

> By day I praised you
> and never knew it.
> By night I stayed with you
> and never knew it.
> I always thought that
> I was me—but no,
> I was you
> and never knew it.
>
> —*Rumi*

The journey I embarked on to understand the emergence of my analytic identity has become closely intertwined with the personal. The patients through whom I developed and grew and my journey through the resistance and acceptance of my own therapy process all informed my clinical identity. The struggles of immigration, assimilation, and reintegration back into my home country, helped to mold this identity as well. Thus, I share with you my personal stories of immigration, doubt and hesitation, and finally my crossings within and between my own realities in order to affirm and appreciate my patient's internal cultural frame and worldview.

Being an Arab in today's world is wrought with layers of stereotype, fear, and defamation, for which even I struggle to discern between the media's sensationalism and reality. When a clinician's primary aim is to alleviate the suffering and distress of an individual, and you for them embody that terror, your words remain of questionable and even dangerous intent. That was my predicament at the beginning of my internship year in New York City, staring at the television screen propped against the ceiling in the recreation room of the inpatient unit, witnessing the 9/11 attacks. I was looking up, immobilized, as panic, psychotic disintegration, and cries surrounded me. I stood and prayed that the source of this terror not be *Arab*. I turned to my analytic supervisor standing next to me, and in desperate attempt to separate myself from what had just happened and relieve myself of the guilt I was feeling, I asked her, "Is this psychopathy?"

To my surprise, she replied with a matter-of-fact smile, "This is humanity." And so, I let out a sigh of relief knowing on some fundamental level I was safe. We immediately gathered the patients and were instructed to lead a group to contain their fears, and I, trembling on the inside, accommodated. In the coming weeks throughout the hospital, we did the same, but as the news progressed and the identities of the hijackers became known, I became the target of interrogation and mistrust by my own patients.

> *"Where are you from?"* was the first remark I received from a lady glaring at me from across the circle of an outpatient group. I answered. Immediate self-disclosure at that point I thought would be the safest bet. But before I had a chance to discuss the group's felt terror and fear, I was asked another question.
>
> *"Do you agree with them, the terrorists?"* another woman remarked. I knew where I had just been placed. *"Because if you do,"* she said, *"then we can't have you in this group with us."* I was co-leading the group with my supervisor whose empathic look I felt silently upon me, awaiting my response. But before I knew it, I reacted in defense of my own humanity and ethics.
>
> *"Just as you do not believe in murder and destruction neither do I, and just as you do not feel safe today neither do I."*

The patients were soothed by my response, able then to integrate me back into the group. This, after all, was all that I wanted. But my supervisor was not entirely pleased with my reaction. I was told that I had acted upon my countertransference at the confrontation I received. But was this a transferential mistrust and anger at authority or was this real world, present day politics entering the therapy room? Suddenly, there were two of me in the room. The therapist and the Arab: the therapist who missed an opportunity to fully process the group's anger and fear, and the Arab, who felt that while analytic theory protected the therapist, it did not protect me.

The experience of migration from the social collective to the individual

I was a young Lebanese-Iraqi girl growing up in Saudi Arabia. I identified more broadly as an Arab and as a Muslim but I also rejected much of the societal restrictions placed on me. I was averse to the black *abaya* that concealed my body and the culture that forced me to conceal myself. I developed over time, what Dwairy (2002) called the "private" and "public" selves of Arab collective culture; the "public" self to ensure the essential harmony and support needed to function each day, and the private self to allow the expression of forbidden desires away from watchful eyes. Despite an otherwise comfortable and pleasant childhood, I waited eagerly for travel to the United States that was promised to me by my parents who had both earned their higher degrees abroad. I longed for the freedom and independence that I believed being in the United States would offer me.

I arrived to my doctoral program in 1996, at the age of twenty-one, to study and earn my PhD in clinical psychology. My program was one of few in the US that could boast an eclectic model of therapeutic modalities, offering didactic courses in both cognitive behavioral theory and psychoanalytic theory and supervision of cases in both orientations. However, courses in analytic theory particularly intrigued me, guiding me at the time towards further independent study. I recall my captivation with the concept of narcissism as being one of the first times I felt the possible intersection between analytic theory and culture, which eventually led me to my dissertation study on the role of culture in shame and guilt.

I was filled with anticipation and excitement when my first clinical cases were assigned to me, as finally, I was pursuing a practice that I had previously known only through books and Hollywood films. At that point, my clinical identity was neither layered with politics nor the stigma that I was later to know, as most patients I worked with were neither aware of my background nor did they appear too concerned. My accent was unnoticeable and thus they willingly ignored my otherness. Yet, I naturally could not ignore theirs. Sitting face to face in front of my first patient was personally and culturally, exceptionally foreign to me. I suddenly became a legitimate explorer of others' individual pain, and yet, the pains I heard from across the room emerged from difficulties so different from the ones I was familiar with. I listened to struggles of heartbreak, divorce, and of substance use, all taboo in the social context I had come from. Both my parents came from countries devastated by war and both were living in an estranged country as a result. The legitimate pain I had known was a social, political, and collective pain, and to me at the time, it was *only* that, that made pain real and valid.

This changed in 1998 when my mother passed away after years of battling cancer. In support, my analytic supervisor at the time said to me, "You should begin your therapy now." So I did, but admittedly with great resistance. The process of therapy initially felt intrusive and indulgent to me. I struggled with divulging myself and when I did, I struggled with the enormous amount of time, effort, and money that was being consumed on my behalf. My analyst interpreted it as an issue of self-worth, yet I wondered if it was an issue of culture. In my experience, individual pain, outside of the context of the larger and more important narrative of national struggle was minimized and never provided its own space and time. I thus, in reaction, undermined the very role of my analyst who sat in what I felt was an overbearing chair, placed at enormous distance from my couch, trying to grant me that space and time.

I eventually crossed this barrier. I crossed the space, I took the time and I paid the money. With each interaction in which my personal sadness was felt and validated by my therapist, I moved one step towards the process and towards a new culture that highlighted the kinds of pain I never allowed myself. With time, just as I allowed my therapist into my most private layers, I became captivated by the depth of experience and emotions that I was able to reach with my own patients, most of whom were American. I felt an intimacy with them that I never thought could exist in a space that initially appeared to me so contrived and foreign, and yet it began to feel real.

Back to the collective: the patient, the therapist, the supervisor, and the realities in between

In 1999, I was referred a patient through my externship program. He was a thirty-year-old man from Iran who battled against the Iraqi regime, and who was now seeking refuge and asylum in America. He deeply despised the Iraqi regime and the American regime. He described the Empire State Building as American weaponry, and the streets below as the blood of his people. He experienced intense survivor's guilt, separation guilt, and feelings of betrayal and shame upon his arrival to the United States. It was here that I noticed for the first time my two identities in the room: the personal one that embodied my values and political positions, some of which we shared, and the clinical one, who was to introduce him to the therapy process. Yet the interpersonal dynamic of two Middle Eastern immigrants engaged in a therapy relationship in the United States was threatening to me, as I felt the comfortable boundaries that were previously so easily drawn between me and my American patients were no longer clearly discernable. My patient felt an enormous loyalty to family, friends, and fellow combatants back home, and in the name of neutrality, I suddenly found myself overtaken by feelings of betrayal and abandonment of my own values, connections, and political allegiances that once defined my very being.

When my patient described his cause and his losses since coming to America, he would look at me with the assumption that I understood, and I did. It would become a relationship of understanding and a mourning together of family connections, causes, and meaning as he once knew it. My supervisor at the time however called it *collusion* and challenged my clinical sense. Humored by his political remarks, she rejected my patient, describing him as manipulative. But this collusion gave him permission to process his hate, anger, and fear in an environment so safe that it ultimately allowed him in this new environment to attend to his personal needs of finding work and trusting his new relations.

One year later 9/11 publically branded me as an Arab in America. I felt suffocated by the media, which further triggered a complex array of emotions that I needed to divulge to someone. I reached out to my

Iraqi relatives who were horrified by the foreign news reportages and who were bracing themselves for an imminent war. I remember my therapist, after I had asked her to disclose her political position, said to me, "This situation is new to me and I am open to hear what you have to say." But I was silent, because in order to feel safe I needed that same collusion that I once gave my patient. I knew our differences were certain to create an irreparable clash, as it had already done with others in my life at the time. Although I knew that I had rage and fear to process, this rage stemmed from a collective and political anger that I felt had no place in individual, interpersonal therapy. As the rhetoric of George Bush, in his State of the Union address in January 2002, began to reveal his plan for a "pre-emptive" invasion of Iraq, I found myself ready to terminate therapy. To this day, I do not know what would have made me feel safe enough to continue the process. But I do know that my termination was the most significant phase of my therapy because in those last sessions, I deeply mourned my mother *and* her country that was also about to be terminated.

An evolving clinical identity: the collective within the individual

Upon graduating, I noticed that my clinical identity and consequently my work had shifted again when I took these experiences to my new employment where I remained for almost three years working with predominantly African Americans patients. Here, I felt somewhat at home—a minority working with minorities, but whose plight was surely different from my own, thus allowing enough objective space within the intersubjectivity of the relationship. However by now, every individual to me was one within a context of community and country. I considered African Americans as individuals within their collective cause. These patients were struggling to survive amidst the harshest of circumstances. Many lived in shelters, many had children in prison, and many had current or past substance abuse; while most were unemployed and dependent on food stamps. These patients needed safety, they needed skills, they needed to process their losses and their pain, they needed to develop hope and vision, and to me, they needed to connect to their very essential identity, culture and what they believed in as a community.

When George Bush was re-elected in 2004, I was again leading an outpatient group. My most empowered group member demanded to know if I was a conservative or democrat. This time, confident of the connection I had built with my patients and the development of my clinical identity, and despite my immediate eagerness to further divulge my distaste for Bush's re-election, I allowed them to bond in anger towards me as a suspected "white conservative." They discussed my separateness as a "wealthy" woman living in Manhattan while they resided in the ghetto. It became both political and personal, and in my life, it had been both political and personal, so it had to be in therapy also. They sat face to face with some of the real challenges in front of them, as poor African American mothers and fathers who lived in impoverished communities that were neither going to be saved by their government, nor by me. I shared their anger, I as their therapist, and I as an Arab. I felt that the responsibilities and expectations that were placed on these patients to improve their lives were unfair, but they needed empowerment to do just that. Empowerment became the theme of our sessions thereafter.

Perhaps it was my own anger and a need for empowerment that brought me back to my country. In 2005, I terminated with all my patients and told them I was returning home to Lebanon. One of my patients flatly told me she was envious. "And where do I go?" she asked me. She was not only sad and angry in anticipation of being left, but she also felt neither rooted nor protected anywhere.

Navigating the space between countries, cultures, and selves

I was returning to my "roots," and I was to take the clinical identity that I had nurtured and developed throughout the past nine years, with me. I had no idea at the time, what it really meant to take a practice, born in the West, to an Arab country. I reviewed the literature that had been written about psychotherapy in the Arab world and discovered there were views in the region that objected to insight oriented or psychodynamic work with traditional or conservative Arabs. Yet, I was committed to discovering if this was true on my own.

Within the first year of my practice, I was branded the atypical Lebanese woman and the gay friendly therapist and was thus, immediately placed outside of the cultural and political boxes within which the

Lebanese were so accustomed to categorizing each other. As such, my very familiar sense of otherness remained with me. I shifted between the Arabic and English language despite my patients speaking to me predominantly in Arabic. Again, I experienced the social and cultural divide that I recalled from my childhood, which after years of living independently in the United States, now became strikingly apparent to myself and my patients.

Emotional curiosity on my part was met with silence and struggle on their part. My patients' feelings were threatened, not only by internal conflict, but also by social meaning and social consequences as well. This made my work with them particularly challenging. A forty-year-old female patient explained that feeling and expressing anger in session in reaction to her childhood experiences with her father would undermine her father's necessarily dominant position in the family. Even her imagined weaknesses of him would serve to dethrone him. This dethroning deeply threatened her very existence and sense of safety, despite having endured and survived her father's physical abuse for years. One year into therapy, although the patient could process her own anguish at being beaten, she could not allow herself any negative feelings towards her father, leaving me to carry the heavy weight of injustice and defiance on my own.

Similarly, a thirty-year-old male patient felt that the expression of his sadness and lack of fulfillment would only serve to separate himself from his family and community. Fantasies of success and feelings of pride were experienced as arrogance and in turn would create intolerable distance from his family and further feelings of guilt. He worked in a family business and yearned to leave in order to grow, but could not walk away. My patients were so very bound and loyal to their families; it felt to me that the space I had to work within was uncomfortably narrow and restricting, and potentially destabilizing for them.

I became acutely aware of and afraid of importing Western values to a society that could potentially reject them. From women not permitted a divorce, to young professionals prevented from living on their own, to youth who could not love whom they wished; I was the therapist with whom they would seek solace and through whom they would struggle against. I began to feel that with each patient, the rules *had* to be positioned at the start of the therapy. Was divorce, employment, cohabitation, independent residence or travel abroad an option?

I discovered over time that the natural inclination I had to assist patients to move closer to themselves at the expense of their social context was not always the path of greater well-being. Boundaries between themselves and their families were blurred, and values related to reputation, image, honor, and allegiance were also meaningful to them. Though the destination was not guaranteed, the consequences of veering off path had to be clarified. Sometimes they veered and sometimes they did not, and I have realised over time that each direction is met with its own set of bumps and roadblocks.

The harmony of here and there

Yasmine

Yasmine was a forty-year-old married woman and a dedicated mother of two children. She was a teacher at a local school and thus also financially self-sufficient. She reported symptoms of anxiety and depression triggered by her oldest child leaving home for university, but Yasmine had also endured years of emotional and sexual abuse at the hands of her husband. Over the first few months of therapy, Yasmine began to discuss her aversion to the idea of living alone again with her husband, once her two children had left home. She also began to divulge intimate details of experiences in her marriage that she described as humiliating. Yet, Yasmine was very uncertain of how to understand her predicament. She would freeze upon hearing me use the term *abuse* as she would claim that all forms of sexual activity and occasional physical force in marriage were legitimate within her belief system. Nonetheless, I felt I had an ethical responsibility to label for Yasmine what I had heard, while also validating her consequent feelings of pain, humiliation, and sadness.

Yasmine's struggle with dependency became very clear in the therapy relationship. She sought answers from me to her many questions on love, marriage, and sexuality and wanted direct guidance on the best ways of managing and avoiding her husband. With every decision she took she looked to me for permission, and so, I became intent on empowering her. Yasmine had a difficult childhood, one filled with themes of abandonment and emotional neglect. She came from a religiously conservative background and thus, did not have any significant relationship experiences before marriage. As a shy, withdrawn young adult, she was thrilled to gain the attention of the man who was to become her husband. In sessions, Yasmine took great pains in discussing her past, yet the process led her to claim her deep insecurities of being unlovable and unworthy that further opened awareness to the many signs of threat from her then husband-to-be that she had ignored.

Gradually, Yasmine became more personally intent on gaining confidence in herself and I applauded her desire to do so. I praised her as she took steps to protect herself financially, to create space for herself to do the things she loved most, and to value her accomplishments in life. While I felt I was only *mirroring* her, I was also apprehensive. When Yasmine began to express relief from her depression and reported experiencing greater self-satisfaction throughout her days, she started drawing closer to a desire to be single again given her children were no longer young. Here, although privately pleased, I began to tread very carefully as I knew that our society looked upon divorce as a tragic demise. When several weeks later Yasmine acknowledged this wish more fully, I supported her. We carefully weighed the pros and the cons of a separation from her husband and the ways in which she could approach him on the subject. Until one day, Yasmine phoned and canceled her session due to deadlines at work; and since, I have not seen her.

"Which lens had I used?" I continue to ask myself. Was it the one from here or the one from there? Was Yasmine's sudden termination of therapy a consequence of culture or more simply a classic case of battered woman's syndrome? Had her decision come only through me? And what prevented her from a greater openness with me? Had I become my patient's enemy just as my own therapist had become to me? These kinds of questions invade many of my clinical experiences in Lebanon as I am persistently confronted by my realities of here and there.

Yara

Yara was a patient whom I had similarly wanted to protect from the "intrusions" of our society. She was a twenty-five-year-old single, female patient who presented with panic attacks and multiple somatic symptoms. The oldest of three sisters, Yara lived with her parents within a very conservative, rural community. She graduated with distinction from the top university in Lebanon and went on to work as a graphic designer. She was the go-to person in her family, but also a triangulated, *parentified* child (Bowen, 1966). Her mother relied heavily on Yara to resolve the many conflicts between herself and her husband, to offer advice and to make family decisions. Yara strove for perfection in everything she did, but she was also deeply unhappy. She felt she had nobody she could depend on and struggled with deep feelings of alienation and aloneness. Yara revealed that the generations of women in her family were uneducated, disempowered, self-sacrificing and neglected. She took great pride in her academic success and work, yet still feared ending up like these women. Despite her parent's clear objection to her living independently or studying abroad, Yara dreamt of a day that she would travel and leave everything behind. Yet she believed that if she were ever to walk away from the dysfunction at home, that the family would indeed fragment.

Adhering to Yara's initial transferential need to be guided, for she was in search of someone else who would take charge, I initially opened a discussion with her about family boundaries. We discussed the fluidity of boundaries in our culture that both served a positive communal purpose, but that could also result in emotional overload. Yara listened intently and from the start of therapy enjoyed the concrete guidance she was receiving. She worked very hard at refraining from behaviors at home that compensated for others' lack of initiative, which greatly liberated her from an exaggerated sense of responsibility and promoted more assistance from her siblings. She also began to learn to differentiate between her needs and emotions and those of each member of the family. It was not long before her panic attacks and much of her somatic pain subsided and Yara began to feel in control again.

However, what remained with Yara were sleepless nights of heavy tears. She still felt trapped and overwhelmed. On the one hand, she mocked her community as narrow and regressive, and on the other, maintained very valuable, traditional views. When we discussed her disappointment at a rigid and unforgiving society, it opened a space for her to aspire to what she wished: to date freely, marry whomever she loved, and travel abroad. *Then* we were in harmony. At other times she would reproach herself for not planning for the life her family and society expected of her. At these instances, when I would repeatedly make the mistake of questioning the ideals of society, Yara would in turn cling to them, expressing a vital need to be part of her community and live in harmony with it. Here, I would become the outsider.

Once I stepped outside of this struggle, we began to appreciate that Yara had a healthy dependent self, defiant self and very autonomous self, a traditional self that valued her community, but also a progressive self that wanted to leave it, I realised that Yara also needed to feel cared for, protected, and loved. She needed to connect to her family and she needed a more fulfilling connection with them. That reality could not be undermined. She also needed to take charge in her own therapy. Yara expressed a wish to more authentically reveal herself to her family just as she had been doing in therapy, and she courageously took the steps to do so. With this openness, Yara discovered a mutual understanding between herself and her younger sister as well as an unexpected ease of communication with her mother and her father, both of which were liberating and deeply meaningful to her.

What initially felt like opposing and conflicting forces became a coexistence of several "self-states" that Yara needed to feel whole (Bromberg, 1998). Her longing for the opportunity to experience her values and aspirations outside the boundaries of her own community now took priority. One year into therapy, Yara was accepted into a graduate program abroad and she was to go. She knew if she left, she would be taking her pain with her, the anticipated isolation, the sadness of her mother and the disapproval of her father, yet she now had the calm and conviction to do so along with the internal harmony of her realities. After months of deliberation and reflection on all feared outcomes both abroad and at home, and many sessions of self-disclosure around my experiences of immigration, Yara left happily and eagerly, in a state that reminded me so much of myself twenty years earlier.

Points of departure

I still struggle with these points of departure that my patients arrive to. With every departure from the familiar, there is something vital gained, but also lost in the process. We can no longer deny what we bring into each session through our words, expressions, and appearances. I find myself secretly aspiring for many things with my patients. I continue to grapple with what it really means to be "individuated" in a social, collective context, and how to strike that balance between dependence and autonomy, or rather move freely between them. The Arab's sense of communal connectedness that provides a sense of safety and stability also provides a self-integration and completeness that cannot be reached independently. Sometimes this harmonious belonging appears as an illusion, yet nonetheless, it reflects the reality that each individual self in the Arab world is made up of multiple selves and thus multiple realities and multiple needs (Shehadeh, 2008).

I was challenged in New York to step outside myself and lean into the internal frame of my patient, to see the validity and reality of each individual pain or conflict. Here in Lebanon, I feel more so challenged by my cultural pull towards "autonomy," not in the analytic sense of wanting patients to give up infantile aims, but in a cultural sense of wanting them to separate from states of dependency. Yet I have come to realise that if a patient's desire for change is to be viewed from within his or her cultural context, the patient needs not only individual affirmation before change can occur (Watchel, 2008), but also cultural affirmation for all that the current context is and provides for the patient. While patients often seek out new experiences, and in many cases, new cultural experiences, we become what Bromberg describes as participators in the "here and now act of constructing a negotiated reality [within the patient's inner reality]" (Bromberg, 1993, p. 160), despite the challenges of there being two different realities and often times more in the room. In my case, this dynamic brings about opposing personal and cultural motivations, shifting both me and my patients not forward and backward but in and out of new experiences, new realities and most certainly, new ways of seeing things.

References

Bowen, M. (1966). The use of family theory in clinical practice. *Comprehensive Psychiatry, 7*: 345–374.

Bromberg, P. M. (1993). Shadow and substance. *Psychoanalytic Psychology, 10*: 147–168.

Bromberg, P. M. (1998). *Standing in the Spaces: Essays on Clinical Process, Trauma and Dissociation*. Hillsdale, NJ: Analytic Press.

Dwairy, M. (2002). Foundations of psychosocial dynamic personality theory of collective people. *Clinical Psychology Review, 22*: 343–360.

Shehadeh, S. (2008). Psychoanalytic exploration into the Arab self and implications for therapy with Arabs in the United States. Unpublished Doctoral Dissertation. Rutgers University, United States of America.

Watchel, P. L. (2008). *Relational Theory and the Practice of Psychotherapy*. New York, NY: The Guilford Press.

CHAPTER FIVE

De dónde eres? Finding a "from" in psychoanalysis

Norka T. Malberg

> If there is a knower of tongues here, fetch him;
> There's a stranger in the city / And he has many things to say.
>
> —*Mirza Asadullah Khan Ghalib*

As I begin this journey with you, the reader, the words of an old Puerto Rican song: "In my old San Juan" resonate in my mind: "… but time passed by and destiny mocked my terrible nostalgia, and I couldn't return to the San Juan that I loved, little piece of my land …" (Estrada, 1942). My family left San Juan, Puerto Rico during the summer of 1978 for what was supposed to be a three-year expat assignment to San Jose, Costa Rica a great opportunity for my father's career and our family's financial future. "In my old San Juan" encapsulates the sadness that surrounded our departure the day we said our goodbyes. Eight years old at the time, I almost caused us to miss the flight by hiding in the closet of my grandmother's room and struggling to avoid being torn away from her arms. Well over thirty years later and having never returned to live in Puerto Rico, my mother still becomes overwhelmed with sadness when she hears "In my old

San Juan." My two children heard the same lyrics sung to them at bedtime and experienced the broken quality of their mothers' nostalgic tone. I recently realized the strength of the generational transmission of loss carried in these lyrics when my oldest son, now seventeen, spoke of feeling inexplicably sad when he heard the song during a family gathering.

Children never choose to migrate. Their parents/caregivers decide for them, potentially imposing on them experiences of loss, but also offering the hope of wonderful opportunities for growth and creativity. The experience of migration will challenge their emerging sense of self and the developmental process of psychic organization. However, my own personal experiences of migration as a child and my work as a child psychoanalyst have informed my firm belief in the central role of the caregiver in this process. The caregiver's can provide both a protective shield and a secure base, a home from which to experience and integrate the multiple "migrations" we experience externally and internally. How a parent experiences and manages migration and the way in which he/she helps the child create a coherent narrative about this potentially traumatic event weighs heavily on how the child integrates the experience and its effect on the child's emerging internal picture of the world. There are many ways in which we communicate our thoughts and feelings of difference, loss and hope to our children in the context of migration. Similarly, these verbal and non-verbal ways of communication enter the psychotherapeutic relationship and can have both the potential to hinder or facilitate the growth of its development and the process it seeks to foster.

I chose to begin this chapter with a personal story that depicts the generational transmission of the loss of a geographical home, a song that means different things to each of the three generations. My mother is reminded of her ambivalence at having left and choosing not to return to her motherland. My son, who has only experienced San Juan through the stories of his mother and grandmother and occasional tourist excursions, connects it with his own experience of having left several lands behind in his young life as well as the transmission of an idealized place that is hoped and longed for. For my part, the song encapsulates the experience of mourning the many lands that have been given to me, but that have never been fully mine. I can only imagine what it meant for my Estonian father, who was exiled as an infant from his land to see the sadness in his family's eyes the day he left Puerto Rico, one of his adoptive lands.

> To arrive at a place inside us that feels it is home is a long and hazardous journey, beginning in the place we have in the minds of our parents as we are conceived of consciously and unconsciously by them. So even before we are infants, the external setting of our being is preparing the kind of home that we will inhabit, which will profoundly affect the home that we create inside ourselves. (Joyce, 2013, p. 3)

My search for a "from," a place where I might still be a foreigner to others, but not to myself has and continues to be as defined by Joyce a long and hazardous journey that has influenced deeply my personal and professional choices.

In this chapter, I hope to share with the reader how the construction of my own ever-developing identity as a multicultural woman informs my work as a psychoanalyst. I have spent my life living and working in different countries in Europe and the American continent, never staying in one place longer than ten years. So, for me, the term multicultural represents the multiple transitions, both external and internal, which I have experienced throughout my life, and the impact they have had in the construction of that internal home. My multiculturalism consists not only of the mixed ethnic roots of my parents but also of the acquired cultural identities that I have integrated in the course of my journey so far. One might suspect that at times this might constitute a source of disintegration and dislocation and in fact, there is some truth to this. Nevertheless, there is also a certain level of genuine flexibility, curiosity, and openness that emerges from having to develop within such a context, one which I feel positively informs my role as a psychoanalyst.

As a result of my "global nomad" existence I have been fortunate to have come into contact with children, adolescents, and their families in diverse cultural contexts, both in the consulting room and in outreach settings such as schools, hospitals, and other community venues. My journey as a psychoanalyst has been influenced by my early experiences and continues to be re-defined by the narratives of those who choose to trust me with them. I hope to be able to interweave my own experiences with those that I have listened to and provide the reader with a story filled with multiple meanings and voices.

María Elena: De dónde eres nena?

Early and often in my career I have made the decision to abandon the safety of the consulting room for the outreach setting. I have spent significant portions of my career attempting to translate psychoanalytic thinking to the needs of diverse community settings. This choice has been influenced by a strong tradition in my maternal family of service to the community through education. At a personal level, what drives this work is my own desire to help those being silenced by poverty and other forms of invisible oppression to experience the feeling of being heard. My work as a psychotherapist in home visiting programs has proven to be one of the most challenging, but also rewarding experiences of my career. The following vignette, I hope illustrates my experience as a multicultural community psychoanalyst working with families from my ethnic heritage.

> Maria Elena opens the door of her apartment with her three-year-old son hanging off her waist and an eight-month-old baby girl being tightly held to her chest. The three-year-old scans me with his large dark brown eyes populated by large eyelashes as he hides behind his mother who also looks at me with suspicion. I introduce myself in Spanish as the therapist from the local guidance clinic, she visibly relaxes, the door opens wider, and she smiles. As we enter the small living room filled with toys and the loud sound of the "novella" (soap opera) playing on the TV, I comment on the plot of the show and ask about the name of the actor. Mom looks at me in surprise and tells me the name. I can see I have awakened curiosity in her and as we sit to talk about the program I represent, and she asks:
>
> "De dónde eres tu nena?" [where are you from girl?].
>
> I smiled and reply: "yo soy Boricua" (meaning from Puerto Rico).
>
> Maria pauses and after making a funny face, a big smile is followed by: "de verdad? Tu no pareces!" [really, you don't look it].
>
> I replied: "pues si!" [Well, yes] and a conversation about the towns our families come from ensues.
>
> Little Enrique (age three) is running around the room and Elisa lies happily in mom's arms. Mom looks relaxed and ready to engage, and I breathe a sigh of relief as once more I have survived

that dreaded question: Where are you from? And most importantly: "I passed!"

Altman (1995) speaks of a psychoanalysis in which a dialectically driven process includes the analyst, the analysand, and the social system which structures both psyches. By doing so, he proposes a framework in which the psychotherapist can work with both culture and self as continually mutual and mutative lived experiences. From this point of view, culture begins as a relationship, one created by both the therapist and the client. (Bodnar, 2004)

Maria Elena and I went on to build a strong therapeutic alliance. Together, we were able to understand what lied behind Enrique's difficult behavior and what it meant for Maria in the context of her own history of trauma and geographical dislocation. That first afternoon, I had introduced myself as a Puerto Rican woman and showed Maria that I shared a basic understanding of where she came from. Maria had grown up in a small town in the center of the Island and had moved to the United States following her high school sweetheart. As our work evolved, tough, she discovered how foreign certain aspects of the Puerto Rican experience were to me as I had left the Island at the age of eight and only returned during the summertime to be with my extended family. Although I had answered, "of course I am Puerto Rican," that afternoon, later on in our work Maria continued to enquire about my ethnic origins. Why my accent sounded different? Why did I use words that were more South American? I could have given her my well-rehearsed story about where I was from (as I have been doing since a very young age), however, it was more important for our work that together we understood how difficult it was for Maria to trust and to take a leap of faith with a "Puerto Rican who did not look or sound like one." Why was it important for her that we were alike? What was the meaning of this in the context of having two mixed race children? As it often happens, the puzzling nature of my ethnicity could potentially become both an obstacle and a window into the multiple meanings that inform someone's internal representations. And, so, I remained mindful of finding a balance between my desire to be recognized and my capacity for therapeutic abstinence which would allow me and my client to explore the fantasies and resistances resulting from being presented with such a puzzle.

This book, so wisely titled *Identities in Transition*, is all about puzzles, our own and those of our patients. Preparing to write this chapter, I found myself experiencing the familiar feeling of conflict between the multiple cultural pieces that inhabit my internal world. The field of psychoanalysis is another one of those cultures but also a way to re-visit those puzzles from a brand new perspective. The psychoanalytic process allowed me to integrate both the past and the present into a more coherent narrative that belongs to me, but which honors the multiple meanings given to me. In my work as a psychoanalyst, I strive to provide this experience to others whilst acknowledging the intersubjective space in which my own experiences and those of my patient interact and at times become conflicting and struggle in the process of translation.

Where do I come from? Generational transmission of otherness and cultural identities in transition

I have lived in multiple countries since my birth. My mother tongue is Spanish, but often (as illustrated by the clinical vignette shared early on in this chapter) the origin of my accent is impossible to identify by other native Spanish speakers as it represents a "melting pot" of regional expressions. My physical appearance can be confusing as well, as I am a mix of two very different ethnic backgrounds: Caribbean and Eastern European. As a result, when I am asked, "Where are you from?" I often find myself choosing my answer depending on the circumstance or the person asking. For example, if I am asked by a White American, I often reply, "Puerto Rican." The reason being, a large sector of the US population still does not know that Puerto Ricans are US citizens by birth and that we represent, like many Caribbean nations, a wonderful rainbow of ethnicities, often all belonging to one family tree. As a result, I hope to break the chains of ignorance and stereotyping and educate others about the wonderful richness of the island where I was born. Many outstanding Puerto Ricans have contributed to the greatness of the United States, but they often remain a silent minority drowned by the tales of gangs and inner city violence that afflict a large number of the Puerto Rican community. Where I come from has influenced my professional choices and my development as a psychoanalyst. So, I have chosen to share some of the pieces of my puzzle in this chapter as a way of framing and introducing the home where I began my journey.

My father was born towards the end of the Second World War in Tallin, Estonia, a small and proud country (as my grandmother used to describe it). Both his parents were of German descent and had stayed during the German occupation, but had decided to leave once the Russian troops began to make their way in, and most of my grandmother's family was exterminated or had fled the country. My grandfather's family had stayed, but once things got dangerous, my grandfather sent his young wife and their two twin boys (one was my father) with his sister and her children to Austria where they hoped to get passage to the American Continent. As it happens, my grandmother met her parents in Austria and remained safe after a treacherous journey, leaving behind her life in Estonia.

Once in Austria, her parents managed to get a Visa to South America, so one day my grandfather arrived to see his children and they were gone forever. I grew up with a completely different story told by my grandmother, who had remarried shortly after she arrived in Venezuela. My grandmother's story had my grandfather dying fighting the Russian troops, I used to love listening to the story as she would become uncharacteristically alive. Thinking about him, her face would light up and then she would lose herself in some mindless task such as watching the TV as if she needed to close again a forbidden gate that had been closed forever. It was not until after her death and fifty years later that my father's cousin found him via the internet and told him the truth. My father had grown up speaking Spanish and German; the Estonian language had been lost together with the truth about his biological father. I don't think I understood the extent of my grandmothers' sadness and grief until much later in life. I was for her the daughter she never had, so she gave me her stories about her life before the war and about her great love affair with my grandfather. I still hold in a small book the pictures of her home in Tallin before the war, her dog, her living room, pictures of places that held significance only for her. My grandmother gave me her Estonia and I made it mine during my trips to Tallin after its independence from Russia. My Estonia is a land of proud and hard-working people who sang and held hands in order to achieve freedom; it fills me with pride. However, I also carry the sorrow of my grandmother who never returned. To this day, a sense of "not belonging" invades me when I walk into the Estonian Consulate as I don't speak the language and once more I become "the other" in one of the lands given to me.

Some time ago I came across a paper by Chodorow (2002) exploring the process of listening and interpreting the stories of people born towards the end of World War Two. I have always admired my father's resilience in light of the history of relational trauma he grew up in. Dr. Chodorow's paper further confirmed my respect and appreciation for the way in which my father had managed to provide me and my siblings with an emotional home to depart to despite his own experience of having grown up with parents whose main purpose was to survive psychically in the aftermath of unthinkable loss, grief, and guilt whilst keeping their children physically nourished but emotionally starved. My father's story informs my belief in the power of new identifications throughout the developmental continuum and on the importance of social supports in the community for children at risk.

My mother was born in Puerto Rico. Both her parents were second generation born in the island after a massive migration from Spain at the turn of the century. Both my grandparents were school principals. My grandfather was the principal of one of the toughest high schools in the Metropolitan area, so I grew up hearing people thanking my grandfather for having "straightened them out." My grandparents had a strong sense of service to the community and an unwavering belief that education was the way to achieve what you wanted in life. The same as my paternal grandmother, my maternal grandmother cultivated in me since a young age, the love for reading and studying. My grandfather was one of the best storytellers I have ever known and I was his favorite audience. As a result, my own children have grown up hearing my grandpa's stories as told by me and my mother (the other storyteller in the family). Telling stories was the way in which my grandfather gave me Puerto Rico to take with me. As a result, in my work as a psychoanalyst I carry the conviction that listening to others' stories and helping them to make sense of them is the best way to help someone grow and develop their sense of coherence and agency over their lives. It certainly has helped me, so let me tell you a story ...

> The year was 1979, I was nine years old and my younger sister was four. We were sitting in the playground of our new school in San Jose, Costa Rica. We had arrived three days earlier in an early morning flight to be confronted for the first time in our lives with the need to wear a sweater. We were living off a suitcase as we still had not moved into our new home, so the feeling of being lost

and a tremendous sense of longing for my grandfather's afternoon delivery of "pan mojao" (soft and warm bread) populated my stomach and my heart.

My sister and I were sitting in the swings talking and a group of girls passed by and overheard our conversation. One of the girls began to laugh and screamed "gringas" and laughed. Another older girl uttered some words as to make fun of our accents to which my sister responded with a punch in the stomach as mighty as a five-year-old can produce. I sat on the swing, frozen, still puzzled by the attack. Why were they calling us "gringas?" We did not speak English and we were from Puerto Rico. Completely ignorant of the tense political situation inhabiting Central America at the time, we got home that afternoon and relayed the story to our mother who proceeded to tell my father for an hour all the reasons we should leave the country the next morning. I was left with a feeling of guilt over causing such an argument at home and begged my mother not to complain to the school and promised we would sort it out. However, weeks of agony and loneliness followed this incident. I spent all my school breaks in the library or the nurses' office. This was followed by an immense feeling of rage towards the country— I refused to stand during the signing of the national anthem, I refused to participate during class activities, and I retreated into my books and the world of imagination. This, I believe was my first conscious experience as "the other."

Eventually, I made friends with other children like me, who liked talking about their parents' country of origin, who spoke in weird accents, and who felt like second-class citizens as I did. The reminders of being a foreigner were everywhere and I worked hard at finding them too. Every year after having spent Christmas and New Year's and the summer months in Puerto Rico, I would return to Costa Rica to relive that process all over again and with it, to consolidate my identity as a perpetual foreigner. I believe that my parents' own conflicts regarding their lands of origin influenced in many ways my own difficulties claiming what I now think of as one of my adoptive lands. However, this experience helped me clinically in supporting immigrant parents support their children and help them reflect and honor their own conflicts with the new culture they encounter and how they impact their children's own process of adaptation.

Melanie: on losing, remembering, and finding

People who do not manage to become assimilated, who take refuge behind a fence that encloses their memories and distant affections, seem to be condemned to view life as something that always happens in a "garden next door" on someone else's property into which they peer without being able to participate in the activities taking place there. (Grinberg & Grinberg, 1989, p. 89)

Melanie was a successful lawyer in the United States who had moved to Chile following a good job opportunity for her husband. Initially, the family was supposed to be away for two years but Melanie had recently learned that the contract had been extended for three more years. She had reacted with a sudden bout of the flu after learning the news and had remained in bed for a week. Following her illness, she had found herself staying in bed for another two weeks. She would drive her two children to and from school but otherwise spent most of her days watching re-runs of American soap operas. Her oldest, Virginia, age twelve, seemed thrilled with the news of the extension, whereas her youngest Bonnie, age three, seemed sad and disappointed about not return to the US (according to Melanie). Melanie felt puzzled by Bonnie's reaction and sudden regressive behavior (she had begun to wet the bed, occasionally having daytime accidents and sucked her thumb again). Melanie's husband seemed unsympathetic to the difficulties experienced by both her and Bonnie and had created what Melanie described as "a united front" with Virginia against them.

Melanie and Bonnie were referred to me by the local American school, as they thought it would be helpful for Melanie to speak to a therapist who was a "fellow American." The school had concerns about Bonnie's sudden regressive behavior, which manifested itself at school in difficulty separating from mom in the morning and during transitions throughout the day, with Bonnie becoming frozen and clingy. Our first encounter was colored by Melanie's awareness of my strong Spanish accent, and she began by trying to figure out how much I really shared her "American experience." She made reference to popular shows and restaurants, to stores and items that are thought of as "typically American." I listened and chose to "pass" most of the tests as I could see how important it was for Melanie that I understood all that she missed and felt she had lost.

I met with Melanie first to get Bonnie's social and developmental history as she was the referred patient. However, rather quickly I realized how unsupported and lonely Melanie felt and became aware of my own identification with the side of her that felt she did not have the strength to, in her words "put on the show for another three years." Once again, I resisted my own need to show Melanie that I understood, as my own process of adaptation to Chile had been less than ideal, also influenced by my own sense of cultural dislocation. I chose to stay with Melanie's curiosity and feeling that although I had "passed" many of the "American tests" she still had decided in her mind that I was a "returned" Chilean who could not possibly understand how difficult it was for a Mid-Western American to live in Chile. Towards the end of our first meeting, I posed a question to Melanie, "what did she think Bonnie's behaviors were trying to communicate?" Melanie shrugged at first but after a few minutes said she thought Bonnie was as sad and frustrated as she was. I comment on how difficult it was sometimes to be able to differentiate which feelings belong to us and which ones to our kids. She agreed, but defensively replied, "A mother knows, you will understand soon" (as she acknowledged my pregnancy for the first time in the session). Melanie showed no further interest in my pregnancy, but did comment that it was tough moving with babies and wondered if I was staying in Chile or was I also an expat. I commented on feeling that one of the most painful aspects of moving and starting in a new place was knowing you will eventually say goodbye.

It was at this time, with only ten minutes remaining of our initial meeting that Melanie shared that her mother had died of cancer just a year after she had moved with her family to Chile and that she often felt this was one of the reasons she hated this place. I said I could see how my comment about loss brought this to her mind and wondered if we could have a second meeting to explore further these issues prior to my diagnostic meeting with Bonnie. Melanie agreed. However, two days prior to our next meeting, Melanie called to cancel and said that she wanted to try medication for her depression first and that Bonnie seemed to be getting back to normal. Melanie felt that having spoken to me had helped her realize that Bonnie was just "copying" her sadness and since then she had been hiding it better and Bonnie was "back on track." I was left feeling puzzled but mostly wondered if somehow, my therapeutic abstinence had made Melanie feel foreign in my presence.

A month and a half after our initial meeting, Melanie called again requesting a meeting for herself. This time, Melanie had self-referred and came in to "work on herself." Melanie spoke of having frequent dreams about her mother since our first encounter and feeling sad in a "different way." Melanie and I worked together for several months on her unresolved mourning over her mother's sudden death. During our work, we spent a significant amount of time working in the negative transference, with me representing the foreign country, the one that takes things away. During our work together I endured at times strong feelings in the countertransference as it was difficult to resist Melanie's need for an ally against "the insensitive Chileans." She would often sit in the corner of my waiting room staring at the Chileans waiting for other professionals and complain about me not having English language magazines. She was often rude to my receptionist who tried desperately to speak English to her. Meanwhile, my pregnancy continued to advance and with it the threat of losing me. Melanie made a trip to the US and came back with lots of American magazines and the book, *What to Expect When You Are Expecting*, beautifully wrapped and lovingly delivered during her returning session. This gesture provided an opportunity for a phase of "rapprochement" between Melanie and her "ethnically mysterious psychotherapist." Melanie had found a common ground between us, feeling she could support me in my experience as a new mother.

This new phase of our work consisted of Melanie revisiting her feelings of loss of her identity as a lawyer and independent woman and the difficult transition into a dependent, stay at home, expat mom who often felt as a "stupid gringa" in a foreign land. Melanie was able to make links between her ways of coping with this reality and her daughters' reactions and overall feelings regarding the extension of the job assignment. For instance, Virginia her oldest, who had spent the first years of her life in a daycare and then with a nanny, loved the fact that Melanie was so available to her now and enjoyed several mother–daughter trips to neighboring Argentina with her.

A month before my due date, Melanie came to our session reporting significant improvement in her mood, her marriage, and her relationship with both girls. Bonnie was doing very well, in fact Melanie felt that in many ways Bonnie had always been mourning a bit with her and now that she had done the work, she noticed this had freed Bonnie who was much more independent and happy. Melanie felt she was ready to stop our work for a while and wish me good luck with the baby. I understood this as Melanie's defensive way of protecting herself from the experience of me leaving her, but I chose not to name it. As it turns out, I had just found out two days prior that I would be leaving Chile with my young family, so I struggled with my response.

Eventually, after giving birth to my first child, I wrote a letter to Melanie letting her know everything was ok and thanking her for all the advice about the baby. I also let her know that I would be leaving the country. Melanie called and asked for a meeting. We met a few weeks before my departure and she brought a card with all her numbers and contact information in the US and said she hoped we could stay in touch. She added, "Go figure, we are not so different after all." I smiled and thanked her for trusting me with her story and allowing me to be of support during a tough time. By allowing herself to say goodbye to me and surviving the sadness of the moment together, we both grew and found a new way of being with another in the midst of loss and challenging transitions internally and externally. I believe that our work provided Melanie with a transitional space where to integrate her internal and external worlds and recover a sense of balance, a stronger internal home from which to support and facilitate her daughter's own journey separate from hers.

Working and living in multiple languages

> Loss of language and culture, and adjustment to a new language and culture, create broken links to childhood and within the inner world. Language develops, grows, and is learned in the social, cultural, or psychological conditions and structures in which is generated, so each "natural language" grows out of a particular way of living, seeing, and describing the world. (Flynn, 2013, p. 65)

My first encounter with Freud's writing was at the age of fourteen. A rather colorful and enthusiastic Psychology teacher in my high school asked for a short essay on Freud. I decided to read *The Interpretation of Dreams* in my native Spanish and proceeded to write a fifteen-page essay. I worked for weeks, reading the text over and over. The day the grades were given, my psychology teacher gave me an A, but most importantly, he wrote a cover letter in which he explained how moved he had been by my effort and how much he hoped I would consider psychology as my professional choice. This was my first attempt to understand the language of psychoanalysis, which later on in my life became one of my languages. I was always proud of my capacity to write and think in my mother tongue. My school did not teach English, but French, so at eighteen when I transferred to the United States as a junior in college I found myself completely stripped of my capacity to express my thoughts and ideas in an eloquent fashion. My sense of being a foreigner, an outsider, became further consolidated through the multitude of linguistic transitions throughout my life from Spanish to English, then to German, to British English; even in Chile the use of vocabulary was different.

I believe becoming a mother helped me to reflect on my relationship to language and to tolerate and manage racism and discrimination in general for the sake of my children's adaptation. Interestingly enough, both my children consider English as their mother tongue. Painful as it is, I seem to have repeated the same sin as my paternal grandmother who did not speak Estonian to my father. This theme, central to my own training analysis is one that I feel I can address with a significant level of insight, sensitivity and genuine curiosity in my clinical work. Furthermore, through my work with very young children I have come to understand how these experiences become internal organizers very early on and are often evidenced and experienced in implicit ways in our work with adults.

Joy, Tom, and Brenda: learning to understand each other

Joy and Brenda were referred to me by a local pediatrician. Joy was fifteen months old when Brenda and Tom adopted her from China. Joy had been cared for by an elderly foster couple. They loved Joy and were happy she had found a "forever family." When Brenda and Tom arrived to take Joy home, she had been ill with a terrible stomach virus, so on the way home she slept most of the journey and seemed very calm. However, once they arrived in the United States, Tom and Brenda noticed a change, Joy seemed lost and afraid all the time. The family was referred to me for parent–child psychotherapy and an evaluation of Joy's development.

My first impression of Joy brought to mind the American expression "a deer caught in the headlights." Indeed, she looked lost and afraid, but so did her new parents. Joy responded to my invitation to play compliantly. She sat on the floor and followed my play with blocks. She did not reference any of the adults in the room initially, however, as the tower got taller and fell she walked to me and sat on my lap hiding her head on my shoulder. Brenda looked heartbroken and I felt guilty for allowing myself to be the better parent in the room. Immediately, I re-directed Joy towards her new parents. I had read that Chinese children are kept very close to their mother's bodies in certain geographical areas and Tom and Brenda confirmed that Joy had slept with her foster parents until recently. They were concerned because Joy did not want to sleep alone and cried inconsolably all night. Together, we came up with some basic ideas on how to make Joy's new environment more familiar to her. Both Tom and Brenda were extremely loving, and dedicated new parents, always following up on the ideas that emerged from the sessions. However, there was always a certain divide between Joy and Brenda that I could not understand yet, but I could feel. The invisible wall was much more than a cultural one, it was an emotional barrier which had no words yet.

As my work with both parents and Joy continued, Joy's sleep became more regular and Brenda began to feel more competent as a mother. However, during moments of distress, Joy would reference and seek Tom but not Brenda. I decided to name what I was experiencing and spoke of how much time and effort we had put into honoring Joy's early cultural environment by trying to help her transition in the midst of such a delicate developmental period. However, I added, there was a different kind of work to do which I felt we were all running away from, that of facing the fact that adopting Joy had been a last resort for them. I wondered if they had time, in the middle of all the paperwork and the emotional rollercoaster of waiting for a child, to stop and think about how to move forward in making Joy truly theirs. Tom noted that Brenda had lousy parents so this was more difficult for her. Brenda was able to speak about her fear of feeling rejected by Joy; she was afraid of feeling close and also felt guilty for feeling so disconnected and foreign with Joy. Tom spoke of feeling irritated with Brenda when Joy cried and Brenda laughed and said she looked funny. He felt that Brenda thought of Joy as an object and not a person at times. Brenda became defensive at first, but said she felt relief that someone had noticed and that she was afraid to talk to Tom about this. What kind of a woman is not moved by a small child's cry? The following months of our work together focused on finding ways to promote Joy and Brenda's bond and to help Brenda speak of her feelings of disappointment, shame, and sadness.

Having worked with adoptive children and their families for many years, I have come to understand the impact of certain silenced feelings. At times, it is easier as a psychotherapist to become seduced by the obvious cultural, physical, and in some instances linguistic differences between adopted children and their parents. It is easy to collude with parents by focusing on these and to try to offer concrete refuge with suggestions and all sorts of "culturally sensitive" practices. For the multicultural psychotherapist who has experienced the feeling of being lost in translation, these situations can prove particularly challenging in the countertransference. Often, Joy's face reminded me of my first days in the United States when I would try to understand my professors or my experiences in a Germanic country as a new mother trying to shop for diapers and formula. I felt the urge to make it all ok for Tom and Brenda and to speak Joy's language to let her know it was ok, and all was not lost, and perhaps, that is one of the most challenging tasks of working with very young children and their parents, how they awaken our own primitive feelings and often our implicit memories.

Months into my work with this family, I was visiting my parents in their home and I found some pictures of my first weeks in my father's adoptive country, Venezuela. I had moved there with my parents as an infant shortly after my birth, my mother confessed how difficult the three years we spent there were for her and showed me pictures of me helping her clean the house and playing with a group of Japanese children who lived in the building, whose mother had become a support for my mother. I wondered how much of my early experience had been often activated during my work with young adopted children and how it has impacted my work, my understanding, and my responses to the multiple meanings and needs in the room.

The work of Amati-Mehler, Argentieri and Canestri (1993) in their book *The Babel of the Unconscious* elegantly explores how speaking and working in a foreign language can facilitate the creation of a safety barrier against primitive emotions, sensations, and affects in which the mother tongue is deeply rooted. I am often mindful of those moments in my psychotherapeutic work where I find myself "not finding the words" in my adoptive language as they usually signal important countertransference reactions and can lead to turning points in the therapeutic relationship in which repressive forbidden content can be interpreted and understood.

Sofia: leaving and coming home

Sofia was referred to me by her college advisor. An exemplary student, she had arrived in the UK at the age of nineteen to pursue her college education. It was important to her to find a psychotherapist who understood how it feels to be a foreigner, so her advisor thought of me, as she was familiar with my background and the fact that I spoke Spanish like Sofia.

Sofia was the only child of older parents. They had married late in life and had decided to have only one child who they could be devoted to. Both her parents were academics and so they prioritized this aspect of Sofia's development. In her own words "sometimes I felt like a trained monkey." However, they were loving and extremely protective of her in many ways. At the time of referral, Sofia was struggling with issues of separation from her parents and adaptation to the UK. She found people cold and mean and missed her mother's food, her room, and her friends.

Sofia found my therapeutic abstinence regarding disclosure of my country of origin and my experiences as a foreigner frustrating and uncaring. However, rather quickly she turned her distress into a playful, almost manic game of guessing about my life. I often felt invaded by her questions and her constant curiosity. She rejected or defended against my interpretations regarding the possibility of feeling afraid of what kind of person I was, could she trust me? In response, she became obsessed with correcting my Spanish and picking up on the "lack of consistency" of it. She began to speak rather angrily about Caribbean women coming to Spain and stealing the men from the local girls with their treachery. I wondered about Sofia's oedipal experience in the context of an aging couple.

Sofia had a very close relationship with her father and had become recently quite infatuated with an older colleague of mine who she used to see coming out of his office to greet a patient who had the same time slot as hers. As our work in twice weekly psychotherapy progressed, so did Sofia's anxiety over losing me parallel to her continuous attacks in displacement. Interestingly, during moments when her rage seemed to become overwhelming, her perfect Spanish would start to suffer and she would begin to speak in English. I could identify with this experience as I had been able to observe it during my own analysis. I waited and just named it, withholding any possible interpretation. Eventually, Sofia and I came to understand this as a way to distance herself from me and to protect me from her rage. It was during this period that associations about her relationship with her mother as a young girl helped us understand the role of aggression in Sofia's relationship with her mother. A highly educated and accomplished woman; Sofia's mom never really wanted children, but had succumbed to years of requests by her husband. Sofia had always felt like the one that had come to steal her father from her mother and had understood her mother's insistence on her studying abroad as a way of getting rid of her, the rival.

Our understanding of this was a turning point in Sofia's treatment that facilitated her process of separation and individuation. Sofia continued to work with me for two years, in the transference; I became the mother who accepted and claimed Sofia in her mother tongue. Her relationship with her mother became more open and she developed a more age appropriate relationship with her father. Towards the end of our work together, nearly three years later, Sofia had nearly finished her studies and had decided to "go home." She wondered if the UK was my home and said she wished me lots of luck going home if it wasn't. My young patient was able to address and separate my own longing from hers without fearing or attacking me.

Finding a home in one's passions: dance and psychoanalysis

As the reader has gathered by now, my life, first as a child and now as an adult has been a series of migrations from one country to another. This has required constant re-organization and the capacity to adapt to new ways of being with others while retaining the essence of where I come from, where I started. Perhaps as a result, I longed for communities that encourage and respect both my passion and creativity and that are also transferrable, that "I can take with me." I found in the worlds of dance and psychoanalysis "containers" for my experience and wonderful "transitional spaces" where to process and integrate my ongoing experiences of internal and external migration.

Very early on in my life I found in the world of dance a place to call home. When I was four years old, my mother took me to my first ballet class to help with some orthopedic issues. By the time I was nine years old I was taking ballet class every day. I felt like a native in the world of dance, in fact, to this day, every time I move to a new city the first thing I look up is a dance class. As an adolescent, I became enamored with everything about dance, particularly its history and its European roots. Dance was a wonderful bridge between the two predominant cultures in my life, both my mother's and father's countries have been under the control of other nations most of their existence, however, you can reach into the collective soul of both countries by listening to their songs and their dancing. Dancing lends itself to the expression of multiple affects and the telling of stories without words; it helps to translate the internal into an external coherent story, very much like the dance we engage in during the psychotherapeutic encounter.

In the same fashion, I found my passion in child and adolescent psychoanalysis; in my opinion, an often undervalued area of psychoanalysis which is currently in danger as a field. The psycho-analytic community has provided a place where my diversity and the challenge it represents are embraced by most. I found a home in the collective passion existing in psychoanalysis for facilitating the development of new perspectives and ways of connecting through the telling and retelling of our stories and those of our patients. In my work, I strive to create a safe environment where thoughts and feelings can be explored and clients can learn to develop their self-observing capacities and emerge with a stronger sense of agency over their lives and find their own road "home." In this context, I truly value the flexibility, genuine curiosity, and passion that I have developed as a result of my own life journey.

References

Altman, N. (1995). *The Analyst in the Inner City*. Hillsdale, NJ: The Analytic Press.

Amati-Mehler, J., Argentieri, S. & Canestri, J. (1993). *The Babel of the Unconscious: Mother Tongue and Foreign Languages in the Psychoanalytic Dimension*. Connecticut, US: International Universities Press.

Bodnar, S. (2004). Remember where you come from: dissociative process in multicultural individuals. *Psychoanalytic Dialogues, 14*: 581–603.

Chodorow, N. J. (2002). Born into a world at war: Listening for affect and personal meaning. *American Imago, 59*: 297–315.

Estrada, N. (1942). *En Mi Viejo San Juen* [In my old San Juen]. New York.

Flynn, D. (2013). Migration, loss and connectedness: two analytic cases. In: A. Varchevker & E. McGinley (Eds.), *Enduring Migration through the Life Cycle* (pp. 61–87). London: Karnac.

Grinberg, L. & Grinberg, R. (1989). *Psychoanalytic Perspectives on Migration and Exile*. New Haven, CT: Yale University Press.

Joyce, A. (2013). Internal and external migration in infancy and childhood: the representation of absence in a mother–baby couple—a case study in psychoanalytic parent–infant psychotherapy, In: A. Varchevker & E. McGinley (Eds.), *Enduring Migration Through the Life Cycle* (pp. 3–59). London: Karnac.

CHAPTER SIX

A wound of no return: in search of self, loss, and transformation

Monisha Nayar-Akhtar

> But I find that thy will knows no end in me. And when old words die out on the tongue, new melodies break forth from the heart; and where the old tracks are lost, new country is revealed with its wonders.
>
> —Rabindranath Tagore, *Gitanjali*

Meeting of waters/confluence of identities

In the northern part of India, in the Kullu Manali region of the Himalayan Mountains, the Beas River rises and flows for some 290 miles to the Sutlej River in the Indian state of Punjab. The river is imbued with mythological history as it was named after the sage Vasistha, (Beas is a derivative of the original name) who despondent by the death of his hundred sons tried to end his life by jumping into the river. However, the river, touched by this sage's sorrow, safely carried him to the banks. The river also figures prominently in India's history, serving to thwart Alexander's conquests in India. Today, the waters of the Beas River traverse through the mountainous landscape, clear as crystal making its way down the countryside. Its gushing waters enthrall and beckon the brave of heart to run the river's course as it moves rapidly through the mountainous territory. Similarly, the Parvati River also rises in that region of the land, and flows into the Beas River at Bhuntar. The Beas and Parvati rivers are both fed by waters from the glaciers that gleam in the sunlight from the distant Himalayan range. But in contrast to the Beas River, the waters of the Parvati are darker, muddied with silt and traverse down the mountainside steadily and stealthily. The confluence of the two rivers at Bhuntar is striking. The clear water of the Beas becomes muddy, the turbulence increases and an unsuspecting underlying current can often catch someone off guard. The dramatic shift in nature and composition often finds itself in local folklore that alerts travelers to the deadly seduction of these two rivers when they meet.

Now, crossing several continents and practically on the other side of the globe, in the deep Amazon basin of Brazil, there occurs another "meeting of waters." This refers to the confluence between the Rio Negro, a river that is characterized by dark (almost black in color) water and the sandy-colored Amazon River, known as the Rio Solimoes, in that region. For about 3.7 miles, the two rivers run side by side without mixing.

These two meetings of waters serve as a backdrop for this paper in which I explore and highlight key experiences that served as precursors to shape, mold, and eventually transform the trajectory of my analytic identity. This "meeting of waters" represents symbolically how I came to conceptualize and understand the manner, often unconscious, in which my various identities transitioned over time and came to define the way I work and think today as an analyst. At times like the rivers Beas and Parvati, indistinguishable from each other and at times like the rivers Rio Negro and Rio Solimoes, running parallel, side-by-side, in uneasy harmony. In using the analogy of these four rivers, I am also referencing the multilingual, multicultural, as well as secular aspects of my motherland, India.

Unknown to many in the Western world, the diversity of India can be overwhelming as the definition of what defines an Indian, remaining nebulous and confusing at best. As a secular country, Indians represent the largest population of Hindus in the world with the Muslim population being the second largest in the world after Indonesia. One additional caveat bears mentioning at this point. While many are familiar with Bollywood, the largest producer of movies in the world (made famous in the movie *Slumdog Millionaire*, released 2008) my personal cinematic history was shaped by Satyajit Ray, an exemplary Bengalee film-maker whose movies won international acclaim and recognition and posthumously an Oscar award as well. My story is therefore complex, strewn with strands of ruptures and integration, as confusing and fragmented in the beginning, as it will appear to be in the end. It is and continues to be an identity that remains in a state of transition. This then is the story of my journey, my "meeting of waters," a discovery in the end, of myself.

Analytic identity

The transformation of a therapist who thinks dynamically and works with a certain theoretical and technical perspective is eventually an amalgamation of many internal and external forces that impact the individual during the course of their training and beyond. This journey, whether undertaken in a formal analytic institute training program or encountered during an individual's graduate clinical training, is long and arduous, at times difficult and challenging. In the end, it is a life-altering course for most people. Much has been written about the analytic identity that continues to evolve long after one has completed training (Klauber, 1986; Wille, 2008) with thoughtful discourse on the role of challenging life events, the widening scope of analysis, the surge of relational and intersubjective thinking in theory and technique, and the influx of cultural diversity in our programs.

For an immigrant, the impact of cultural diversity and the literary discourse around this subject is significant. Perhaps my referencing the confluences of the Rivers Beas and Parvati and the Rivers Negro and Amazon, conveys the dilemmas of identities in transition particularly that of mine, as I emigrated from my country of origin to the country I now call home. Inherent in this dilemma are the origins of my several identities and the confluence of significant threads with developmental impact in my life.

Early history

The story of immigration and the language of adjustment and assimilation of a new culture shaped much of my young childhood, adolescent, and adult life and is deeply embedded in my mind, body, and soul. My ancestral history from both my paternal and maternal side can be traced to what is now known as Bangladesh. India's history is rich with strife and partitions, either of kingdoms or that of countries. India's independence from the British, who ruled for over 300 years, resulted in a partition of the land along religious lines. On the Western border, the country split with the formation of West Pakistan whereas in the East, a smaller split occurred with East Bengal being renamed as East Pakistan. Hindus who resided in East Bengal/East Pakistan were forced to flee and make their way into India, surreptitiously, traveling sometimes in the middle of the night with little to sustain them other than their will to live and survive. My father belonged to one of many such families that migrated and made their way into India, fighting off those that would accost them along the way and hauling as much of their wealth as they could. This was little considering the abundant life-style they originally had as landowners. My mother was more fortunate as her family had left East Bengal many years ago to Calcutta, a thriving city that welcomed intellectuals and businesses in those days. Once seen as the capital of India by the British, Calcutta offered an intellectual and financial refuge for many. My maternal grandfather was an example of that having served for most of his adult life as the Dean of Philosophy in the prestigious Calcutta University. His writings on time, space, and Brahma are well-known in Eastern philosophy and vestiges of that have found their way into my thinking as well as you will gradually see.

But despite my mother's relatively privileged life, she was not immune to the impact of partition. As a young girl, she participated actively in the youth Congress movement and rose to the occasion when Mahatma Gandhi, the Nation's father during these times, called upon all to boycott Western goods as part of the non-violent movement. But Bengal was by no means a compliant participant in such movements having sired a National Hero of its own. Subhas Chandra Bose, a noted military man, led many a Bengalee youth to bear arms and retaliate militarily against the British in defiance of Gandhi's non-violent move-ment. Both movements marked my development and characterized my developing adolescent years as I listened intently to the stories of struggle and valor recounted by my parents, echoed by my relatives who had managed to survive the massacre that accompanied the pain-ful partition of India and the formation of Pakistan. Political discourse often accompanied our evening meals and social discourse about where the country was heading was part of our daily diet. Needless to say, these became embedded in my identity, as internal objects, defining it to some degree and certainly finding expression in my clinical work later in life. Not surprisingly, as has been noted in the psychoanalytic literature, the agonizing impact of partition and the division of the country is now emerging in a body of work undertaken by a prominent psychoanalytically oriented author and critical theorist, Ashish Nandy (1983, 2007). Nandy's examination of several personal accounts of struggle related to this period underscores the lingering impact of trauma. As a child of such a struggle, my journey was colored by verbal and non-verbal accounts of such trauma and the accompanying geographical displacement. These eventually became part of my personal narrative and my core identity.

Family history

I grew up enveloped by an ancestral history of forced migration and relocation. Very early in life I became aware of the losses encountered by our family, and the struggles that ensued. The struggles were both economic and emotional. My father's status as the oldest son made him responsible for the well-being of his parents and siblings and these were not taken lightly. This often limited the funds that were available for his family that was now growing. I entered my adolescent years, with several questions regarding my purpose in life, perhaps more existential in nature. India was in a state of political flux at that time and the seeds of Marxism and the Naxalite movement (that became more pronounced in the coming decades) were being sown, particularly in the State of Bengal.

Several skeins of sociocultural, political, and familial influences appear in my transition to a young adolescent. Psychoanalysis in the mid-1900s was flourishing and as a psychiatrist, my father was not immune to this. In pursuit of knowledge, my father quite early in his career, moved to London accompanied by his wife and young children. Early writings by Freud now found their way into our library just as strands of intense political and social discourse. My father devoured these books with fervor and I at a very early age was introduced to key psychoanalytic concepts, though I viewed them with a mixture of suspicion and curiosity. Psychoanalysis and psychiatry for that matter was a brand new medical discipline in India and for the most part, my family with my father at the helm was viewed with a modicum of disapproval and concern. Stigma associated with the diagnosis of mental illness and ignorance in the community marked my father's entry into the field of psychiatry and psychoanalytic thinking. This mixture of derision, suspicion, some admiration and considerable alarm in the community influenced me as a young girl, as I remained ambivalent about my college aspirations as my time to leave home became imminent. It was only with considerable physical distance (though not emotional!) between myself and my family of origin (after migration) could I loosen the burden of ambivalence and self-doubt and embark on a training program that culminated in analytic training and practice. Such is the power of cultural mores and norms and the world we grow up in!

Yet, my father's psychiatric/psychoanalytic bent of mind was not the only influence in my life, as I grew up surrounded by family where political discourse was a steady diet liberally sprinkled with socialistic thinking and Marxist ideas, especially during social gatherings. All strands appear in my adult life in one form or the other, forcing a merger of choices, of identities and ultimately a confluence of separate parts of myself. My mother's, often silent presence marked many life experiences and transitions for me. She was a gifted musician and dancer and a poetic writer as well. She derived solace from hours of practice on her sitar in the wee hours of the morning. Unable to change the world she found herself in, my mother imparted to me the wisdom of silence, the gift of music and dance and the power to heal oneself through perseverance and dedicated practice. Vestiges of both maternal and paternal influences appear in how I live my life, a steady reminder that the "apple never falls too far from the tree."

Migration

My immigration to the United States in my late teens put in motion the process of what Salman Akhtar (1995) has called "the third individuation," and set the stage for further exploration of myself and my identity. One could say that migration was in my blood and though the move was traumatic, I could not have lived my life in any other fashion. Now faced with choices and opportunities hitherto unavailable for me for various reasons (much like my father in his pursuit of academic training) I began to consciously carve out a path for myself, with my unconscious motivations for the most part remaining quite unclear. Perhaps this paper is an attempt to pull together different strands of sociocultural and political influences that once merged and have now emerged in the ongoing consolidation of my analytic identity.

However, there were clear periods (with some overlap) during which my identity as a therapist and analyst began to coalesce more rapidly and with clarity. These periods for me were marked with papers that I wrote to pull together different skeins of my identity, grappling with feelings and thoughts that I could not effectively voice. As I reflect on the various papers that I have written, they mark transition points for me. In the development of my identity, in the working through of powerful affects and in consolidating split of parts of myself, I am reminded of the use of writing as an essential adjunct to the process of self-analysis (Griffin, 2004) in addition, to being a powerful identification with my mother who often wrote poetry and prose to work through difficult self-states. One can say that the confluence between my professional and personal journeys bear the mark of various strands of maternal and paternal influences, at times distinct and at times indistinguishable from each other.

Upon further reflection, I am able to identify three distinct periods (again with overlap) that defines this developmental trajectory. These are characterized by distinct attitudes, beliefs, values, and conduct accompanied by an unconscious and conscious world. I identify the three periods as:

- **Identity of acquisition** is defined by a feverish wish and desire to acquire as much theoretical and technical knowledge. Often this period is marked with considerable self-doubt, with a certain awkwardness of thought and being, and a desire to emulate one's training analyst, supervisor, and collectively the training institute.
- **Identity of assimilation/adjustment** is defined by one's imminent graduation from a training program. With the analysis of transferences, the helpful exploration of de-identifying with one's analyst and training program, and in conjunction with the successful (hopefully) completion of candidate requirements, the candidate is able to relax and assume a more informed stand towards their training. This frees them to broaden their thinking, expand their associations, and eventually find expression in an analytic voice and attitude that is more comfortable and in sync with different parts of their identity. However, some struggles still emerge and the desire and wish to conform are sometimes at odds with their newfound position in cultural

communities and various settings. The process of adjustment to the outside world, and the questioning of internal constructs can now begin. This period can continue for many years after graduation till the young analyst through self-reflection and exploratory conduct finds a path that is acceptable.

- **Identity of acceptance** is the culmination of an individual's gradual acceptance of themselves, how they work and relate internally to notions of psychoanalytic function in both thought and action. This period lasts throughout life as the developmental trajectory for identities in transition extends well into our twilight years. Witness the growing semi-autobiographical accounts of the personal journeys of some analysts (Parens, 2004) who later in life reveal poignant and heart wrenching details of their personal struggle that define them and are embedded in their souls.

Having defined these three distinct (with overlap) periods of development, I will elaborate on how I worked through the internal dialectic tensions that appeared between who I was and how I lived and thought.

Identity of acquisition

Steeped in coursework as a beginning candidate, I spent hours devouring psychoanalytic books and articles. The *Standard Edition* acquired quickly symbolized my entry into the field of psychoanalysis and was proudly displayed in my library. My progression into clinical psychoanalytic practice marked another entry point, as did the supervisions that were now introduced into my weekly work routine. My training analysis was also progressing and I encased by my institutes ever-watchful eye, I grew.

I was fortunate to have received my training in an institute that is considered one of the strongest in the country and I was part of a cohort of seven seasoned therapists. While they were professionally diverse (social workers, psychologists, and psychiatrists) ethnic and cultural diversity was nonexistent. I was the only woman of color and an immigrant to boot. Although, awareness of this limitation and its impact on me did not occur till much later in my personal analysis and professional development. Ensconced safely within the holding environment of an analysis that was progressing and caught in the throes of a "transference" that Bollas (1979) has referred to as the use of the analyst as a "transformational object," it was a few years into my candidacy that I wrote my first paper on an issue relating to cultural diversity. My paper on silence was presented in Nice, France in 2002 during an International Psychoanalytic Conference and described how prevailing attitudes regarding silence within the analytic space did not adequately capture Eastern notions of silence or how it manifested itself in my own personal analysis. This paper marked my entry into working through professional and sometimes personal culturally imbued dilemmas by writing about them. Yet, during my early years as a candidate, I was still intent on acquiring knowledge, denying for the most part my ethnicity and cultural diversity and early rumblings of dissent were somewhat muted and obscure.

My second attempt to pull together culturally diverse aspects of my identity and self emerged towards the end of my candidacy. Prominent in my self-exploration (during analysis) was the role that mythological icons and religious figures played during my early childhood and adolescent years. For my graduation paper, I chose to write on mythology albeit with some trepidation (concern was conveyed to me by senior culturally diverse colleagues). My paper titled "Psychoanalytic perspectives on the role of religious icons and mythology in working with trauma," highlighted how patients use such cultural icons as organizing constructs to conceptualize, frame, and understand (often unconsciously) their narratives of trauma. These two papers marked the beginning of my journey into incorporating various dimensions of my cultural identity into my professional life. Having completed one journey, I now embarked on another—to find and give expression to that while strangely familiar, had remained unfamiliar for so long. As such, I entered my second stage of identity exploration.

Identity of assimilation/adjustment

I graduated in 2005 from the adult psychoanalytic training program and in my graduation speech I acknowledged the love bestowed upon me by my mother and the dreams evoked and nourished by my father. This was a conscious acknowledgement and acceptance of my past and a preliminary exploration of other emerging cultural trends and traits. My analytic practice especially with a culturally diverse population was growing, and I found this both challenging and satisfying. The absence of a structured regimen of studies, coursework, and supervision freed me to work more creatively accompanied initially with a great deal of anxiety. Perhaps one of the initial markers of this shift appeared in the inclusion of more ethnically designed scarves and attire in my daily wardrobe. Scarves had always been part of my Western attire, but the inclusion of culturally motivated motifs and designs was a shift that did not go unnoticed by my patients.

In addition, I noted shifts in technical practice as well. Toward the end of my candidacy, I had been invited to join a trauma study group led by Richard Hertel, an Ann Arbor based analyst whose discussion group on trauma continues to be part of the American Psychoanalytic Meetings held in January in New York. Richard's ideas and thoughts on trauma influenced me profoundly and served as the impetus for my ongoing work in trauma and later in attachment. It was, with some trepidation, that I began to incorporate creative ways of working with my patients, especially those that had suffered indescribable trauma in early childhood and during their adolescent years. Exploring these challenges in a paper on this subject, I wrote about a patient whose distress upon my leaving (to go to New Delhi) was palpable and concerning. My response to that was to provide her with enough information, including geographical location that would allow her to remember and place me when I was absent. I have found this to be particularly useful with patients whose inner experience of psychic pain is so profound that holding on to our work and maintaining object constancy is easily threatened. Interestingly, the only time I informed this patient was when I left for India. Though there were other vacations, usually short, which I took from time to time and I never found the need to contain and hold her in a similar manner. As I reflect on this enactment, which occurred several years ago, I wonder if when it came to my travels to my motherland, that my agony of parting was experienced more acutely by me and in identification with her loss (and my history of migration), I felt a need to ease our mutual sorrow at that time.

Identity of acceptance

In 2007, for personal reasons, I relocated to the East Coast and joined the Psychoanalytic Center of Philadelphia whose institutional culture was markedly different from the one I had trained in. The cultural shock that ensued profoundly compounded my grieving process as memories of several other losses, past and present, now emerged in full force. In addition, my move also resulted in several forced terminations as I went through the process of closing down my over twenty-year-old practice. In preparation for my move, I had begun informing my patients almost a year in advance of my anticipated date of departure. Once again, I turned to writing about my move in an effort to cope with the feelings of pain, loss, and guilt. Presenting my paper on termination, in a discussion group on termination, held during the winter meetings of the American Psychoanalytic Association in 2008, I spoke about the agony of loss of relationships with certain patients, whose work was now interrupted. At that juncture of my analytic identity, I still remained deeply entrenched within the walls of "classical psychoanalytic orthodoxy," though attempts to incorporate different parts of my identity could clearly be seen from time to time overtly in my appearance and with occasional forays into my clinical work as well in my writing. Yet, these were rare and often accompanied by considerable guilt and anxiety. Still, in my paper on termination and its impact on me and my patients, I stepped outside my internal frame to explore how deeply this move resonated with my early experience of immigration and my subsequent attempts during my training to hide painful affects associated with my initial move. One patient in particular came to mind.

I had been working with Marjorie for over four years. She was now eighty-two and though our three times psychoanalytically oriented work had been productive; there were a few more issues that needed further exploration. Majorie listened to me with stoic silence when I informed her of my impending departure and remained unresponsive when I suggested that she could benefit from seeing someone else for a while after we discontinued. When the time came for me to leave, she chose not to take me up on my offer for a suitable referral, stating that she had come as far she possibly could and was able to go on with her life without needing further therapy. I have often wondered about Marjorie (as I do so even today) and how she is faring. Perhaps these thoughts had something to do with my thoughts about my ailing mother who lived in New Delhi. My access to her was limited to bi-yearly visits and periodic phone calls. She had passed away a few years prior to my relocation, but thoughts of her would sporadically appear and occupy my mind. I was also thinking of Marjorie (and feeling very guilty about holding onto her in this manner) when Joseph Schachter (1990, 1992) who was the discussant and whose work on termination is well-known, enquired if I had ever thought of contacting her either with a phone call or letter. We debated this issue, my discomfort evident in my reticence to pursue this further at that time. Perhaps my response today would be different.

Later, in 2010, I had an opportunity to present a paper in China titled "The impact of culture on the work ego." This paper was fuelled in part by my increasing visits to New Delhi, India during which I presented frequently on the topic of child and adolescent analysis to psychology graduate students enrolled in Delhi University. My paper on work ego emerged from my observation (and the observation of my patients) that I appeared different and worked differently whenever I returned from such trips! I had not thought about this consciously and the paper allowed me the luxury of self-reflection and enquiry. The slight differences in how I handled time (not as bound by Western notions of when to exactly begin or end sessions) or money (with one analytic patient, I waited six months to receive payment as she was in a dire financial crunch!). Though I do not for a moment think that these are all a product of cultural differences, I do concur with the observation of some analysts (Akhtar, 2006) that these are imbued with cultural nuances and meanings that appear in our clinical work in subtle and sometimes in not so subtle ways.

Since my move to the East Coast, a few life-changing events have also altered the trajectory of my professional and personal life and facilitated my identity of acceptance. Of these, my frequent trips to New Delhi stand out as markers of another developmental phase in my professional life. My desire to reconnect with my country of origin has of course multiple meanings, from sharing the language, clothing, ease of communication and feeling "at home" the moment I step off the airplane. The irony of this profoundly deep connection is that within ten days (the usual length of my stay) I am ready to return home to my adopted land! During my brief stay however, I have found ways to connect, contribute to, and shape some of the mental health care provided in orphanages and elsewhere.

Case vignettes

My frequent trips to India to take care of an ailing mother during my candidacy, one day led to the following exchange with a patient. Laura, a twenty-six-year-old woman who had lost her mother in a car accident when she was five, experienced severe anxiety every time we had a break in our work. It appeared the day we began our analytic work, when Laura experienced difficulty leaving my office and reported the next day that she had spent half an hour, sitting in the stairwell, crying. As these diminished, Laura became more comfortable for my shorter breaks and eventually began to show more irritation and anger that could be then analyzed. However, longer breaks (usually scheduled in advance) were always more difficult. When my mother suddenly passed away, it necessitated a sudden and imminent departure on my part. I did not have time to explain, as I had to leave in the middle of the night.

Upon my return, Laura looking visibly shaken up and asked me if I had gone to India. I replied in the affirmative and when she asked why I had left so suddenly, I replied, my mother passed away. My decision to reveal this information was a function of my abject grief and an inability to contain my painful affects. Though somewhat shielded by the couch on which she lay, I could not hide the tremble of tears in my voice and was grateful for the fact that the she did not turn around and look at me at this time.

I found this exchange extremely uncomfortable though many today from a relational perspective, would describe it as a moment of deep connection. But shrouded as I was at the time by a cloak of "psychoanalytic orthodoxy," and bound by the rigidities of frame and structure, I suffered internally with what I had felt to be grave technical transgression. The analysis of this moment was ongoing and imbued with concern, care, and some hostility on Laura's part for being burdened with this knowledge. In due time, we could begin to understand the profound implications of the loss of her mother at that age.

Some thirteen years later, working with Jamie, a woman in her fifties, I suffered another personal loss. The unexpected passing away of my sister who lived locally led to an immediate cancellation of all my patients for that day. Having received the information about half an hour before the arrival of Jamie, I did not have time to reflect and craft out a suitable neutral response. Instead, calling my analytic patient on the phone, my voice trembling with tears, I informed her that I would have to cancel all her appointments with me for the following three days. The patient, who had been previously diagnosed as borderline, insisted on knowing why. I informed her of my loss and we agreed to meet in three days.

Jamie's response to my loss was deeply sympathetic, but anger at having been inconvenienced (as she was close to my office), wondering if I was able to help her, as well as envy and a longing to be my sister, all emerged in due course and was subjected to analytic enquiry. My internal response was contained and I considered what appeared to be "grist for the mill."

Needless to say, my reactions with Laura and Jamie were quite different and colored by experience, time, and a sense of my identity as an analyst. With Laura, I was a candidate in training, eager to conduct the work in analysis with clarity, anonymity, and considerable neutrality. I adhered keenly to the key tenets of my discipline and institutional character. But, vestiges of my cultural self would peek through from time to time. My initial reluctance to disclose anything about myself gradually eased (aided by a growing relational and intersubjective theoretical and technical stance in the field) and found its way into my work. Nonetheless, my anxiety and discomfort remained ego dystonic and I questioned such departures in technique frequently. Attempting to resolve this internal struggle and not entirely satisfied with what I read in the psychoanalytic literature, I sought answers from writers, outside the field. Drawing from the writings of critical cultural theorists (Bhabha, 1994; Chakraborty Spivak, 1988) and engaged in dialogues with my bicultural daughters, I sought refuge in terminology such as "liminal space, hybridity" (Bhabha, 1994), which captured for me the complex internal dynamics associated with being an immigrant and "subalternity" (Chakraborty, 1988) that explores and broadens understanding of postcolonial mentality and class structure. These terms deepened my understanding, resonated with my sociocultural and political soul and seemed to intuitively capture the various skeins of my several identities and the space that was now being created.

Several years later, in my work with Jamie, self-disclosure (sometimes around issues of culture) was no longer self-exploration, but an exchange between myself and Jamie that deepened the analytic process, enhanced our work, and eventually allowed her to access split off parts of her own identity. During a Division 39 conference held in Boston, 2013, I examined Jamie's exploration of her own migration from the Mid-West region of this country to the East Coast. During the course of our analytic journey, Jamie has begun to reclaim split off parts of her own sociocultural and political history which is quite different, as she puts it, from the East Coast mentality!

Meeting of the waters

My opening metaphor of the river Beas and Parvati and that of the Amazon River reflects and captures the undulating nature of my struggle to find my identity as an analyst, to hear my voice laced by the voice of my parental imagoes, and the voices of my ancestors before them, to practice with an ethos that comes from the depths of my soul. Like my father, my personal history *is* imbued with my history of migration and subsequent migrations to other parts of my adopted country. The narratives of my ancestors and the yearning in their voices as they spoke of the lost land, the demise of dignity, and the accompanying affect of shame, seeped into my being as I grew surrounded by my people who were now refugees in a foreign land. They had been shaped by world events and now they in turn would shape those who were in their care. The story cannot be told any other way. Experiences, like the individual water molecules of a river, link together, blending and fusing in till they become indistinguishable from each other. They link us to our past and provide the blueprint of our future. During the course of understanding ourselves, these experiences become delinked and come under self-analytic enquiry. I am reminded, here, of the intergenerational transmission of trauma and the narratives that live beyond one's personal experience. Psychoanalytic perspectives on the history of Holocaust survivors (Brenner, 1997; Kestenberg & Brenner, 1986) highlight poignantly, the story of trauma and its transmission to the next generation. It is rich with the painful narratives of survivors and the agony of their children who continue to bear, often silently, the multitude of losses inherent in their individual yet collective struggles.

This along with sociocultural and political strife shaped much of my personal history, as did my desire for social justice and personal growth. As a mid-career analyst, I find myself with a newfound freedom. Informed by my personal development and reflecting on the path that I chose, with conscious and unconscious influences, to integrate various aspects of myself, I have gone beyond the confines of "psychoanalytic orthodoxy," while paradoxically adhering to it even more tenaciously. The paradox for me lies in the knowledge that it takes years for an analytic identity to evolve and as some would say, it never stops. The psychoanalytic culture is in a state of flux. Not unlike the impact of globalization on the experience of personal space and identity, the development and experience of analytic identity is in a state of jeopardy.

Perhaps in adhering to it and examining it we also allow ourselves to become more integrated and eventually free.

In summary, the consolidation of my analytic identity is a work in progress, though several threads of early sociocultural and political influences appear more consistently now in my work and in my writing. Experience and expressions of sociocultural discord are not limited to immigrants as I have found. Individuals who migrate from one part of the country to another, bear the marks of traumatic and *geographic* dislocation as well. One may speak the same language, but one hears and feels in markedly different ways, as Jamie in her mid-Western dialect once commented to me. Perhaps it was a consolidation of various parts of my identity, informed by immigration and cultural displacement that led to this following exchange with a patient.

Carol was nearing the end of her seven year analysis during which we had uncovered and worked through an early childhood history of abandonment complicated and informed by the presence of black caretakers that had been responsible for her care. Carol often declared her love for me, though this felt "contaminated," in some ways. She could not keep me with her and had to check me at the door when she entered her white world. As my termination work continues with Carol, we will examine the profound unconscious meanings behind this split. Perhaps similarly in the trajectory of my "analytic identity," I along with many others like me, will not have to check something at the door when we enter our consulting rooms! Instead, we will have the courage to take them along with us and give expression consciously or unconsciously to the profound meanings of our inner experiences.

References

Akhtar, S. (1995). A third individuation: immigration, identity and the psychoanalytic process. *Journal of the American Psychoanalytic Association, 43*: 1051–1084.

Akhtar, S. (2006). Technical challenges faced by the immigrant analyst. *Psychoanalytic Quarterly, 75*: 21–43.

Beaufoy, S. (Producer), & Boyle, D. & Tandan, L. (Director). (2008). *Slumdog Millionaire* [Motion Picture]. UK and India: Warner Brother's, Celador Films, Film4, & Pathe Pictures International.

Bhabha, H. (1994). *The Location of Culture*. London and New York: Routledge.

Bollas, C. (1979). The transformational object. *International Journal of Psychoanalysis, 60*: 97–107.

Brenner, I. (1997). Recovered memories of abuse. *Journal of the American Psychoanalytic Association, 45*: 1285–1287.

Chakraborty Spivak, G. (1988). Can the subaltern speak. In: C. Nelson & L. Grossberg (Eds.), *Marxism and the Interpretation of Culture*. Chicago, IL: University of Illinois Press.

Griffin, F. L. (2004). One form of self-analysis. *The Psychoanalytic Quarterly, 73*: 683–715.

Kestenberg, J. S. & Brenner, I. (1986). Children who survived the Holocaust—the role of rules and routines in the development of the superego. *International Journal of Psychoanalysis, 67*: 309–316.

Klauber, J. (1986). *Difficulties in the Analytic Encounter*. London: Free Association.

Nandy, A. (1983). *The Intimate Enemy: Loss and Recovery of Self under Colonialism*. Oxford, United Kingdom and New Delhi: Oxford India Paperbacks (Oxford University Press).

Nandy, A. (2007). *A Very Popular Exile*. Oxford, United Kingdom and New Delhi: Oxford University Press.

Parens, H. (2004). *Renewal of Life: Healing from the Holocaust*. Rockville, MD: Schreiber Publications.

Schachter, J. (1990). Post-termination patient-analyst contact: I. analysts' attitudes and experience; II impact on patients. *International Journal of Psychoanalysis, 71*: 475–485.

Schachter, J. (1992). Concepts of termination and post-termination patient-analyst contact. *International Journal of Psychoanalysis, 73*: 137–154.

Wille, R. S. (2008). Psychoanalytic identity: Psychoanalysis as an internal object. *Psychoanalytic Quarterly, 77*: 1193–1229.

CHAPTER SEVEN

A demand for training

Marco Posadas

Because one believes in oneself, one doesn't try to convince others. Because one is content with oneself, one doesn't need others' approval. Because one accepts oneself, the whole world accepts him or her.

—*Lao Tzu*

The present is a personal account of a journey to pursue psychoanalytic training. I would like to compare this journey to the journey a patient takes when he or she decides to express a demand for analysis. My journey has conscious and unconscious motivations that led me to formulate a demand for training. This is an account of some of the conscious ones. I think that my journey may or may not be like any other journey to become an analyst. The fact that is, part of this book speaks more about the need to reflect about the trials and tribulations that an aspiring analyst has to go through, and the importance of sharing psychoanalytic stories than to any specific aspect of my story.

I believe our profession needs to be more open about the challenges that psychoanalysis is facing today. Sharing the struggles inherent in becoming an analyst and the way aspiring candidates work through these challenges can help to unveil the human side of the person that sits behind the couch. In fact, part of our skill set and identity as psychoanalysts are rooted in the analyst's personal history, personal obstacles, and the way we overcome them. Through storytelling, we can find a powerful tool to foster a holding environment for future psychoanalysts in training.

Origins

Through my work in the International Psychoanalytical Studies Organization (IPSO) I have heard many stories of candidates that had to break systemic barriers to be able to go after their dreams to practice the "Talking Cure," as Bertha Pappenheim once coined. Moving to a different country to have access to better opportunities is not a new thing. I am convinced that almost everyone has heard someone talk about this, but we rarely have a chance to reflect on the things that the practitioners had to do to be able to conduct analysis. I would like to share my story, and the things that helped me to find a space within the psychoanalytic realm. I hope by sharing my story I can help in carving a territory to think about diversity within psychoanalysis and the importance of challenging the status quo. I hope my story resonates with someone and that it provides a voice for them.

"We do not train homosexuals to *be* psychoanalysts." That was the response I received when I asked what the admission requirements were to pursue psychoanalytic training in an International Psychoanalytical Association (IPA) affiliated institute. I tried to keep my cool and to appear as if the statement had not fazed me. After all, I was in the middle of one of my classes during my psychology training in a well-known university in Mexico City in the late 1990s, but truly I was stunned. I was not totally *out* to my peers back then, so the nonchalant manner the professor used to address my question in front of the class took me by surprise. Just like that, my long-standing desire to become a psychoanalyst was officially put to the test.

Perhaps it may be useful to provide some history of my journey to become a psychoanalyst before telling you about how I ended up training and practicing psychoanalysis and psychoanalytic psychotherapy in Toronto, Canada. I wanted to become an analyst ever since I had my first encounter with psychotherapy at the age of ten. My family, like many other Mexican middle-class family, was going through a difficult period of adaption and it was decided that we all had to go to therapy. Of course I resented this decision, and I felt ashamed of and worried that my peers would think that I was a "crazy person." I did not know what to expect, and I was not able to articulate my doubts and tribulations about psychotherapy back then. I was convinced that nothing good could come out of this decision, but I had to go.

X-Men

When I first met Alma (pseudonym), the child analyst I was referred to by my parents' psychotherapist, I did not like her. I had determined that she was the enemy and the person that was forcing me to do this thing that *crazy* people do. The sessions seemed endless, her questions were boring, and I could not bring myself to trust her. The interesting thing was that I could not *hate* her either. She was also warm and fun to be with, and she seemed genuinely interested in the way I drew people, houses, and trees. She was particularly invested in me telling her stories about my drawings.

I thought she made me anxious, but as time went by I realized that she was helping me to identify when I was anxious. Alma seemed sincerely curious about me and her patience intrigued me. She did a standardized battery of tests before proceeding to twice per week psychotherapy. I remember spending most of the first few sessions sitting in silence and looking at my watch to see how time went by and it could not go fast enough.

Alma's strong presence and gentle demeanor, her attunement, and her skills created a shift for me. I began to notice a profound sense of calm after some of her interventions. This experience left an important imprint in my mind. I became fascinated by her way of speaking and what I later understood as her way of listening. It helped me to shape my understanding of my inner world. It aided me in putting words to my fears, doubts, and resentments. I felt better about myself and about my family. Even though I had struggled during the first few months and *hated* the treatment, I was very impressed by how she rolled with the punches and was able to develop a caring connection with me. I felt cared for and contained.

I remember the exact moment after a particularly difficult session when I thought as I was leaving her office, "I want to do this when I grow up." At the time, I did not know what *this* meant. I just knew I wanted to be able to have *those* conversations with people. I wanted to be able to make people calm and make them feel better about themselves after they talked to me. I asked her a lot of questions about her profession, and that was when I heard for the first time the word *psychoanalysis*. I learned about psychologists and that psychotherapy was a way to help people *weave* stories together, something similar to making a puzzle with someone's help. I did not know how to weave, and I was not fond of puzzles so she lost me there, but I understood the idea. I understood that psychotherapy was something like figuring things out and I liked that. To me I thought of her as a superhero. I have always loved superheroes and I thought about Alma as some kind of an X-Man. To me it was the only a logical decision; I wanted to be one of the X-Men too and develop those same powers. I wanted to be a psychoanalyst and have the power to soothe people by listening to them.

Evolution

Since then, I started to read every book that I came across about psychotherapy, psychoanalysis, and psychology. At that time in Mexico City, the predominant theory in the mental health field was psychoanalysis and its presence in universities continues to be very well established. I knew I had to be a psychologist in order to train as an analyst. I was in my teens when I started to read Freud and Lacan for my psychology class in high school and became obsessed with them. It was at the same time when I was beginning to articulate my own sexual identity, and both Freud and Lacan's theories helped in my coming out process. Through reading their work I felt less ashamed of identifying as a gay man.

I began volunteering at an AIDS Hospice and HIV-related mental health clinic in my late teens to find out more about homosexuality, and gain some skills that could help me get in the psychology program that I wanted. It was there that I took my first training in HIV counseling, and volunteered in their buddy program to help people die with dignity. The model used was humanistic and person-centered counseling. The clinical team would train participating in role-plays, re-enacting how to prepare people to get tested, and how to support them through a positive diagnosis of HIV. The program's clinical supervisor was a Jungian analyst and his focus was very psychodynamic with a particular emphasis on drive theory and ego-psychology. During those years

I provided therapeutic accompaniment for people in the last stages of the HIV infection, and supported family members through the process of losing their loved ones to HIV/AIDS.

I participated in personal development groups, workshops, retreats … you name it. In my mind, every single step I took academically was an attempt to get me closer to my goal to become an analyst. I felt very proud of myself when my undergrad teachers would praise my skills and passion for psychoanalysis as a *psychotherapist-wanna-be*. You can imagine how shocked I was when I was told that homosexuals could not be practicing psychoanalysts. I had not anticipated that. It took me a couple of hours after that class ended to really take in what had just transpired. I had no idea what this could mean to my imaginary and idealized professional career. All I knew was that I felt very passionate about psychoanalysis and refused to believe that there were intrinsic differences in the way heterosexual analysts and homosexual analysts listened to the unconscious.

I already knew that psychoanalytic training would be challenging. Even though psychoanalysis continues to be a well established profession in Mexico, and like Argentina psychoanalysis is part of the cultural milieu, pursuing analytic training can be costly, emotionally taxing, and not rewarding when you are in the beginning stages of your career and trying to build up an analytic practice. Halfway through my psychology degree, I began to look for psychoanalytic institutes that would allow gay people to train, and began to hear the horror stories about homophobia within psychoanalysis. The analytic scene in Mexico City was confusing and closeted regarding their stance on homosexuality. When it came to homosexuality, there were mixed messages and blurred ethics.

I heard about unspoken rules that banned homosexuals from training as they were compared to all sorts of psychopathic mental structures due to their choice of love object.

> A professor once said in class "A homosexual structure is exactly the same as a rapist … you don't want a rapist analyzing people …"
>
> In another class where I attempted to question what seemed to be a misconception about homosexuality I was told, "If a homosexual was an analyst, he or she would only be able to properly analyze homosexuals, and wouldn't be able to properly analyze heterosexual people."

I thought "What? How?" I was too embarrassed to challenge this professor's view about homosexuality. I was already rocking the boat too much with my questions, and it was starting to look obvious that I was gay. I did not want to be the target of homophobic attacks that could jeopardize my credibility as a student and as psychologist in training. The outlook was grim, and I seem to find obstacles every step of the way.

I felt deflated, but continued to look for support amongst my network. Someone told me that I might be able to train if I found a training analyst who was open-minded enough and would not report me to the institute for being gay. This seemed more like a threat to me rather than an option. I was asked to perhaps consider keeping myself in the closet with their ethics, while participating in other institute activities outside of my personal analysis. I could not imagine how to do that. I witnessed how psychoanalytic institutes perpetuated homophobia through friends of mine that had been shamed back into the closet to be able to be admitted for training. A friend of mine disclosed how her own analyst deterred her from speaking about her sexual identity as the analyst did not feel comfortable with that material. I learned how people were expelled from institutes if someone found out about their sexual identity. I could not fathom how someone could undergo training analysis *inside of the closet*. I struggled imagining how a person could free associate and still be able to avoid discussing the experience of being gay. It all seemed unfair to me.

At the time I did not know how, but this lit a fire in me. My understanding of sexual identity was not as developed yet, but I was now somewhat aware of what I was up against. As I learned about the complex and often contradictory views about homosexuality that existed within psychoanalytic discourse, I continued to feel disappointed and enraged. I was now becoming aware of how psychoanalytic institutions were in fact famous for being homophobic. Curiously enough, I was both warned and encouraged by mentors to not give up on my quest to become a psychoanalyst. I had to find my way and my place. The only consolation I had was that I could not really afford to pursue analytic training at that time, so I did not have to worry about dealing with rejection then. I started to take different courses in Lacanian psychoanalysis as I watched from the sidelines how some of my straight friends applied successfully to psychoanalytic training institutes, while

I worked in human resources in the corporate world to save money for training.

The only psychoanalytic institutions in Mexico that were open to training openly gay people were a couple of non-IPA institutes, and neither of those options could provide a homophobic free environment for training. By then I felt extremely invested in the idea of belonging to a larger international community of analysts where my voice could help open up a space for *queer* thinking. I liked the historical tradition of it and the possibility of actually making some real change. I became very passionate about being able to contribute to diversity within psychoanalysis. The more I thought about it, the more I realized that if I wanted to become an analyst and practice I would have to leave my hometown. That possibility scared me. I felt saddened that I would have to sacrifice my friends, family, my favorite foods and favorite places in order to achieve my dreams. I would have to move to a country that provided a civil rights platform that prevented academic institutions from rejecting its applicants based on sexual identity and sexual orientation. This felt very exciting. That was how Canada came into play.

Why Canada?

There are two amazing things about Canada (besides universal access to health care and poutine); the *Canadian Charter of Rights and Freedoms* (1982) and the *Civil Marriage Act* (2005). In Canada same sex marriage was legalized in three provinces, in 2002 Ontario and Quebec, and in 2003, British Columbia. On 20 July 2005 the *Civil Marriage Act* was enacted, and with it Canada became the fourth country in the world to legalize same-sex marriage, and the first one outside of Europe. The act provided a gender-neutral definition of marriage, which supported same sex unions. The *Canadian Charter of Rights and Freedoms* (1982) prevents discrimination against any person and more specifically any disadvantaged population. Additionally, there is the Toronto Psychoanalytic Society and Institute (TPS&I) in Toronto. This sealed the deal for me. I had already lived outside of Mexico before, in London, UK for almost a year in my early twenties, so moving to another country did not seem too scary for me. On 1 July 2005 my partner and I moved to Toronto after spending almost a year in Miami where I was working for a crisis intervention and suicide hotline.

The *Canadian Charter of Rights and Freedoms* (1982) made rejecting any applicant from an academic or professional institute based on his/her sexual identity illegal in Canada. That was hopeful. Of course this did not mean that homophobic attitudes inside psychoanalytic institutes ceased to exist, but it certainly provided a safer space to challenge prejudice and to question the status quo. In hindsight, my application process to start a two-year training in psychoanalytic psychotherapy (The Advanced Training Program and Psychoanalytic Psychotherapy or ATPPP) at the TPS&I was a breeze. They were more curious about my clinical experience than my sexual orientation. In September 2005 I started my psychotherapy training at the ATPPP, and in September 2009 I started my analytic training both at the TPS&I. This is where the fun began.

Translation: building my identity as a Mexican immigrant analyst candidate in Toronto

My experience of migrating to Toronto to pursue psychoanalytic training and to practice psychotherapy has been one of the most challenging and most rewarding decisions I have ever made. It helped me grow as a person and as a clinician, and I am very grateful for the challenges and opportunities that I have encountered in my journey. The experience of undergoing a geographic dislocation provides the opportunity to experience a moment of crisis where change is the only constant. Everything but my email account, my relationship, and my personal information changed. As many have said before me, it is true that there is a change in the sense of self after a person moves to a different culture. It felt as if I did not belong to either country, but I know now that I belong to both of them at the same time. It felt like a massive metaphor that helped to ground me clinically and to understand deeply the concept of ambivalence.

This moment of crisis allowed me to value the challenges of pursuing psychoanalytic training in a different country and in a different language. It provided a reason to stay motivated to withstand the tremendous amount of anxiety attached to any and all grieving processes triggered by the move away from home. The sense of loss, the anxiety attached to the adaptation process, and the learning curve for the geographic dislocation was compensated by the incredible learning opportunities that I had access to ever since I moved to Toronto.

The resentment for having to give up my life in Mexico and profound sense of loss that I felt after leaving everything behind due to my sexual identity was the fuel that ignited and motivated me to jump through every hoop and hurdle that I encountered during my first few years in Canada. It helped me to find sense and meaning in every challenge.

Based on my personal experience, I knew that things were not going to be easy in Toronto. Unlike Latin America and Europe, psychoanalysis is not mainstream and is severely misunderstood, misrepresented, and misread in the United States and Canada. In addition to the professional differences, there were also many challenges that came with the label of "immigrant" or "newcomer" in Canada. For instance, all the cultural references attached to my clinical credentials were *lost in translation*. No one in Toronto knew that the university where I did my degree in Mexico City has one of the most respected psychoanalytically oriented clinical programs in the country. They were not familiar with what a clinical internship or building a private practice looked like in Mexico City.

I experienced these losses as narcissistic losses attached to my professional identity and my sense of competence as a clinician. It felt as if the required "Canadian experience" weighed more than the clinical experience that I accrued throughout my career before arriving to Toronto. I was not familiar with being defined as an "other." In Toronto I learned that I was a person of color. I had an accent, I was different, but suddenly that difference was valued as an asset. I believe that the experience of training and practicing outside of my hometown and in a language different than my mother tongue can be summarized in one word—*Translation*. I had to translate the struggle into hope. At least I was being judged and valued based on my skills as a clinician and not based on my sexual identity. The admission processes, the job interviews, and any initial assessment with a new patient felt refreshing. It was worth the struggle and the difficulty of practicing in another language.

In addition to the natural stressors of building an identity as a psychoanalyst, there were many fears that needed to be addressed and overcome as an immigrant analyst. The most immediate of them was practicing in English while my mother tongue was Spanish. I decided to start working in English in Toronto to overcome my fear of "how am I going to practice psychotherapy in a different language?" I knew that speaking Spanish would be an asset at some point in Toronto and that Spanish-speaking patients would eventually find their way to my office. So I wanted to address my fear head on. I chose to undergo my training analysis in English too, that way I could use my analysis as a scaffolding to allow me to build a sense of comfort and safety with English. As my personal analysis progressed, I began to notice how English became more and more prominent in my mind, especially in the way I could think about psychoanalysis.

I believed that if I had no choice but to work in English, it would feel easier to practice in that language at some point. It was not easy and I was terrified when I got my first English-speaking referral. Being attuned to the nuances of a foreign language can be a daunting task, and most of the time my struggle with English added to the load of insecurity that I felt as a psychoanalytic candidate. Picking up slips of the tongue made in English were very difficult tasks. I would try to point them out, just to see my patients dismiss them because I was not a native English speaker. My patient's dismissals resonated strongly with my own insecurities and anxieties. As I sifted through those anxieties both in supervision and in my own analysis, I was able to gain more confidence with being an ESL (English as a Second Language) candidate. As I realized that, the insecurity I felt during my work began to look very similar to the uncertainty inherent in psychoanalysis. I became more and more comfortable sitting with that uncertainty, and the trust in my skills strengthened.

Although access to metaphors, puns, jokes, and cultural references may seemed restricted in a second language, the way I started to experience language in my consulting room and in my personal analysis felt constructive and liberating. Simply put, I could not take language for granted. Even though working in Spanish felt like eating an awesome desert, English began to have a place of its own in my mind and in my heart. Insecurity turned into curiosity, and as I walked that path I felt more settled, and my patients reacted to that. I would associate to my patients' material and notice my associations were both in English and Spanish. It felt as if my internal repertoire to experience, contain, translate, and use my countertransference had expanded. It was very gratifying to notice how being a native Spanish-speaker became an asset while I was working with English-speaking patients.

Soon enough I was setting up a spare bedroom with a separate entrance in my house as my first office. I was interviewing my first few patients and tripping over how to negotiate a sliding scale fee, desperately trying to be able to believe that I was worthy of my full fee, but struggling trying to charge for cancellations and missed sessions. My chair felt too big for me, as if I was playing "dress-up grown-up" and could not play the part. In hindsight, I think that I simply could not believe that I was finally working and making a living as a psychotherapist.

The training program and my psychoanalytic community made a big difference for me. I remembered in my first class on a series of "Classic Freud" feeling awe when I heard the one of my professors discuss from a very inclusive, anti-homophobic, and anti-oppressive view his thoughts about how the oedipus complex could be structured when the child had same sex parents. I thought I was in psychoanalytic heaven. I felt I was born to do this type of work, and I could see how I was starting to build a small supportive community in my institute.

Practicing practicalities

While my internal struggle with language continued, I was also trying to adapt to the cultural differences of Canada. There are countless cultural differences in both countries (Canada and Mexico), and I would like to share my understanding of some of them to help the reader get a better picture of my process of creating my own identity as an immigrant psychoanalytic candidate. For example, psychotherapy is not a regulated profession in Mexico and had just started to become regulated in the province of Ontario. Both scenarios have their pros and cons. In Mexico there are a lot of people without any professional training or credentials that can call themselves a "psychotherapist." On the upside, this lack of regulation can be translated into flexibility in the system which provides the possibility for partnerships between universities and community based centers that enhance the learning opportunities for undergraduate psychologists, social workers, and physicians. In addition to the great clinical experiences that psychology students get in Mexico, psychoanalytic institutes have the possibility of conferring academic degrees with a professional psychoanalytic training.

Aside from how both countries regulate the profession or not, there are also serious differences in how mental health is conceptualized and understood in Canada *vs*. Mexico, and how psychoanalysis is understood and thought about in both countries. For instance, access to mental health services stigma, misunderstanding and misconceptions about psychoanalysis as an effective form of treatment, professional regulations, and the perceived "unleveled" psychotherapeutic playing field. In Toronto, medical psychotherapists are covered under the province's health insurance as part of the province's universal access to health care, while non-medical private practitioners have to bill the patient directly for their services.

This unleveled playing field provided an opportunity for me as a Mexican. In Mexico psychotherapists are trained from the beginning on how to build a referral network and the business side of running a private practice. We would role-play how to negotiate a fee, and these exercises helped to feel a little bit more competent in my skills as a clinician. These are some of the most striking differences that I encountered as I started to set up my private practice in Toronto.

Based on my clinical experience working in Mexico City, London (UK), Miami (US), and Toronto, I believe it is the immigrant analyst's capacity to listen to the cultural differences that can either hinder or enhance the therapeutic action of the analytic dyad where there is an analyst practicing in a different country than their place of origin. The immigrant analyst's identity, their capacity to adapt to the geographic dislocation, and his/her creativity to translate the cultural differences into a common play space for the analytic encounter are crucial to the development of a solid therapeutic alliance.

In my perception there seems to be more shame in accessing mental health care in Toronto than what I saw in Mexico City. Clinically speaking, I would spend more time in the initial interviews carving a space for feelings of shame and embarrassment to come to the forefront in my work in Toronto. I would actively try to address the inherent shame and embarrassment from seeking help, and focus on providing a little bit more support to tolerate the narcissistic wound of "needing help." It took me a while to notice the difference in time spent addressing shame and stigma connected to mental health with my Canadian patients than with my Latin American ones.

With my Canadian patients I spent more time actively encouraging the patient to talk about feelings of shame in connection to treatment and stigma associated to mental health, and it would pay off. It became easier for the patient to settle and begin associating more freely during the session in the beginning stages of the treatment. Another interesting difference is that psychoanalysis seems to me to be a younger profession in Latin American countries where the average age of a candidate is fifteen to twenty years younger than in North America. Every time I entered a classroom, a scientific meeting, or an event organized by the society I would realize that I was one of the younger, if not the youngest person in the room. In my consulting office, I would often encounter in several first sessions that my patients would disclose with embarrassment how they expected to be greeted by an "older man with white hair" than a "football player."

Being the youngest in my cohort in Toronto basically translated into being able to actively participate more intensely in other aspects of my training, and be very active in psychoanalytic community development. The opportunities started to arrive one after the other and not too long after, I began to be acknowledged and offered opportunities to which I could contribute. I had a voice and my "being different," was valued.

Today I feel very proud and satisfied with my decision to take the risk to leave my hometown to pursue my analytic training. Although psychoanalytic institutes in Mexico are now accepting homosexual candidates, there is still a lot of work to be done to work through the internalized homophobia within the psychoanalytic community at international levels. As I said at the beginning, leaving everything was not an easy choice, but the learning and professional opportunities, the personal and professional growth, and the possibility of really making an impact at a higher systemic level that can drive change became attached with this decision, making a big difference for me.

Web resources

Canadian Charter of Rights and Freedoms. (1982). Downloaded from: www.laws-lois.justice.gc.ca/eng/const/page-15.html (last accessed 17 October 2014).

Civil Marriage Act. (2005). Downloaded from: www.laws-lois.justice.gc.ca/eng/acts/c-31.5/page-1.html (last accessed 17 October 2014).

CHAPTER EIGHT

Stolen freedom

Deborah A. Reeves

Thoreau talks about ("being") in our dreams awake … surely this
is what psychoanalysis brings to bear; those otherwise unknown
identities and truths through everyone … that kind of translucent
information that runs like a river reshaping the land.

—Deborah A. Reeves

Just how is an analytic identity established? Marginality and
distance, coupled with certain sensory and perceptual qualities
are most probably requisites. To these should likely be added the
capacity for detachment, a truncated biography, and a personality
structure imprinted with massive overlays of alienation, estrangement,
and anomie. In the following pages I recount, both chronologically and
conceptually, the establishment—or assembly—of analytic capacities.
What follows is a narrative of sorts in which the occasional theoretical
excursus at times interrupts, and hopefully enhances, the discussion.

* * *

It was likely not for nothing that most of the early psychoanalysts (and
their patients) were German or Austrian Jews. If groups of people are

ghettoized for half a millennium, excluded from agricultural pursuits in an overwhelmingly rural continent, badged, branded, and reviled as ritual murderers and enemies of Christ, occasionally massacred, and forced into a restrictive, exhausted gene pool, it is hardly unpredictable that curious and extraordinary human beings will result. The distance and marginality of this nation, and the sufferings—selfinflicted and otherwise—that it endured, made possible the genesis of the Psychoanalytic Chosen People. Despite Edward Hine's scrambled and confused thesis that the English are in fact the Lost Tribe of Ephraim (Hine, 2003) this writer can claim no such heritage as that elaborated in the erroneous and notorious *England's Coming Glories*. But in the case of a British teenager rather abruptly transplanted to an isolated, provincial community in the American Midwest, a region described by the Coen Brothers as "Siberia with Family Restaurants," a pronounced marginality obtains. Certainly not of the caliber of Jewish Diaspora or persecution, but nonetheless a small, private case of anomic displacement, uncannily invisible—translucent as it were—and hence contributory to an identity that ultimately developed within the psychoanalytic paradigm.

Departure from England and emigration to the United States was not prompted by anything as dramatic as religious, ethnic, or racial persecution; we were voluntary economic immigrants of the mid 1970s, on the one hand fleeing high interest rates, labor unrest, and taxes and on the other looking to expand upon industrial business. However, prior to the overseas journey was an internal migration, which was in some ways nearly as unsettling and abrupt.

Yorkshire is a northern farming county in England; the city of York is surrounded by a Roman wall, where it sits cupped in the hands of the Yorkshire Dales. Once ruled by a reputedly illtempered king named Erik Bloodaxe, the county and city have more recently become quieter, mellower, and more comfortable. The place fosters a feeling of deep kinship to the people and the environment. Yorkshire is a place where the rain was more often horizontal than vertical, where the cold mist swept gently across the hills and over the moors and where the hedgerows of the farming fields were the last divide between the countryside and the village people.

Through boroughs, villages, cities, counties and districts, we migrated south to the Midlands where we lived for several years in the county of Staffordshire, in a town called Wolverhampton, formerly known for its industry, especially the manufacture of traffic signals and bicycles.

Now, much decayed, it's held together with hues of grayness; a musky industrial skyscape that seems to visually flatten the scaffolding, chimneys, long wide roads, and concrete slabs. Today there is an enormous population of nonwhite immigrants, resulting in racial tension. The city is short of space, with fences on the outside and fences on the inside. Looking back after thirty years, I still recall a kinesthetic feeling of strain in response to this environment.

Business concerns drove us to Surrey in the South of England, an area utterly different from whence we had moved. Undulating hills, a wellcomposed landscape, and a small upper class town called Farnham, an old market town with roots established in the Bronze Age when merchants travelled through a pre-historic settlement to trade with the people in the East. It has grown and flourished throughout the centuries. The most prominent period in the history of the town is Medieval, and the town of today owes its growth to the development of agriculture during the middle ages. Farnham is surrounded by smaller subdivided areas which for many years and probably still does, consists of a village green, a cricket field, a post office, a place to buy sundries, and a sweet shop. Each subdivided area was established with names reflective of the particular lay of the land.

After a decade of living in the county of Surrey, not long enough to become natives by any stretch of the imagination, but with enough time to partially acquire its distinctive accent (an accent thought by not a few to be haughty, exclusive and proper, otherwise referred to as the Queen's English, Received Pronunciation (RP) or BBC English). This is an old hat linguistic decorum used in elocution lessons with the objective to teach the so-called Standard English accent, commercially advertised as making it much easier for others to understand and to better assist with one's professional goals. Little did I know at the time that I had just been signed up for a pre-emptive course in the lifelong lessons of the adhesive effects and reactions towards stereotypes and signifiers.

Bound on the outside and the inside, the counties seemed worlds away from one another; each with their own character that contains its own ethnic identity along with its own style of sameness and difference. Like separate cohesive historically defined "familial characters," each with a "different" English language, born out of specific combinations and patterns that reflect the environmental history, the traditions, values and social mores. These were signature dialects that could at times be so foreign to the ear; understanding at times was barely possible. Yet, there was still a strong cultural sense of an empathic knowing as referential greetings tended not to be about industry nor dialect, but more about who the person is, where they have been, and where they are going. In England, people tend to be identified by their regional origins, which are also hierarchically ranked. Today, the emphasis is a less formalized social class system than in the past.

It's likely that most who immigrate to the United States do so to escape frightful and oppressive conditions. Apart from the shock of adjustment and learning a new language, I wonder if perhaps they experience greater degrees of freedom? My experience was the opposite. Immersion in American values, culture, and customs was at times painful, frequently disconcerting, and entailed a loss of freedoms. Liberties that I had enjoyed in England were stolen from me.

Stolen freedom

Of importance to me during this period, and likely formative in building an analytic identity, was the advantage of a British education. I was fortunate to have spent several years in my mid to late teens at a sixth form college studying subjects of choice for O level and A level examinations. (The sixth form college in the UK is vaguely equivalent to the first two years in the American university system. The O and A level examinations, now obsolete, measured educational achievement at the conclusion of the sixth form; further study was contingent on performance in these).

Individual choice was encouraged, just as much as personal autonomy and student–teacher relationships. By contrast, the American schools tended to mirror that nation's historic emphasis on industrial mass production, unregulated competition, and an every-man-for-himself ethic. There seemed to be an expectation, or rather an admonition, to join different kinds of highly structured interest groups that appeared to be undifferentiated and socially distant. I was puzzled, frustrated and bored by the seeming lack of independence, freedom, and emotional expression.

Perhaps the most dramatic of these experiences was mandatory attendance at a pieeating contest I witnessed in my senior year of high school. There, I experienced this as a form of collective infantile regression. This isn't to say that I hadn't endured the predictable adolescent peer group pressures and antics back in England where differences in values, opinions, interests and ideology deemed social bonding experiences and reflections of cultural hierarchy. But this American variety was something else again, a nearly Freudian image of the primal horde devouring gooey desserts, as if I was witnessing some regression to a herd instinct, such as Freud discussed in his *Group Psychology and the Analysis of the Ego* (Greisman, 1979). In this situation, I felt my own, somewhat newish identity to be threatened with being dragged toward the dark objects of a distant past ... Olde England? It would appear that America is so hungry to own a history that personal identity seems to be cultivated artificially like a hothouse plant. This was accomplished through education and the merciless imposition of peer group conformity.

When I finally attended college in the States, it seemed to me just a vapid rite of passage, and compared to my prior education, a rather oppressive conveyor belt process. The British tradition emphasized authentic discipline in a collective and inspirational atmosphere driven by interest and curiosity; in this setting, one needn't acquiesce to a culture where the insistence on gaining personal identity gets confused with fitting into the market of industrialized consumerism. The cloying phrases, "Be all you can be," "Dare to be great," "The sky's the limit," and so on, are really about dreams born out of a history in a country that has had perhaps, too much too soon. A British transplant is inevitably reminded of Oscar Wilde's *bon mot*, that America is a nation that's gone directly from barbarism to decadence without once reaching civilization. It's a place where a certain dialogic dependency on bulletproof accounts of existence enslave one to phrases like, "you can be anything you want when you grow up"; this just breeds destructive optimism with its illusions of self-sufficiency and pseudo-intimacy. What results is an extension of childhood bound with cultural limits and expectations that avoids creativity and confuses creativity with chaos (Bion, 1961).

When we arrived in the midwestern United States of America during the year of the American Bicentennial, it was as a family whose internal migration had already put some mileage on it. That month of February was shockingly frigid with temperatures well below zero degrees. We drove through carved walls of snow in an automobile that seemed to mimic a ride in a hovercraft across the Atlantic on a calm day. The landscape with its icebergcovered lakes and drifted walls of snow seemed wildly desolate. The neighbors were nowhere to be seen at least not until spring. As people began to emerge from the depths of winter, I discovered a generally pervasive pattern of rather personal questions. These were expressed in words so alien, in phrases so intrusive, in a context so utterly surreal, and in a linguistic derivative so unknown that the establishment of intimacy was rendered virtually impossible. Not to put too fine a point on it, many of these encounters would be considered "not in good form" back home.

During the month of April, I entered for a brief period of time the first of a few high schools in which I would be enrolled. On my first day, I entered the women's bathroom and witnessed something utterly alien and primitive; legions of chattering teenage girls elbowing each other for space at the mirrors, the better to make themselves up with cosmetics and hairspray. I listened over the buzz of hairdryers to unfamiliar conversations in which emphasis on the anticipations of occupational success, marriage, money, competition, and status symbols were illuminated in a fashion that to me appeared both crass and horrific. These vocal noises had a different sound from what I was accustomed to. It was structured, organized, and bulletproof. In a very short time, I came to see such values as repulsive and surreal. From this point onwards, my status as an outsider, an alien, and a foreigner was irrevocably established. In a way, my AngloSaxon origins and my northern European appearance made it all worse. My peers expected conformity, an expectation that I was unable to fulfill and unwilling to attempt.

* * *

In the mid seventies, it seemed not uncommon at least in the area in which we lived to meet other students who had never been outside the state let alone held a passport. I got the impression that I was somehow assigned to transport these people to a realm not unknown, foreign but still familiar, different, but nonthreatening. Certain esteem was accorded British culture, an attitude that often felt stereotyped with a sort of kennel club mentality that I abhorred. In some social circles foreigners were asked to attend various gatherings; these likely constituted a welcome change for the natives, whose lives perhaps might have been fleetingly enlivened by exposure to outsiders. So much the better if the person in question could claim attributes that were partially familiar, vaguely hybrid, and, most of all, nonthreatening. After all, it's not I that had an accent; it is You.

Within a matter of months I had moved up in ranks from an immigrant to certified resident alien and foreign mascot; a partially stateless cultural mutant. In peer groups I became the invisible watcher and a different player; a hidden stranger whose vocal noises carried the demarcation of being an outsider. I recall in those early days that the Anglophiles gravitated toward me, hungry to gain some knowledge they had missed in their studies about "the mother country." It was as if they were searching for a part of themselves that they didn't yet know. To boot, they generally had a far better academically historical knowledge of my homeland than I did, especially silly details about obscure English royals. These linguistic bouts spawned curiosity, and a seemingly apparent wanting to discover that after all, the transatlantic emigrational passage to America surely can't be that complex: *After all we do speak the same language don't we?* In those more often than not awkward moments of learning to reengage, it was as if a lunar eclipse had just taken place and in the manner of minuets a "nonanalytic third" had arrived, clothed in mystery, with a group of ideational images waiting to become players in an effort to find a common ground and be revealed.

In those early years, interpersonal migratory experiences of cultural discordance were at times painful, lonely, and difficult, but nonetheless compelling. It is this setting, in which I was a person of ambiguous, multiple identities, that I credit with the genesis of an analytic perspective. My peers became exhibits, individuals to be observed at a certain remove, and examined as specimens. Rather than being acquaintances, friends, or classmates, they became material for study: Their carriage, dress, and taboos, their humor and erotic awareness (or notable lack thereof) took on an anthropological cast. Whoever said transference isn't a real event? I'm inclined to think that this was a watershed of sorts, the crossing of which began the development of an analytic identity. Another crucial element—that of music, appeared in my life somewhat earlier on.

Listening

Many years prior to my immigration to the United States of America, on a sunny Spring day at a small primary school in the County of Surrey, England, I was seated in the lunchroom eating Bacon butties: For the uninitiated, these are slices of spongy white bread, dipped in bacon grease; it contains a meaty cut of pork from the loin of the pig, commonly referred to in North America as back bacon. The flavor is at once sweet, smoky, and salty. The consistency is mushy, chewy, and gooey. It's best consumed on a Welsh beach in the summer, wrapped in a wet wool blanket, when the rain is intermittently, gently spitting.

During lunchtime at school, we were commonly entertained by various selections of classical music transmitted and heard through one of the most brilliant contributions to Western culture and society, the phonograph. On this particular day, amidst the usual cacophonic bee-hive buzz of children's voices arrived something unbeknownst to me yet pleasurably familiar; Barenboim's performance of the Beethoven's "Moonlight Sonata". Like an autumn leaf that gently tumbles and glides to the ground on a warm late summer's evening, so did this extraordinary experience carry me. I was transported from the place I was in to an intimate, private sphere of personal experience that seemed far more sophisticated than any experience I had ever had. It was in this transitional place where listening and hearing was spiritually exalted. It was an experience that determined my internal landscape. Much like the child in E. M. Forster's *Celestial Omnibus* (Forster, 1976, pp. 49–57) this elevating space was characterized by curiosity, exploration, and discovery. Without exaggeration, it was a profound experience—life-changing in fact.

The listening experience can likely be traced to one of first bird songs I learned to recognize as a child and which to this very day I still find upon recall to be most soothing; the English Cuckoo's song. Evidence that I am not alone in recognizing the allure of this birdsong can be heard in Frederick Delius' 1912 composition, "On Hearing the First Cuckoo in Spring." Two separate tones are sung with the first higher tone being echoed in response by a lower tone and then there is a long pause before it repeats. A case of repetition compulsion? Hardly so! A demonstration of the sounds defined through graduated tones and when heard in groups of two or more, constitutes music. Music, like the song of the cuckoo, doesn't change; it's always music, a national relational anthem that is ours. Music experientially binds and transports communicative, hereditary meaning, rendering many interpretations to the historical epoch and cultural surround. If it's good we listen, if it's really good "we" don't forget, and the sounds become embodied.

Listening for the otherness within is advantageously carried through into my work in a manner consistent with my British education and musical studies. Positive memories abound with the freedom of speech bringing about heated debates and discussions of differences, and an intimacy that connected the students and the teachers. We became a collectively composed symphony of people, a culturally rich body of knowledge.

I have become familiar with the many perspective levels of relational consciousness from which I have identified as an immigrant. I feel most at home in my counterpart country when amongst other immigrants or simply those non-immigrants who have not forgotten about their own generational past. I feel a certain sense of delight in getting to know them and hearing about their cultural experiences. Together, we keep our differences and our memories alive. I prefer to use more words as this reminds me of the importance of remembering: It is a latent power that is brought with a conscious intentionality to the surface. Witnessed in the fullest light possible, so too may the contents of the psyche be widened and shaped. What was once abstract or blurred becomes in its own right, defined and yielding further inspiration and knowledge.

It is through this experience that I view listening consciously as essential to the basic intelligence of an analytic identity; not only is it vital, it is a tool of necessity. Listening is an advocate of the yet unknown experience, which compels the analyst toward further enquiry and understanding through reconnecting.

It's become my opinion that certain composers are "mediumistic" in Duchamp's (1957) sense of the word, and that such music doesn't attempt to make itself heard, but makes understanding a possibility. In this fashion, to listen to patients is a privilege, and one comparable to hearing good classical music, well played. The kind you can feel.

Following this analogy to the therapeutic context, during initial sessions, I pay attention to various nonverbal cues, becoming attuned to the non-verbal and verbal patterns that develop. I learn to recognize a tempo, a modulation of tone, or a silence perhaps, a break in a rhythmic sequence, so many expressions that words cannot tell. I listen to recognize the sounds of consonance and dissonance, the culturally imbued sounds, the foundation, as it were, of harmonic music. As I examine and reexamine, as I listen and then listen again, only this time with more knowledge, I find respective inflections that bear more meaning, purpose, information, and order as they are repeatedly worked through. This entails immersion in a murky, agonizing chaos that is doubtless familiar to those in the profession: this experience is not infrequently deeply moving. Then, in the light of a day's residue, like a screen memory, once a wish to remember and another, a wish to forget, what has been added today might be subtracted tomorrow.

Translucent

I discovered that developing an analytic identity as an immigrant in the United States was not for the fainthearted. I did not want to conform to the societal standard of "do-gooder looking for a happy ending."

Happiness in America is a mass-produced product of forced labor, the ghastliest example of which is the industry that manufactures motivational seminars and retreats. This pandemic need to feel happy is an instinctual defense against feeling uncomfortable, the terrifying void of character deficits, cultural inadequacy, the fear of mourning, and the fear of allowing grief to be alive and well. It is no accident that the first draft of the American Declaration of Independence from England guaranteed the "the pursuit of property." It's likely that the exaggerated adherence towards social compliances is an attempt (failed) to try to compensate for the absence of the loss of the mother country. Furthermore, it's not for nothing that, recognizing this, Jean Baudrillard described the United States as "… the only remaining primitive society" (Verso Books, 2010). In an atmosphere of aggressive self-improvement, those immune to the fraudulent promises, fake cures, and bogus remedies must perforce find themselves drifting and becoming distant, disinterested, disengaged, alienated, and utterly alone.

Upon revisiting my home country I reconnect with new threads of time and I am reminded of a contextual discontinuity that feels ruthless; an illumination of the temporal order of life. Each time I go back, I gain new knowledge which would have otherwise been unknown if it were not for the opportunity of listening and observing again. Each time, old memories are superimposed with a new layer of experience and brought forth into a different contextual light to be re-experienced and known from a different psychic perspective in place and time. This nostalgic experience brings feelings interwoven with memories reminiscent of an unforgettable past, a fertile ground for mourning and new growth along with experiential aspects of the foreign and the strange, all taking on new layers of identity in the present. It reminds me of playing some of the works by Bach, which demands the dexterity of ten fingers that work independently of one another. And, if they are brought together they can create a whole; like an amalgam of integrated memories, hopes, and dreams, a rich nostalgic memorable experience.

While the analogy of musical listening is valuable, it shouldn't be too closely identified with clinical practice. Music inherently brings sounds to the fore in a veridical manner, illuminating what's to be heard without being dominated by the whole composition. It is like an experiential listening exercise in field independence. Musicianship is more about expression to the composition at hand; it is not about working to express the self. This discernment of identity demands the work required for an autonomous interpretation by each musician mastering a new piece of music. In many ways this unique translation is the responsibility of the musician to the culture at large. Likewise, I feel it a responsibility to define some ideas about my own cultural identifications and disidentifications for those readers, who are perhaps curious about their cultural backgrounds and the intrinsic value this brings to our work.

These ideas in field theory bring to mind how relatively easy it is to unconsciously lapse into becoming extensions of our patients. Maintaining the analytic work at the task level and being efficiently field independent are paramount to empathic attunement. This entails being distinctly different from the patient's pathological inner world and past pathogenic figures, allowing for cultural differences to be heard and understood. Similarly, music transmitted through interpretation has a way of creating an internally audible transitional space where thoughts, reflections, associations, and feelings may be recognized on a different perceptual level. In a sense, this is an invitation to hear; an invitation that can hardly be refused when one begins to recognize authentic and intimate responses that can change through a stream of consciousness. Thus, it is that music assists the analyst. In order to empathize with a patient's inner world, we must listen in the most highly defined analytically disciplined manner, both to ourselves and to the material our patients bring to the sessions.

Parallel to the analytic dyad, the transitional space, or location of cultural experience is created through the structural position of listening and the process of responding with empathic attunement. It is through the culturally transportable skill of listening that we can enable the transformation of identity through understanding; the unconscious aspect of protecting identity. By observing in a non-judgmental manner and openly to nonverbal cues we may examine and learn about unconscious communication. Phantasies, memories, reflections, thoughts, and feelings are stirred, and, as in a concert performance, it is as if the musician and the audience share a kind of temporary oceanic suspension, followed by a sensational shift, perhaps conscious or unconscious to the listener. It is not unheard of for audiences, following the conclusion of a truly moving concert, to report sensations of release, calm, and inner satisfaction, something that Freud might have described as "post-coital" bliss. This has been reliably confirmed in instances where the audience has sat in rapt attention during such pieces as the Tristan "Liebestod," or even more so, the final, triumphal chorus of Schoenberg's "Guerrelieder". The listener like the patient is in a kind of analytic holding pattern, thus establishing an environment in which it is safe enough to associate freely.

In this regard, it has been established (Damasio, 2000) that out of the whole sensory apparatus the auditory system is physically the closest to the brain, affectively regulating life at the highest level. The capacity to listen well is no doubt an acquired skill and music was my accompaniment to such learning. It is through listening that we perceive what we are hearing. Similarly, through application of theoretical constructs which are based upon listening and hearing, we are able to access and open doors to the unconscious. A motif, an embellishment, a loud or quieted silent pause are important in this context. Sounds bound to the ego bring so many sensory elements, pulling and pushing, light and dark, bringing values that color the mind to a place within a certain affectively attuned neurological state of mind. Sufficiently and informatively we respond to our patients' internal worlds; this serves to resolve intrapsychic conflicts, realign the past and the present, distinguish reality from phantasy, and allow for spontaneity and freedom. Just as an analysand learns the language of psychoanalysis through a richly culturally imbued education, this combination of science and art, the constituent ingredients of the current culture being the medium, renders an emotional and intellectual understanding; an order that is based in reality. Listening is a transportable skill across all cultures initiating states of responsiveness whilst strengthening the ego. It teaches emotional expressions that alter with meaning through evolutionary cultural identity.

Summary

It's not for nothing that psychoanalysis has been termed in Janet Malcom's (1982) book, *The Impossible Profession* where failure is expected and chaos is tolerated.

I am often asked what advice do I give people. They seem utterly disappointed when I tell them, none at all. All one can hope for is that repairs are made and to the greatest extent effectively possible, within a flexible discipline of capacities and limitations. Then, disappointment turns to anger when I defend that my work helps people to discover their worth through their identity, rather than manufacture one, as is often the case with those who churn out solutions, taking advantage when people are desperate for any relief at all. In a way, these free enterprise clinical entrepreneurs embody the very worst of what's wrong with the mental health practice in the US. Mass production and aggressive marketing that victimizes and exploit those who are in genuine need of help. The result is, people just keep getting sicker and sicker.

By contrast, analytic identity is a result of contextual experience more than a learned technique that may reflect a certain cultural compliance. It is no less the personal qualifications that factor into the type of work we do, the type of theories to which we may resonate and the diagnostic population we treat. Analytic work is about building and restoring identity, not manufacturing a bogus one on order. Theories bring together different kinds of languages to explain clinical phenomena. Differing perspectives are born out of a metaphoric language, whether talking about part-object representations or vertical and horizontal splitting, or the paranoid or depressive positions. The identity of the analytic lexicon is molded and shaped through increasingly defined sense of culturally attuned defined empathy.

I recall in the mid-nineties a psychoanalyst/academic distinctly made the point that the diagnostic spectrum was widening from treating those able to develop an analyzable transference neurosis to increasing disorder of the personality and ego dysfunctions. In other words people are getting sicker. Reflective of radically changing external environment we confront more formal and temporal regressive states. As sociocultural realities become less defined, then treatment too, becomes less predictable. If we examine culture as the frame from which we may proceed analytically, it may be argued that interest in analytic treatment can be extended to wider audiences as opposed to becoming increasingly limited. Yet as denigrated and debased as culture has become, without a culture, societies die (Dalrymple, 2007). The term "culture" has its elitist meaning, a Culture with a capital "C." It can also be seen as a society as a whole via its intrinsic values. Culture forms an integral dimension of treatment and this paradigm is especially relevant for those who are members of a generation that grew up listening to wartime atrocity narratives and that experienced fragmented familial histories, where "looking forward" was heralded as virtue and "looking backward" was dismissed as a moral failure and cultural treason. What results is the infamous double bind cocktail, a chalice brimming with toxic values: "Don't listen when I'm angry!" A nascent message of perpetual illness sheltered under the umbrella of shame. This kind of tenacious repudiation results in the illusion of a comfortable anaesthetic immersion called denial. The real world is disengaged from the phantasy world, the inside from the outside. Sick families thrive on secrets and even their manifesto of mental illness must perforce secret; Denial of memory is a death sentence, and analysis provides understanding and change if not, at least a temporary reprieve.

References

Bion, W. R. (1961). *Experiences in Groups*. London: Tavistock.
Dalrymple, T. (2007). *Our Culture: What's Left of it*. Lanham, MD: Ivan Dee.
Damasio, A. (2000). *The Feeling of What Happens*. New York, NY: Mariner.
Duchamp, M. (1957). The creative act (audio). Retrieved from https://soundcloud.com/brainpicker/marcel-duchamp-the-creative-act (last accessed 16 November 2014).
Forster, E. M. (1976). *The Celestial Omnibus*. New York, NY: Vintage Books/Random House. (Original publication 1911).
Freud, S. (1990). *Group Psychology and the Analysis of the Ego*. New York, NY: W. W. Norton. (Original publication 1922).
Greisman, H. C. (1979). Herd instincts and the foundations of biosociology. *Journal of the Behavioral Sciences, 15*: 357–369.
Hine, R. (2003). *England's Coming Glories*. Whitefish, MT: Kessinger Publishing Company, LLC.
Malcom, J. (1982). *Psychoanalysis: The Impossible Profession*. New York, NY: Vintage; 1st Vintage Books ed. Edition.
Verso Books (2010). In: J. Baudrillard. *America*. Retrieved from http://www.versobooks.com/books/550-america (Last accessed 16 November 2014).

CHAPTER NINE

Crossing the border within: migration, transience, and analytic identity

Gabriel Ruiz

Then—in my childhood—in the dawn/Of a most stormy life—was drawn/
From ev'ry depth of good and ill/The mystery which binds me still—

—Edgar Allan Poe, *Alone*

Becoming a psychoanalyst brings forth an ongoing elaboration in one's developing identity. This expansion of one's internal dimensions inevitably includes aspects of culture (Akhtar, 1999). Yet when our inscape is met with the amalgamation of two or more distinct cultures, one's analytic identity stretches the boundaries of this transformation to compelling depths (Akhtar, 2006). Throughout my analytic training I often wondered how my Mexican is weaved into my American as a psychoanalyst? My own analysis and training, as was most of my supervision, were conducted in English, my second language. Where does the migrant farm experience of mine reside? Where does this childhood experience of going from farm to farm, US to Mexico and back migrations resound?

It is not only in the "Mexico" or "US" experience that my analytic identity develops from. I find it arises out of my internalized experience of traveling between the two countries. Actual and internal experiences of transitioning between "Mexican" and "American" culture grounds my ongoing analytic understanding of my patients. In essence, this "to and fro," is the deepest signifier of my ongoing self-definition as an analyst.

My parents were immigrant farm workers from Mexico. While migrating seasonally for work, I spent my early years running in the potato, onion, and strawberry fields with other children of that time. I recall countless hours roaming the rural expanse, the feeling of warm soil underfoot, yelling back and forth in Spanish with other kids. We attended "school" for immigrant children with English as a Second Language (ESL) teachers. School was an "alternate" experience, one encapsulated by English learning. My family lived in barebones migrant housing tracts. This is what I knew and one of the core-self rhythms I internalized (Stern, 1985).

Throughout my childhood, my family migrated between Mexico and the US. In Mexico we would reside with various extended family members in a mix of rural and urban areas. Mexico brought its own rhythms demanding both external and internal adjustments. There was a "Wild West" sense, a lessening of safety, while at the same time a sense of adventure couched in social connectedness. Further, there is a certain allowance for young kids to roam the city unaccompanied for better or worse. In essence, this was the "Mexico" I weaved into my internal landscape, similar to Bollas' (1987) transformational object. Yet, what does this say about the bridging experience of these two rhythms?

* * *

My parents retired from fastidious migrant farm work, eventually settling in El Paso, Texas. In juxtaposition to El Paso is Cuidad Juarez, a place psychoanalytically studied by Ainslie (2013), and given much recent press due to its war-level violence. My high school was half a mile from the border, which I crossed several times a week. At this point I engaged in an almost daily level of "back and forthness" between countries. I recall the distinct suspension of "rules" crossing into Juarez with labyrinth style of roads; so easy to get lost and disoriented. The "Wild West" was even more heightened in this border town. From such great heights I would return back to the US and, in this transition, feel both relief and disappointment. A relief at coming back to a relatively more regulated way of life, yet disappointed the excitement of risk was now on hold until my return.

At a core level (Stern, 1985), my experience from birth throughout adolescence involved a migratory rhythm between neighboring countries, each with their own cultural climates enveloping distinct sights, sounds, and sensations. I offer this as a way of orienting the reader to something about the process of constant migration; the process of transience, especially one that involves the crossing of a border on an almost daily level. What is it in the back and forth moving from farm to farm, town to town, country to country that weaves into my psychic resonances in work with patients?

I hope to shed light on how, as a bilingual/bicultural analyst, the repeated travels between cultures and languages operate as a foreground and background internal "dance" of sorts (Pérez Foster, 1992). This ongoing back and forth can be utilized for analytic work at a process level (Akhtar, 2006; Canestri & Reppen, 2000; Greenson, 1950; Hill, 2008; Javier, 1995; Marcos, 1976). With respect to language, I use English (my second language) as a foreground/conscious level of experience level while Spanish (my native language) as a background/unconscious processing level. The capacity to move back and forth across these "borders" of experience is structured by the internalization of my transient experience.

Although it is a general capacity to move between levels of experience, there is something about this being anchored in "Mexican" and "American" that becomes a personal metaphor (Richmond, 2004) for working with a patient's foreground and background of psychic experience. Crossing to Mexico initiates a transformation of identity in response to rhythms of sounds, tastes, smells, and circulation of people. One can imagine this when traveling, but when one takes up residence it involves a "giving one's self over." This "to and fro" is deeply threaded into my unconscious and, given the analytic field where use of self (Jacobs, 1991) is the ultimate instrument, this very process is active in work with patients.

I believe this internal migration shows up unknowingly and singularly after the moment in which it becomes activated in clinical process. When patients are at their most vulnerable, in depths of experience, resonances of my own transition between states become activated. This is where the Mexican-American resides in my developing analytic identity. The actual moment of travel between "worlds" is part of what historically informs my third individuation (Akhtar, 1995).

While with Spanish speaking patients I am less surprised, it has been with non-Spanish speaking patients where this recognition is startling. How can I be sure that this always means there is a deeper level of process accessed by the patient? I simply cannot. Yet, the following case examples are representative of how this phenomenon is to be reckoned with in the analytic encounter while representing my particular analytic identity. I have chosen two analytic cases for their capacity to illuminate areas of convergence and divergence given that one case took place solely in English with an adult male, while the other was a bilingual treatment with an adolescent.

Lewis

Lewis, a forty-two-year-old, highly intelligent, Eastern-European professional man sought out psychoanalysis in response to states of anxiety and depression in response to his recent breakup of a long-term relationship with a girlfriend. Initially, I recall the direct gaze of Lewis' eyes, in what felt like an anxious, albeit evaluative fashion. Throughout the early face-to-face hours, Lewis shared his history of a previous psychotherapy experience during his mid-twenties. He described this therapeutic experience as "what I needed at the time to get through."

In further discussion, Lewis expressed struggling with feelings regarding his parents' separation after his father abandoned the family when he was ten years old. His eyes watered as he conveyed the difficulties of growing up with an alcoholic father, domestic fights between his parents, and his absence for many years. Lewis saw his father again shortly before his death several years ago. Even though Lewis made it clear to me he had worked through feelings and issues related to his father, there was surprise at his own emotional response in recounting this piece of history.

Lewis conveyed his need to work on his feelings and his relationships. Particularly, he was concerned over getting "too attached" and having difficulty moving on upon separation. Lewis also wanted to explore his own thoughts and feelings in order to "find a way to live that works for me." Lewis especially focused on pursuing an analysis in order to "do a form of therapy that seems more intense, and deeper than what I have done before."

In an hour during the middle phase of analysis, Lewis discussed recent interactions with friends, having heard of their wedding engagements. While these concerns had been on his mind regularly, on this day Lewis goes further into thinking about dating again himself. His associations lead to e-mails he received from two different friends regarding the same news article. This was a "point and counterpoint" on why men remain single. The first author argued that the man was alone for being "picky, and basically a real prick." The second author counters that there are a myriad of reasons, taking an "in defense" position.

In listening to Lewis, I recalled a shift in my internal state. I had the distinct feeling of migrating to a different level of experience, which felt charged, connected, along with an "allowance" to roam more "Wild West" landscape. My sudden internal transience cued me to Lewis embarking on deeper internal travels too. All this led me to intervene:

ANALYST: The difficulty with these articles is that they rarely capture a person's reasons for not being married.

LEWIS: These articles don't really get it (begins to sob). I didn't see that coming, this is making me sad. Who will love me? When I was entering adolescence the whole thing with dating girls began. I was not like the other guys that began dating right away. I struggled a lot; I didn't feel as attractive. All the guys around me developed a lot quicker.

Over the following weeks, Lewis was flooded with earlier memories. Although he does not speak Spanish, from my own deep travels arose resonances, images; counter-responses (Richmond, 2004) in "Spanish." I use the quotes around the word Spanish because I not only mean Spanish language, but Spanish specific to me in Latino-Mexican sights, sounds, and aromas. In other terms, a deeper earlier aspect of my "Mexican" experience sees the light of day as the patient's own deeper traumas and unintegrated aspects emerge in the analysis.

While there are potential concerns of over-identification in such an approach, ultimately we have the working split, using our experience while separating our experience as we "accompany" our patients into their own depths. For Lewis, one of the deeper experiences that came to life was being severely neglected as a young child, resulting in repeated trips to the emergency room.

In fact, as Lewis began to feel safer in our analytic relationship, he allowed himself to wonder about me personally; particularly about my religious beliefs. At this point I begin to hear positive memories with his father for the first time. His father, I learn, pursued contact with Lewis over the years after divorcing his mom. Lewis' father invited him to visit his native country. In hindsight, Lewis tearfully began expressing how meaningful this was.

Strikingly, in reverie (Ogden, 1997) I am traveling back and forth between the US and Mexico with ease, while reflecting on Lewis' travels to see his father. Suddenly, Lewis begins speaking in his father's native tongue. In unconscious communication, both patient and I migrate internally across borders of experience and language to make contact with early object figures. In this case, the patient's paternal object.

Inherently, I am assisting Lewis to stay with his feelings in the face of anxiety, in the context of a holding environment (Winnicott, 1986) in order to engage historically avoided aspects of himself, thus creating the opportunity for a more expanded experience of his internal world. This process is accompanied by my own journey across borders to different states of experience encapsulated by travels between cultures and languages. My internal "to and fro," so familiar, becomes a reference point to formulate unconscious data, while simultaneously expresses my analytic identity.

Juan

The second case is Juan, a sixteen-year-old Mexican-American adolescent residing with both parents, Lupe and Manuel. He is the oldest of four and his parents are immigrants from Mexico. Juan, was referred to me during his freshman year by his school for attendance and behavioral issues. He had been truant most of his freshman year along with verbal and physical altercations with other students. Despite Juan's intelligence, his school threatened to kick him out indefinitely. His parents expressed desperation in wanting to preserve Juan's school placement. Initially, they hoped after a one-time interview I would be able to change the school's mind. In fact, the school had already made their decision and Juan was transferred to a local public high school.

During the early months of analysis, Juan questioned the privacy of his analysis. He felt surprised at how this was truly his space as he reflected on the fact that I take him and his thoughts seriously. It was paramount that I see him as a person with his own thoughts and initiative, something he has gone without during his early years. Much of his life up to this point has been to function as an additional parent to his younger siblings.

As the analysis moved forward, Juan began to get in touch with his deep hunger and need for mirroring, idealization (Kohut, 1971), and early missed developmental experiences. In a pivotal session, Juan reports the following dream:

> I am at a fancy dinner. There's all this good food, and a lot of it. I am there with a girl and I think I am dating her. I am there because she is part of your family and it's a family dinner or holiday. There are kids running around the dining table and you have this chandelier. We are about to sit down to eat and I wake up.

As Juan and I explored the dream, he is struck by the abundance of food, the connection to a girl he then realizes was "beautiful," but specifically the fanciness of the chandelier. Juan reports the dream in a mix of English and Spanish, but chandelier is in Spanish. In the midst of my resonances, I begin to notice the sensation of my mouthing "candelabra" (chandelier), complete with the feeling of rolling the "r" which feels first-nature. Not only the fact that this word has come to me and my patient in Spanish, but also the mouth-tongue sensation of verbalizing "candelabra" that is of interest.

In light of the word "candelabra," I now think of early vocalizations and the distinct quality of languages where one rolls the "r." My associations take me back to Juan and his earliest experiences conditioned by the quality of the rolling "r" in its sensational aspects. In my back and forth between the English "r" and Spanish "r," I am cued to his earliest yearnings being reignited via our analytic work.

As Juan elaborated his dream, he found it rich, and described a sense of "enough to go around." This is a dream of hunger for attachment, emotional nourishment, and his transference wish that these yearnings, long ago sequestered, can be met. They begin to see the light of day in the analysis.

In other words, while early needs, identifications, and self-protective functions become mobilized, the fact that Juan is mobilized in the "mother" tongue (Casement, 1982; Greenson, 1950) on both verbal and sensory via verbal processes is attenuated by my own "mother" tongue on both verbal and sensory levels. This becomes a tool for "cueing" me to the emergence of deeper, unintegrated aspects of his psychological being.

Following this period of analysis, Juan settled into a rhythm where the analysis, as transitional space (Winnicott, 1971), could allow for his deeper needs and unintegrated affects to emerge. As Juan and I travel across "internal borders" of experience, Juan begins to articulate his need for a father figure whom he could identify with and organize himself around. In concordance with this theme, Juan and I encounter his struggles with what kind of man he wants to be. As he engages his search to find a model to look up to, Juan confronts a dilemma. On the one hand he sees me as having power and respect. On the other hand, if I haven't been through what he's been through, then how could I possibly know how to help him?

At this point in the analysis, I had been reflecting on the issue of "making" it across the border involving the commonly held fantasy that once you are in the US, you have now "made it." You now have money, power, and access that is unavailable in Mexico. This theme as experienced in the crossing of the US Mexican border infiltrates itself into the self-experience of many Latinos. In this regard, it comes to life for me as it does my patient. As I go back and forth across this metaphorical, historical, and psychic border, so does my patient into deeper aspects of his experience, history, and relational experience.

One day Juan's friends ditched school while he stayed behind to make up a test. During this period of analysis Juan was working through issues of power, respect, and self-agency. Juan decided to meet up with his friends downtown just prior to his session with me. As the peer pressure mounts, Juan confided:

JUAN: R kept pressuring me to go party with them, but she finally let up after I told her I wasn't going to go. It made it hard, and I wanted to party with them, but I want to come here too. I will see them tomorrow anyways.

ANALYST: You were really torn between ditching or not, partying with them or coming here.

JUAN: I held my ground. I'm my own man and I need to have some power in what I do. Plus, I have been thinking; I want to cut down on the partying. You said to me one time that I used to get high because it feels good in the moment, but really it's to get away from feeling so bad. I end up not really taking care of what's going bad for me. That's the thing, the bad stuff is always there waiting for me after the parties, after getting high, and after being with girls. I couldn't say this to them. I think I smoked to not feel sad, to not feel so shitty about my parents not having money, going to a ghetto school, and my mom and dad always being gone. I basically raised my little brothers and sister man. Then I think of my uncle making all that money and when he comes and visits he's got all that stuff, all flashy, pimp-car. I know it's really not a life. I want to do military or go to college. I feel funny even saying that, is college really for me? Do I really have what it takes? I think I am smart and I'm not ditching right now. I'm actually passing my classes. I do good on the tests, but I don't turn in my homework all the time. But hey if I can pass the tests, that's not too bad.

ANALYST: You mean to tell me you have a brain? (the theme of making it, as well as making it across the border.)

JUAN: (switches to Spanish, begins to laugh) I guess I am saying that. You can't really go around saying that at school unless you want to get messed with. But I think I am smart. A few teachers have actually told me that if I tried a little more I could do honors. I never thought of it as really possible. They tried to put me in honors English when I took the entrance test, but I told them no. When I saw R today and they were trying to get me to go partying with them, T stayed back a few minutes and asked me what business I come downtown every day after school for. I told him, "hey bro, I will tell you one day, when it's just me and you." He said, "sounds serious." I told him it's big business.

ANALYST: It is important you are allowing yourself to feel and think about your struggle between a life like your friends and family, something you know, and a different life, one where you could actually make a life with your brain and school.

JUAN: You know it's been hard to really believe in myself that way, that I could actually do it.

ANALYST: This is big business.

In this pivotal session, Juan's conflict of partying with his friends or taking care of his responsibilities mirror the internal struggle between following a familiar solution versus a solution that re-engages ongoing development and forges new object identifications (Greenson, 1954). I am struck by Juan choosing to take his test and come to session, as this reflects the engagement of his own needs.

When Juan shifts to Spanish, an indicator that he is engaged at a deeper level of experience, Juan begins to consider internal potentialities that would lead to college. Juan's budding self-agency makes way for the beginning of new self-organizations that are less compromising. The fact that this is occurring while Juan is in "Spanish" speaks to the issue of his working at a core level.

To and fro: internal migrations

Both cases show my use of deeper, culturally bound counter-response material as an organizer and metaphor (Richmond, 2004) for working with my patient's early aspects of experience. Both cases convey how bicultural and bilingual experience can arise and inform clinical process via use of self (Akhtar, 2006; Greenson, 1950; Hill, 2008; Jacobs, 1991; Javier, 1995; Marcos, 1976; Pérez Foster, 1992). My own experience couched in two cultures and languages, along with continual migrations, to and from Mexico metaphorically elucidate the back and forth between various levels of regressive and progressive experience. This is the case for myself internally and in the interpersonal and intrapsychic workings of my patients. To treat these purely as transference or countertransference reactions short changes the psychic potential available for leveraging an expanded and interpretable analytic field. In essence, my facility with internal migrations structured by historical migrations allows me to engage and accompany patients back and forth between levels of experience. Here is where the continual migration and transience is weaved into my developing analytic identity. While the "Mexican" and "American" serve as reference points, it is the "to and fro" that provides a structure reflecting the essence of my analytic identity.

References

Ainslie, R. (2013). *The Fight to Save Juarez: Life in the heart of Mexico's drug war*. Austin, TX: University of Texas Press.

Akhtar, S. (1995). A third individuation: immigration, identity, and the psychoanalytic process. *Journal of the American Psychoanalytic Association, 43*: 1051–1084.

Akhtar, S. (1999). *Immigration and Identity: Turmoil, Treatment, and Transformation*. Northvale, NJ: Aronson.

Akhtar, S. (2006). Technical challenges faced by the immigrant psychoanalyst. *Psychoanalytic Quarterly, 75*: 21–43.

Bollas, C. (1987). *The Shadow of the Object: Psychoanalysis of the Unthought Known*. New York, NY: Columbia University Press.

Canestri, J. & Reppen, J. (2000). Development of affect in bilingual patients. *International Journal of Psychoanalysis, 81*: 153–155.

Casement, P. J. (1982). Samuel Beckett's relationship to his mother-tongue. *International Review of Psychoanalysis, 9*: 35–44.

Greenson, R. R. (1950). The mother tongue and the mother. *International Journal of Psychoanalysis, 31*: 18–23.

Greenson, R. R. (1954). The struggle against identification. *Journal of the American Psychoanalytic Association, 2*: 200–217.

Hill, S. (2008). Language and intersubjectivity: multiplicity in a bilingual treatment. *Psychoanalytic Dialogues, 18*: 437–455.

Jacobs, T. J. (1991). *The Use of Self: Countertransference and Communication in the Analytic Situation*. Madison, CT: International Universities Press.

Javier, R. A. (1995). Vicissitudes of autobiographical memories in bilingual analysis. *Psychoanalytic Psychology, 12*: 429–438.

Kohut, H. (1971). *The Analysis of the Self*. Madison, CT: International Universities Press.

Marcos, L. R. (1976). Linguistic dimensions in the bilingual patient. *American Journal of Psychoanalysis, 36*: 347–354.

Ogden, T. (1997). Reverie and metaphor: some thoughts on how I work as a Psychoanalyst. *International Journal of Psychoanalysis, 78*: 719–732.

Pérez Foster, R. (1992). Psychoanalysis and the bilingual patient: Some observations on the influence of language choice on the transference. *Psychoanalytic Psychology, 9*: 61–76.

Richmond, M. B. (2004). Counter-responses as organizers in adolescent analysis and therapy. *Psychoanalytic Study of the Child, 59*: 145–166.

Stern, D. N. (1985). *The Interpersonal World of the Infant: A View from Psychoanalysis and Developmental Psychology*. London: Karnac, 1998.

Winnicott, D. W. (1971). *Playing and Reality*. London: Tavistock.

Winnicott, D. W. (1986). Holding and interpretation: fragment of an analysis. *The International Psychoanalytic Library, 115*: 1–194.

CHAPTER TEN

The unmatched twin: enactments of otherness and the autobiography of an immigrant clinician

Lara Sheehi

"Don't grieve. Anything you lose comes round in another form."

—*Rumi*

As I entered my kindergarten classroom on my first day of school in rural Killam, Alberta in Western Canada, I noticed that all my classmates were "twins." In my first experience with a room filled with white-Anglos, my child mind coupled each student with another, a partner, a mirror-double, and a friend. I was the odd-child-out, left without a "twin." This memory is entirely mine, unadulterated and unmediated by reconstructions from adults or by photographs. In that moment, I registered fully that I was a "brown" immigrant child in white Canada, an incomplete self without a twinning-double with whom I could identify. On the most rudimentary level, I registered that, somehow, this brownness, that incomplete "foreignness," was tantamount to exclusion, exclusion from social and cultural spaces but also from the paired space of identification.

This poignant memory would become the cornerstone of my experience of *"being raced"* (Ainslie, Tummala-Narra, Harlem, Barbanel & Ruth, 2013, p. 664, italics in original) as a racial subject

137

in North America. The memory of myself as odd-child-out would also eventually lay the groundwork for my clinical understanding of minority identity formation. The vignette serves as a conceptual antecedent to the mechanics and working tenants of what I have termed "enactments of otherness." The impact and later reworking of the othering experiences of my childhood immigration as well as my later immigration as an outspoken, pro-Palestinian, Arab woman in a post-9/11 United States, further sparked my awareness and attentiveness to racially and ethnically laden power constructs in therapeutic dyads, especially when both patient and therapist have experienced an immigration and/or identify with a denigrated internalized object.

This chapter provides insight into two distinct yet interwoven immigration narratives, highlighting the intricacies of my own immigration, especially as it relates to racial identity development. I will also reflect on the role of my immigration experience and how it influences my psychoanalytic clinical identity, as well as how a narrative of otherness (vis-à-vis immigration) may inform practice, and ultimately, a therapeutic dyad.

My immigration story (ies), not unlike many stories of immigration, was initially fraught with pain and alienation. It was punctuated by defensive and self-protective maneuvers that, at first, instigated a long string of self-effacing measures aimed at both organizing and obfuscating my othered experience. Predictably, the internal conflict produced by this process only fueled archaic, self-hating objects that confirmed my "inferiority" as a half-less, incomplete "twin" forced into an asymmetrical social space that threatened to entirely eradicate my subjectivity. That is, my subjectivity was reified as a contingent "other," always conditioned on its relation to majoritarian North American whiteness.

My concept of "othering," is not novel, but rather extrapolated from defining psychoanalytic works of theorists such as Akhtar, Boulanger, Benjamin, Lacan and of course, Freud. In service of this chapter, however, I deploy "otherness" as the process by which one has identified with a sociopolitically and/or culturally subjugated introject, with potential "wrecking effects" (Holmes, 2006) on the ego. Otherness then is constituted through a complex process of identification with and exclusion from a psychic, political, and social self-same (majoritarian culture, class ideals, patriarchal selfhood, etc.). In Canada, for example, identities are mediated by one's immigrant, native, or White status, which ultimately, mitigates one's relation to the State and the social/cultural place which one occupies (see Thobani, 2007). While there are most definitely positive introjects in an othered subjectivity, I primarily explore what Jones (2000) would refer to as "interaction structures"; these structures are power-imbued and instigated by the denigrated introject in the service of self-protection and reacquisition of personal power. The immigration experience for Arabs, for example, is inevitably coupled with a process of becoming a racialized self, a process of identification with a denigrated introject, and an othered space of exclusion that becomes both a space of refuge and alienation.

"Rayhin, Rayhin Mushwar"

My first immigration was familial and occurred in August 1990. The organizing family narrative behind this immigration is one laden with near misses during the sixteen-year Lebanese Civil War, punctuated by a devastating sense of helplessness in my increasingly fatigued parents. While still a child at the time, I have vivid—and happy—images of hide-and-seek games with my brother in our family's bomb shelter, living by candle light, and drives to the local spring because municipal utilities were inoperable. The sectarian fighting had been particularly violent and unrelenting for approximately one full month prior to May of 1989 when my parents decided to immigrate to Canada, where my paternal uncle and his family had emigrated some years before. My mother, who in my adult life confessed of her "hysteric" tendencies at the sound of bombing, has told of our collective cabin fever during this inordinately long period of confinement. Therefore, when the onslaught ceased for several consecutive days, my parents made an ambivalent decision to venture outside the shelter, eventually driving to a nearby relative's home with my maternal grandmother, while my father stayed behind. We tellingly sang a song that represented a magical undoing of constriction and physical, as well as psychic, fear of movement: "rayhin, rayhin mushwar, ta nobrom al-'alam bi nhar" (albeit less nuanced and emotive outside the Mother tongue (Greenson, 1950)—"we're going, we're going on a trip, to circumambulate the world in one day").

The bombing recommenced as soon as we had reached our relative's home with shrapnel raining heavily around us. My brother has a vivid memory—confirmed by my mother and grandmother—of a "bright red" piece of shrapnel whizzing by as my grandmother instinctively enveloped us in a protective hug. While we were fortunately unharmed, a worker inside the home was killed, and my father watched in horror from our own home as dark smoke bellowed from the location at which he knew we were. He now wistfully remarks that his instantaneous decision, marked with guilt and regret at not having left Lebanon sooner was, "if I find them alive, we will leave." So began the first semi-forced immigration process to Killam, Alberta.

S. Akhtar, (1995, 1999) and Grinberg and Grinberg (1984, 1989), have spoken of the mourning process as well as the "losses inherent in immigration" (Akhtar, 1995, p. 1052). Yet, while Grinberg and Grinberg (1989) highlight that children in some ways, are by default exiled inasmuch as the decision to immigrate is made by proxy, the preparation for my own immigration did not immediately include the pre-emptive or active mourning process my parents had to endure. Rather, my brother and I delighted in speaking gibberish prior to our departure, pretending to be fluent English speakers. We also were both incredibly excited to reunite with our cousins who had lived with us prior to their own immigration to Alberta, Canada. One and a half years after my parent's decision to leave, our departure, ironically, coincided with the "conclusion" of the Lebanese Civil War in 1990. The only memories of our journey are reworked constructions based on a photograph of myself next to the Bear at Paddington Station in London, and my parent's recounted frustration, as they could not speak English at the time.

My initial interaction with Killam, the 1,000 population, virtually white, and largely middle class, town in which my family and I found ourselves, was largely positive. My memories from this time were not yet racialized—starkly dissonant from the stories of struggle my brother described. My initial non-racialized existence may have been attributable to my age (five-years-old at the time) (Akhtar, 1995), my light skin, and various other protective factors, including my outgoing nature as well as my being at the developmentally optimal stage for language acquisition (Chomsky, 1986). However, the virtual absence of transitional struggle from my initial memories of Killam (prior to my first day of school) is curious when one considers the tremendous psychic shift that such a move demanded. Namely, I had not only lost my environmental and lingual constants, but also, along with my brother, assumed what Jurkovic, Kuperminc, Perilla, Murphy, Ibanez, and Casey (2004) refer to as "filial responsibility," as we became interlocutors for our parents.

My first racial memory can therefore act as an illustrative vehicle of the primary tenants of racial identity activation and formation, especially within the process of acculturation following immigration. Namely, my child ego did not pose the pain I registered when identifying myself as the odd-child-out among white Anglo counterparts vis-à-vis my *aloneness*, per se. Rather, I instinctively understood my aloneness as a function of *exclusion*, registering this as a function of my brownness in juxtaposition to the other student's whiteness. Even at the young age of five, therefore, a relational reference point of race was activated and an essentializing identity of outside-other was formed.

This necessitated shift in "self-structure," as named by Antokoletz (1994) had the indisputable pain flavor that alienation carries. Fanon (1963) refers to this alienation as the common vulnerability in his patients, an internalized inferiority and self-hatred that almost entirely eradicated their subjectivity. This shift sets the stage for an extensive self-preserving effort to metamorphose into a self-othering subject (Masri, 2009; Sheehi, 2009). That is, while a denigrated self-will outwardly act in retaliatory ways to upset a power imbalance, psychic intrusion, and/or re-oppression, relying on this defensive strategy may also be pre-emptively aimed at oneself in a complex bid for (self)protection, psychically and otherwise. Ferenzci (1993) addresses the denigrated subject's reaction to domination stating, *"The weak and undeveloped personality reacts to sudden unpleasure not by defence, but by anxiety-ridden identification and by introjection of the menacing person or aggressor"* (Ferenzci, 1949, p. 163, italics in original). Ferenzci conceptualized introjection as the psychic, cognitive, and experiential assimilation of the dominating object and held that this abusive object became internally present. Introjection allowed the child—later adult—to anticipate the perpetrator's attack and protect him/herself. While aimed at protection Frankel (2002), in response to Fercenczi's supposition, states that introjection also preserves the trauma, as one is haunted by the internalized image and experience of the subjugator. Less ambiguously, one may subjugate oneself in anticipation of likely subjugation by another/an other. This is the primary mechanism in *enactments of otherness*.

Almost, but not quite

The subsequent post-immigration experiences I had in Canada underscore this tinge of alienation and self-denigration, as my ego-ideal (see Lacan, 1978), even at a young age, strayed from my indigenous roots and quickly became one of white female, marked by a middle to upper middle class lifestyle, slender body, and stick-straight hair. I had instigated a violent process of identification with a culturally/ethnically/racially superior other which, by default, demanded a denial and subjugation of my own racial/ethnic identity. In Fuss's (1994) view, this type of identification is an intrinsically exploitative and self-denying process that re-denigrates the other, as it excises other traits that have potential to compromise the assimilation process. Because my very being was marked by incontrovertible other traits, my identified ego-ideal was at best Sisyphean and, at worst, detrimental to my developing ego as I was time and again entirely rejected by my white counterparts. In a bid to gain legitimacy, therefore, the ego-ideal, as it had come to be constructed and experienced, could only be achieved through an "almost, but not quite" mimicry (Bhabha, 1984).

Beginning in grammar school, I mimicked (and, therefore, identified with) the lifestyle and mannerisms of my Anglo-Canadian peers. Yet despite my own light complexion and blue eyes, I was often reminded of "my foreignness," told and retold, "you're as black as the dirt we walk on." This comment, incidentally, acts as a double-othering process, as I did not even fit the more available black/white divide (see Jones & Shorter-Gooden, 2003; Perea, 1997). Further highlighting the racial divide, were the stories I heard of my brother's own struggle, having been called names ranging from "Paki" to "sand-nigger," as well as my head of coarse, curly hair that would inevitably be butchered into a buzz-cut because the local hairdressers pronounced it too unruly to style. While my hair would later become an incredibly powerful identity marker that facilitated ownership of my racial identity, the initial repudiation of this betraying trait would culminate in a repeated chemical straightening of my hair starting at the age of eleven. These instances punctuated my realization that racial markers were tantamount to exclusion, inviting a self-protective stance of effacement where I could turn passive into active (Ferenczi, 1933) in order to pre-empt further attacks on my ego.

Frankel (2002) illuminates the underpinnings of my pre-emptive stance further, highlighting how, in identifying with the aggressor, we:

> make ourselves disappear … like chameleons, we blend into the world around us, into the very thing that threatens us, in order to

protect ourselves. We stop being ourselves and transform ourselves
into someone else's image of us. (Frankel, 2002, p. 102)

My recourse to *effacement*, therefore, helped maintain my survival and
was promulgated within the primary and organising defensive strategy
of an enactment of otherness.

In the meantime, my maiden name was transformed from its cor-
rect pronunciation of Masri ("muss-ree") to the anglophone "Maazree,"
and my father constructed a new proper name altogether, having been
told that his given name was unpronounceable. I ceased to speak Arabic
with my parents and would spend countless hours in front of the
mirror willing my hair to become long and straight. Recounting these
examples is not in service of a pedantic stance on my perils, especially
as, in comparison to other minorities, my family and I were rather
privileged. However, the examples are necessary so as to explicate the
process of subjugation of self and concomitant desires that accompanies
the experience of enactments of otherness (Masri, 2009; Sheehi, 2009).
Moreover, these examples illustrate further how a denigrated internalized object vis-à-vis one's othered status not only materializes, but also
becomes self-reinforcing in the object's legitimizing effort. In fact, while
I ultimately could never enjoy full membership in majoritarian white
rural Canadian society, my self-effacing efforts were met with capri-
cious reinforcement. Indeed, at times the identification process yielded
returns (e.g., validation by white counterparts); and when they did not,
it fueled a raging fire to ensure they were met with acceptance in the
following round, only to inevitably be rebuffed again.

Native other

Repatriation to Lebanon occurred when I was twelve years old, seven
years after we had immigrated to Canada. The preparation to return
to Lebanon in many ways was not a psychological shock. My parents'
frequent reminders that we would eventually return underscored
our life in rural Canada, serving, far too frequently, as a convenient
excuse, for example, to be repeatedly denied a pet, reminded that the
attachment would ultimately be painful, as I could not take the pet back
to Lebanon. This promise of return was instrumental in keeping the
family entrenched psychologically, socially, and culturally in Lebanon
and Arab culture via what Berry (1990) might describe as relative

"separation." Similarly, I witnessed my mother buying household items that were difficult to come by in Lebanon, storing them away for "when we return."

While psychologically the return may not have been jarring, it initially exploited the established internalization of myself as denigrated other, albeit in a more nuanced manner. Linguistically, my mother tongue had greatly deteriorated, as archaic introjects of otherness fueled my internal conflict and aligned me with my projected ego-ideal of a White North American woman. With this, I spoke my acquired language without a trace of an accent, but my native tongue exposed me as Native other ("mughtaribah"). My initial loss experienced in my immigration to Canada was therefore replicated by and for me, unable yet again, to communicate with my peers and family until re-immersion into Lebanese village life forced me to reacquire fluency rapidly.

There is not a cultural equivalence between immigrating from Lebanon to Canada and moving from Canada to Lebanon. We were returning to post-war Lebanon that was reconstructing itself very comfortably within the mode of globalized, neoliberalism. In this way, the Lebanese were far more conversant with North American culture than the Canadians were with an otherwise exoticized Arab otherness. Within this context, there existed, therefore, a collective projection of a Lebanese ego-ideal, one that also rests on ideals of white primacy (interestingly, both Anglo and Francophone)—akin to "light-skinned" discrimination in other minority communities (Tummala-Narra, 2007). I came to be known as the "ajnabiyah" (foreigner), frequently asked if I had lived "barra" (literally translated as "outside"). Understood as a privilege by others, this title only furthered my experience of alienation and strengthened the "wrecking" objects that inhabited my internal world.

Of course, at thirteen years old, I was negotiating a crucial and normative developmental stage that I would be remiss to overlook as a major contributor to the internal upheaval I experienced at this time. I was actively reconciling conflicts of individuation, emerging adolescence as a woman, body image concerns, and the like. However, the primacy of my racial and cultural conflict vis-à-vis my self-perception as other cannot be dispelled when one considers, for example, how my more "Canadian" or "ajnabiyah" traits (and therefore, at that time, ego-ideal congruent) were lauded by my more accepting, but themselves socially othered and self-effacing, Lebanese counterparts.

Notably, I was voted by my school peers as having the "Best Eyes" for several consecutive years, admittedly owing to the fact that blue/green eyes are, as in many minority communities (e.g., Hurstfield, 1978), collectively considered as a superior racial trait due to their congruence with projected standards of White beauty in a non-white community; what Jones and Shorter-Gooden (2003) refer to as the "lily complex." Indeed, my light skin tone was frequently referenced as a superior trait (I was referred to as "shaqra," meaning simultaneously "light-skinned" and "blonde") in juxtaposition to the archetypal Arab "olive" or dark skin. Thus, while outwardly I may have appeared more at peace, less conflicted, and seemingly working through only normative developmental hurdles, the insidious internal conflict of raced (Ainslie, Tummala-Narra, Harlem, Barbanel & Ruth, 2013) other was steadfast. Indeed, I continued to engage in grossly self-effacing acts such as chemically straightening my hair, especially conspicuous in a country where there were an abundance of appropriate haircare techniques to preserve curls.

Holding environment and curls

Not coincidentally, structural change by way of my ethnic and racial identity was galvanized in a truly meaningful way by my matriculation into the American University of Beirut (AUB) in culturally and historically complex Beirut, Lebanon. For decades, AUB had been the hotbed of political activity, the space for left-wing political movements (e.g., the founding ground for George Habbash's Arab Nationalist Movement (ANM) and later the Popular Front for the Liberation of Palestine; 1960s student protests/occupations), and a powerful agent of social change in Lebanon and the Arab world (Anderson, 2011). I now recognize myself to have been very provincial prior to beginning my education at AUB. Despite my bicultural experience, immigration, and repatriation, I moved between a mountain village to a small prairie town far from the cosmopolitan spaces of Toronto or even Edmonton.

The move to Beirut and more specifically into the dynamic space of AUB, therefore, served multiple purposes for my burgeoning identity, not the least of which was to give me a virtual containing and holding environment (Winnicott, 1960, 1969) to explore, challenge, and experiment with the complexities of identity formation within the latent and manifest elements of Lebanon's (and therefore my) social history and political and sectarian reality. Much like my predecessors, then, the university environment became breeding ground for my political education against the backdrop of globalization and United States' unipolar power, or Empire. That is, my introduction to AUB coincided with the new phase of American political, military, and economic expansion in the region marked by its invasion of Afghanistan and then Iraq, not to mention a heightened neocon political militancy in support of Israel's policies regarding the Palestinians, including the expansion of the "Apartheid Wall."

On a personal-political level, I studied and committed myself to the Palestinian cause ("al-qadiyah"), and became an activist against sectarianism and gender inequality in Lebanon. These were the days of my first marches, demonstrations, and civil actions, first against the American invasion of Iraq and eventually against the Syrian occupation of Lebanon. On a more intellectual and far-reaching structural level, however—fortuitously supported by my academic department as an English Literature major—I turned to psychoanalytic theory and literature as I grappled with my racial identity and sociopolitical role as an Arab woman during this dynamic, yet chaotic, time. With its breadth, psychoanalysis spoke to the complexity of inter- and intra-psychic life, and to possible explanations for outer manifestations of inner turmoil and as such, on the most simple of levels, made my personal process of identity negotiation more tolerable. Within this containing frame, I took my first of many racially affirming decisions in recognizing my hair as physical marker of my personal and ethnic identity, one under which a generation of women before me succumbed to the pressures of patriarchy, "modernity," and the commodification of their womanhood to erase the outward signs of Arabness. I now wore it down, voluminous, and free. My hair, therefore, symbolized an unapologetic embrace of my indigenous traits and a bold demand to be *seen* in this way—as anyone who has seen my hair can attest—it cannot be overlooked, denied, repressed.

The easy way out

With this, I entered into my second immigration, this time to the United States for graduate school. While immigration narratives may always include elements of loss due to reconfigurations of one's role in the new *vs.* indigenous space (Akhtar, 1999; Ainslie, Tummala-Narra,

Harlem, Barbanel & Ruth, 2013) as well as what is left behind, this new wave of immigration in the summer of 2006 was incredibly promising. I had decided to pursue psychology, even more invigorating after being accepted to my top choice in graduate programs at the George Washington University professional psychology program—at that time head by the incredibly adept and race conscious Dorothy E. Holmes. My immigration plans, unfortunately coincided with the beginning of the Israeli invasion in the 2006 war. On 12 July the Lebanese airport tarmac was bombed, all major roads leading out of the country were eviscerated, and Israel imposed a sea blockade on Lebanon as the "Israeli Defense Forces" poured across the border in the South.

Under these conditions, I came to rely on a privilege that I held, along with several thousand others that many Lebanese citizens did not share, namely, dual citzenship. With this came the recognition of my own collusion in the configurations of race, and the tacit agreement one makes with a racialized identity for citizenship in Canada. That is, as Sunera Thobani (2007) noted, citzenship in Canada is mediated, unlike the United States, through its "multi-cultural" policies, where immigrants' relation to the State and their compatriots is always mediated by their ethnic, immigrant status and community. Indeed, the privileges of citizenship from a country founded on a history of sustained abuses and land theft of native peoples come at a high cost for many in Canada. Yet, if the full privleges of citizenship came to me only when outside of Canada, this "privilege" would soonafter be erased as the Parliament of Canada amended the Citizenship Act in 2009, specifically targeting, in the words of Canadian MP Garth Turner, "Canadians of Convenience" (Turner, 2006).

My family and I fled to our mountain hamlet to escape the immediate dangers of warfare. My apartment was left unpacked, my friends unaware of when I had left, and my beloved Beirut flooded with refugees and the activitsts that helped organize their care with whom I wished to join. My family and I spent twelve days and nights under the intrusiveness of night-time drones, listening attentively to not-so-far-off explosions, and on one beautiful summer morning, watched from our balcony as the largest bridge in Lebanon crumbled before our eyes. All the while, we waited on instructions from the Canadian government as to when our evacuation would take place, most concerned about the violence that could be unleashed once the United States government had successfully completed their evacuations. Assuming a parentified role not alien to us, and perhaps in mastery of what had been asked of us as children, my brother and I requested that our parents join us in the evacuation, again leaving their world behind as we had done sixteen years prior.

While we had the privilege, so to speak, to assume another loss via immigration, the rest of my family and friends would remain in Lebanon. Their identities were not hyphenated. They did not have an additional citizenship to aid them in fleeing safely. As such, the internal conflict and recognition of my own collusion was activated, as I had heated discussions with family and close friends about their complex emotions of relief, envy, and disdain for me/us. On the one hand we had the "option," and therefore privilege, to leave, while on the other, we were accused of taking "the easy way out," commentary on a collusive interaction within the West/East binary. Ultimately, this coveted "option" whisked my family and I away from Beirut on a boat along with hundreds of other Lebanese Canadians on 25 July 2006.

Many non-Lebanese friends and colleagues have remarked about how harrowing the evacuation process must have been. Over many years of personal reflection, therapy, and conversations with trusted loved ones, however, I am more likely to highlight the ways in which my identity conflict was activated, especially as it related to my racial and ethnic identity, as potentially the most "dangerous" moments in this upheaval. This is not to detract from the true losses that I incurred and/or the abrupt and unorganized (*vs.* planned for and, hence, contained) path upon which my life had been forced (e.g., we were only allowed to carry approximately twenty pounds of belongings with us when evacuated, causing a true re-examination of my connection to material goods and a reflection on what was *necessary* vs. *desired*, a question that is often indistinguishable in the capitalist and material-driven world in which we currently live). However, my family and I were, and continue to be in many ways, part of the privilged minority: in 2006, we had access to a dual citizenship that helped us escape unharmed; we also had the monetary funds to fly to a relative's home after landing safely; specific to me, I had been accepted to graduate school and had already planned to make this very move, albeit under different circumstances.

This background may help, therefore, contextualize why a reactivation of the internal conflicts about belonging and identity may have been forefront in my consciousness, despite realistic "safety" concerns. While the scope of this paper does not allow for full exploration, this may also help us recognize how our patients may have an entirely different reference point regarding internal activations than where our initial clinical assumptions may lead us. That is, to a first-world clinician/reader, stories of war and evacuation may surface as the most central themes of potential trauma, while those accustomed to political upheavals and/or have forged spaces of normalcy within these frameworks may have the psychic flexibility to go beyond such expected markers, placing their trauma elsewhere. Considerations of racial identity and potential re-collusions with denigrated introjects in this immigration had, therefore, a much more nuanced meaning than the act of expatrtiation itself.

Race traitor

In an intriguing, but perhaps inevitable, way, my process of working through internalized objects of denigration and racial/ethnic inferiority was not yet complete. I entered graduate school at a time of great emotional fluidity. Many manifest factors may mistakingly be highlighted as integral in this fluidity, such as, how this move had been my first visit to the United States, or how I was entirely alone in the process, as my family remained in Canada and I had no relatives or friends in Washington, DC. However, I can non-defensively admit that these were among the less meaningful factors to my internal upheaval, as I quickly grew to love the city, made life-changing connections with fellow women of color, and was able to capitalize on the ferociously independent personality my parents had always encouraged.

Within the landscape of graduate school, I forged some of the most meaningful relationships of my life, both personally and professionally. It is during this time I found in my friends, most of whom were racialized children of immigrants themselves, the twin I lacked as a child. Yet, against these fulfilling relationships, my time in my training program was fraught with sustained racially laden innuendo and direct attacks, largely a consequence of my vocal political activism around the Palestininan solidarity and anti-war movements. Echoing the political atmosphere of the late-Bush era, this politicized atmosphere, a thin guise for the racism of the program's homogeneously white, upper middle class, mostly women, student body, served to reinscribe my recourse to enactments of otherness as a primary means of identity negotiation.

This negotiation did not take the form of racial or ethnic *effacement* in this case, but a psychic rearranging of that space that identifying with the introject, ironically, created. The enactment of otherness materialized in its most productive form, as an unbending enactment that placed me in the role of mouthpiece for racial justice, truth, and political realities, all of which, not coincidentally, simultaneously positioned me as aggressive.

How could the political positions that I assumed be perceived in that hostile, racialized space as anything but aggressive, especially as I was untwinned and chosing to identify with my introjected-other rather than the whiteness projected onto me? This interaction structure (Jones, 2000) was ironic considering my own immigration status and how my ethnic position as an Arab woman in post-9/11 Washington, DC placed me in a vulnerable position of being "too vocal." Such a structure played out in a regular deployment of the racial tropes predicated around brown/black aggression, not in the hallways and classrooms only, but brought up time and time again to the faculty and, in one instance, addressed in a program-wide meeting, referring to me, while I was in the room, without using my name but rather the effacing epithet "she."

In one instance I was pointedly asked, "why are you trying to deny your whiteness?" Not ironically, only the week before, the same white student had defended her "right" to identify as Indian or Black if she felt affinity towards those ethnicities. When my identity politics stood in contrast to my skin tone, the racial privilege that accompanies whiteness became apparent because I was either seen as a race-traitor or a "black" sheep in white fleece. My light skin evoked a rage among my cohort, who, effectively, indicted me for being a bad "twin."

The double-bind and root conflict embedded in both my immigration stories is therefore glaring. I could not fully integrate, as assimilation meant effacement under stringent guidelines of what would and would not be acceptable (Bhabha's, "almost but not quite" mimicry (1984)). On the other hand, when aligned fully with my Arab identity, I was experienced as aggressive, irrational, overstepping my "place," and most poignantly, as a traitor to, at least outwardly appearing, white physical characteristics.

Working through and within

I was fortunate to have the guidance of incredibly supportive and nurturing faculty and loyal friends who encouraged my identity growth and racial working through in the most meaningful of ways. I also spoke about this conflict extensively in my individual therapy.

Most meaningful by way of clinical development, however, was my ability to work within an enactment of otherness between myself and Mr. H, a Middle Eastern immigrant patient, himself a racialized subject (often referred to as "sand nigger") who relied heavily on internalized, aggressive introjects to defend against further psychic intrusion. This emerging clinical work and concomitant countertransferential material with Mr. H, allowed me to theoretically and practically engage the racial power struggle in which I was embroiled. It also has provided a lens through which I could retroactively understand the enactments of otherness that had underscored my own identity negotiation as an immigrant.

The term "enactment" warrants clinical attention. The word implies that both patient and clinician are engaging in a pattern of behavior. Recognition of the therapist's role in this interaction structure is imperative. The minority therapist with his/her own potential introjects (much like my own) cannot be immune to the potential wrecking effects (Holmes, 2006) of the historical and sociopolitical remnants of their direct or indirect subjugation. In other words, the therapist's own vulnerabilities to power-imbued interactions as a result of his/her own introjects and subjugated self-view may influence the mobilized enactments. Once acknowledged and worked through, one's countertransferential susceptibility to power-laden exchanges within the therapeutic dyad can be used as a mobilizing force for therapeutic change.

In other words, the clinic room emerges as the breeding ground for both problem and cure. Mr. H's personal history included a physically and verbally abusive father as well as an unbending affinity to family lore surrounding a very complicated and politically laden immigration history. Mr. H frequently felt subjugated and denigrated within his family, but most especially as a racialized subject in the United States. For example, he recalled being singled out as Muslim, being in constant internal conflict in relation to his traditional Middle Eastern upbringing, and fending off psychic intrusion from an intrusive and denigrating father. In a bid to work through the powerlessness that resulted from these positions, Mr. H would resort to "dominating" others, that is, he referred to women as "conquests," would instigate power maneuvers in relationships, and would avoid feeling "weak" at all costs.

Throughout our work together, my own feeling of racial inferiority (my denigrated introjects) created the circumstance in which I had impulses to retaliate against Mr. H's identification with the aggressor (mainly manifested as subtle as well as direct power maneuvers in our work) to regain my own footing. These impulses would surface as a result of my own vulnerabilities to invisibility and therefore instigate a process by which I could reinstate my presence—in this instance exacting my power as therapist/knower.

What I experienced as the most painful reminders of my own otherness often occurred at times when Mr. H himself felt psychically intruded upon, such as when we delved more deeply into his underlying dynamics. In these instances I often felt relegated to invisible other—a bystander, powerless. Essentially, we would engage in power-centered enactments, instigating what seemed to be a game of out-maneuvering that initially allowed us to escape our alienation, stave off overwhelming affect, and contain and protect our introjected otherness. In this regard, the enactments in which we engaged simultaneously pacified and protected our introjected otherness by gaining dominance over and protection from a perceived onslaught, from each other in this instance. Naming and working within these enactments not only allowed for a deeper understanding of Mr. H's intrapsychic disturbance, but also the intersubjective space created in/through our work.

Like Mr. H, patients will engage relationally in patterns that mimic the larger sociopolitical environment in which they are intertwined. As clinicians, we may be partially responsible for activating these destructive introjects through what Hegarty (2007) refers to as our "psychological power." Namely, we have "the power to name the psychology of another" (Hegarty, 2007, p. 85) in our role as therapist and therefore become the signifier. Acknowledging how otherness may be enacted in the clinical work may allow adequate space, both psychically and interpersonally, for our patients to work through their introjects by exploring the othering experiences within their own autobiography, especially as immigrants and racialized subjects.

References

Ainslie, R. C., Tummala-Narra, P., Harlem, A., Barbanel, L. & Ruth, R. (2013). Contemporary psychoanalytic views on the experience of immigration. *Psychoanalytic Psychology, 30*: 663–679.

Akhtar, S. (1995). A third individuation: Immigration. Identity and the psychoanalytic process. *Journal of the American Psychoanalytic Association*, 43: 1051–1084.

Akhtar, S. (1999). The immigrant, the exile, and the experience of nostalgia. *Journal of Applied Psychoanalytic Studies*, 1: 123–130.

Anderson, B. S. (2011). *The American University of Beirut: Arab Nationalism and Liberal Education.* Austin, TX: University of Texas Press.

Antokoletz, J. C. (1994). Cross-cultural passages. *The American Journal of Psychoanalysis*, 54: 279–281.

Berry, J. W. (1990). Psychology of acculturation. *Applied cross-cultural psychology*, 14: 232–253.

Bhabha, H. K. (1984). Of mimicry and man: The ambivalence of colonial discourse. *October, Discipleship: A Special Issue on Psychoanalysis*, 28: 125–133.

Chomsky, N. (1986). *Knowledge of Language: Its Nature, Origin, and Use.* Portsmouth, NH: Greenwood Publishing Group.

Fanon, F. (1963/2004). *The Wretched of the Earth.* (R. Philcox, Trans). New York, NY: Grove Press.

Ferenczi, S. (1949). Confusion of the tongues between the adults and the child—(The language of tenderness and of passion). *International Journal of Psychoanalysis*, 30 (4): 225–230.

Frankel, J. (2002). Exploring Ferenczi's concept of identification with the aggressor: Its role in trauma, everyday life, and the therapeutic relationship. *Psychoanalytic Dialogues*, 12 (1): 101–139.

Fuss, D. (1994). Frantz Fanon and the politics of identification. *Diacritics*, 24: 20–42.

Greenson, R. (1950). The mother tongue and the mother. *The International Journal of Psychoanalysis*, 31: 19–23.

Grinberg, L. & Grinberg, R. (1984). A psychoanalytic study of migration: Its normal and pathological aspects. *Journal of the American Psychoanalytic Association*, 32: 13–38.

Grinberg, L. & Grinberg, R. (1989). *Psychoanalytic Perspectives on Migration and Exile.* New Haven, CT: Yale University Press.

Hegarty, P. (2007). Getting dirty: Psychology's history of power. *History of Psychology*, 10: 75–91.

Holmes, D. E. (2006). The wrecking effects of race and social class on self and success. *The Psychoanalytic Quarterly*, 75: 215–235.

Hurstfield, J. (1978). "Internal" colonialism: White, black and Chicano self conceptions. *Ethnic and Racial Studies*, 1: 60–79.

Jones, C. & Shorter-Gooden, K. (2003). *Shifting: The Double Lives of Black Women in America.* New York, NY: Harper Collins.

Jones, E. (2000). *Therapeutic Action: A Guide to Psychoanalytic Therapy.* Northvale, NJ: Jason Aronson.

Jurkovic, G. J., Kuperminc, G., Perilla, J., Murphy, A., Ibañez, G. & Casey, S. (2004). Ecological and ethical perspectives on filial responsibility: Implications for primary prevention with immigrant Latino adolescents. *Journal of Primary Prevention, 25* (1): 81–104.

Lacan, J. (1978). *The Four Fundamental Concepts of Psycho-analysis.* New York, NY: W. W. Norton.

Masri, L. (2009). Introjects in the therapeutic dyad: Towards "decolonization." *Unpublished doctoral research.* Washington, DC: The George Washington University.

Perea, J. F. (1997). The Black/White binary paradigm of race: The "normal science" of American racial thought. *California Law Review, 85*: 1213–1258.

Sheehi, L. (2009). Introjects in the therapeutic dyad: Towards "decolonization." *Unpublished doctoral research.* Washington, DC: The George Washington University.

Thobani, S. (2007). Exalted subjects: Studies in the making of race and nation in Canada. Toronto, Canada: University of Toronto Press.

Tummala-Narra, P. (2007). Skin color and the therapeutic relationship. *Psychoanalytic Psychology, 24*: 225–270.

Turner, G. (2006). *Citizens of Convenience.* Retrieved from http://www.garth.ca/2006/09/19/citizens-of-convenience/ (Last accessed 16 November 2014).

Winnicott, D. W. (1960). The theory of the parent–infant relationship. *International Journal of Psychoanalysis, 41*: 585–595.

Winnicott, D. W. (1969). The use of an object. *International Journal of Psychoanalysis, 50*: 711–716.

CHAPTER ELEVEN

Conclusion: change is us

M. Hossein Etezady

> The only means of strengthening one's intellect is to make up
> one's mind about nothing, to let the mind be a thoroughfare for all
> thoughts.
>
> —*John Keats*

W hat do we mean by identity and what about its transition?
Identity may be considered as concrete and static as the card
we carry in our wallet, letting others know, unequivocally, who we are
by name, date of birth, occupation, where we reside, and other such
particulars. This ostensibly sets us aside and apart as a unique individual, unlike any other and far from identical to, anyone else, at any other
time or in any other place. This concrete instrument of identification,
serving to putatively bestow upon us avowed uniqueness and individuality can, at best, go only so far in terms of defining and distinguishing
us, particularly with regards to the salient essence that constitutes the
actuality of what and who we are.

From a psychoanalytic perspective, identity represents a multifaceted
concept that may be regarded from numerous viewpoints and

from many levels of discourse. Far from a simple, well-defined and circumscribed entity, its definition, phenomenology, function, development and vicissitudes, can touch upon nearly every aspect of mental life and is derived from the widest range of our conceptual and principal tenets. If we maintain that the singular subject of psychoanalysis is subjectivity itself, we are then obliged to center our focus on the topic of identity within the domain of subjectivity and the internal universe of psychic reality. This of course is not to deny, downplay or disregard the objective reality of the experienced external world, or the vast field of the universally recognized states of relatedness and intersubjectivity.

While dividing reality into disparate sectors of objective, subjective, and intersubjective is a common exercise, in fact there is but only one singular reality that we might regard from various viewpoints. Each of these points of view originates from the subjective perspective of the beholder of that position. Additionally, as primal constituents of the subjective realm, we would have to emphasize sensory, perceptual, sensual, cognitive, conceptual, affective, and discriminating elements, as well as actual comprehension and eventual appreciation of objective reality. From the viewpoint of representational mental activity, there can be no object in the absence of an experiencing subject. In this context objects do not exist until they are created and virtually constructed anew, incrementally, in layers upon layers of progressive accumulation of successive encounters represented as emerging ingredients of subjective momentary experience.

Psychoanalytic theories of ego psychology, object relations, internalization and separation-individuation, describe the rudimentary psychic apparatus as an undifferentiated global entity within which distinctive characteristics of self *vs.* other have not yet been established. Boundaries separating internal from external, qualitative and functional features of the id *vs.* those of the ego and the constitutive elements of the subject *vs.* those of the object have yet to be formed. This early beginning is known as the undifferentiated phase of psychological development, out of which differentiated structures and functions, distinct boundaries and links, as well as individual elements of relational interaction, transitional experience and intersubjectivity, in time, emerge. The containing vessel of subjectivity and the possessing owner of one's identity, that is, the sense of self, traverses a pre-representational, pre-oedipal, pre-verbal and pre-symbolic course that departs substance, meaning, utility, and purposeful direction to the matter of identity, in its compounded complexity, as it proceeds towards its subsequent way stations of progressive transition during the process of maturation. We therefore, cannot undertake any basic consideration of identity without including specifics that might illuminate areas pertaining to the emergence, establishment, and maintenance of the sense of self.

Having established, in the course of this brief excursion, the primacy of subjectivity as a developmental contextual background, as well as in terms of its centrality as the primary subject of psychoanalysis, we may now return to the examination of identity and various passages of transition or leaps of transformation that it is destined to undergo.

Identity as the containing envelope of the self

Within the containing envelope that holds together the cohesive wholeness of the psycho-physiological continuity of one's subjective experience, over time and through changes in conditions and variability of states, resides the cryptic entity we know as the individual's sense of self. The sense of self begins dimly and globally, in physical and bodily origins that gradually gain increasing mental representations as they coalesce, evolve, combine, and diversify in the course of exposure to, and during interaction with, the environment. Within this containing envelope is deposited the entirety of our conscious or unconscious past, present or the future, drives and motivations, inhibitions and compromise formations, cognition and emotions, hopes and fears, ideals and expectations, with regards to our own life as well as those of others. It is within this containing envelope that we maintain borders of individuality and separation as well as extended connections to others and to the outer world. Also, it is within this cryptic entity that we maintain and utilize a sense of agency, effectiveness, responsibility, duty, commitment, affiliation and devotion. Our mental resources are crucially invested both in realizing wishes, satisfying our needs, and reaching the objectives we aim at by engaging the external world, as well as in maintaining the internal cohesion and homeostatic equilibrium. This allows for and sustains the stability, resiliency, and buoyancy that we need internally in order to go on being, thriving, and preparing for the contingencies of the future, whether in confident expectation or in vigilant anticipation of the unpredictable events yet to unfold.

The sense of self is not only an aspect of one's identity, but it may be considered as its main content. Perhaps it may not be too far off the mark to view identity as the containing envelope that covers, carries inside and holds in whole, the different physical components as well as heterogeneous mental elements of the sense of self along with their interconnections, all together, in unison. Such a metaphorical envelope can be seen as having a naming label or other signifying markers to indicate the nature of part, parts or the whole of what it contains, where it originates, where it may be heading, and how it may be accessed and by whom and under what conditions.

Identity also carries with it external as well as internal indications, implications, and determinants of gender. In fact gender characteristics can be noted almost from about the last quarter of the first year, coinciding with the differentiation sub-phase of separation-individuation and the so-called "dawn of intersubjectivity."

At the age of one year, differences between boys and girls can be recognized by casual observation on the basis of facial and bodily expression or preference for and choices of toys, games and attraction to objects in the surroundings. Not only is this difference is objectively recognized by a casual observer, it usually elicits distinctly different, gender-specific reactions from adults who engage in interaction with infants as young as one year or even earlier. Although we customarily speak of gender identity as though it were an independent entity of its own separate standing, it is worth noting that gender, as such, is but one remarkable constituent of identity that is, for all practical purposes, not possible to isolate from the sense of self and its containing envelope in the metaphorical rendition presented above. Coherence, instability, disintegration or fragmentation as well as conflict, ambivalence or dysphoria, pertaining to gender unavoidably pertain to the sense of self in similar terms. On the other hand, it also goes without saying that pathological versions of the emergence and maintenance of the sense of self and disorders of narcissism will not spare identity or its gender implications.

In the beginning

If we base our understanding of identity on its course of development in terms of the emergence of the sense of self as a psychological process, we would need to begin with the indispensable requirement of secure attachment. Secure attachment is predicated on maternal qualities that have their routes in parenting and environmental aptitudes of the previous generation. These conditions would be closer to optimal when mother's own attachment was secure as a matter of primary prerequisite for her capacity for empathy and attunement. In this context the mother is hopefully capable of seeing the newborn as a separate entity with his own subjective identity, his own needs, urges, and desires and in time, as an agent of his own intentions, emotions, likes, and dislikes. Such a maternal figure is capable of holding, containing, and mirroring the infant and can identify with his needs and emotional states. It is through this empathic attunement that the newborn is able to see, through mother's viewpoint, her mirroring and reflective functions, the objective reality of his true self.

When such an accurate reflection is hindered due to deficit in maternal libidinal availability, or because of trauma, depression or mother's unresolved narcissistic needs, the germinal core of the emerging self does not correspond with the reality of the child's internal experience. This sets the course towards the formation of a false self, failing to establish the capacity for effective self-soothing, self-reflection, and successful self-regulation. This inevitably results in failure of interactive regulation and lifelong disturbance of object relations. Without presence of maternal empathic attunement and her libidinal availability, self object needs remain unmet and are relegated to defensive narcissistic realm of schizoid or paranoid modality and persistence of grandiosity, fantasies of omnipotence, and archaic idealized objects. Splitting of the ego, the objects and affects create a chaotic internal turmoil perpetuated by primitive defensive mechanisms, as affect modulation, via signal-anxiety, repression, reality processing, and symbolic functions, fail to enter the scene. Triadic and oedipal conflicts are unmanageable as paranoid and schizoid positions and coercive, anal sadistic and pre-oedipal modes of relatedness persist. The so-called depressive position cannot be established as this is predicated upon the establishment of a stable and individuated sense of self and upon the capacity for mourning and relinquishment of infantile omnipotence.

The second and third years of life, which we can describe as the years of transition, contain crucial and substantial events that prepare the ground for the emergence of self- and object-libidinal-constancy. It is this acquisition that is indispensable for the establishment of the capacity for a triadic mode of relatedness and oedipal conflict resolution.

These two years therefore, not only coincide with appearance and functional dominance of transitional experience, transitional objects and transitional phenomena, they also provide a developmental context for gradual and progressive transition from primary narcissism and monadic mode of relatedness to a dyadic and later to a triadic mode of secondary narcissism.

From primary process thinking to secondary process, from preverbal and pre-representational to verbal and symbolic representation, and from a pre-oedipal to an oedipal mode of conflict resolution; we might say it is the optimal resolution of the so-called infantile neurosis embedded in the Oedipus Complex that eventuates in identification with each parent and the formation of internalized functions of synthesis, integration, execution, discrimination, and moral judgment. At the end of this period of childhood the individual has achieved a relative degree of autonomy, capacity for socialization, repression, sublimation, and peer relations. With achievement of relative constancy and stability of such internal structure formation, provided that more or less good-enough environmental circumstances have prevailed, the individual has by now arrived at the point of consistently displaying particular personality features and rather distinct character elements and gender expression that constitute a cohesively distinct and unique gestalt that we might consider to be the founding core of his individual identity.

The terrible twos

What makes the terrible twos at times truly terrible, not only from the parents' perspective, but perhaps more unfortunately so for the bewildered and infuriated burgeoning toddler, is the developmental gap that remains in its wake, unless sufficient resolution of its attendant issues can be achieved.

When I ask parents about the status of their children during "the terrible twos," I am frequently told something like "it was not so bad when he was two, but got really bad in his third year." It is therefore my impression that the terrible twos consist of two years, that is, the second as well as the third year. Reflecting upon the frequently reported claim that the third year is significantly more challenging than the second year in these cases, I am reminded of the time sequence involved in the subphases of separation-individuation. While from twenty four months to thirty six months is one whole year of "consolidation" during which the new acquisitions of the preceding sub-phase, are increasingly better integrated, solidified and assimilated, the sub-phase of rapprochement proper and its critical imprint on structure formation coincides only with the second half of the second year, roughly for about six months or so. This period follows the practicing sub-phase which is normally characterized by the junior toddler's elated mood, his love affair with the world, his triumphant attitude of being impervious to knocks and falls and his daring feats of darting away from the mother, to be frantically chased by her and swooped up into her arms.

By the fifteenth or sixteenth month, when this state of buoyancy and darting takes a dramatic turn to an anxious retreat to mother's lap after each brief distancing venture, and the need for mother's close participation and comforting reassurance, this dramatic retreat can create considerable confusion and unsettling bewilderment for many mothers. When mothers respond to this unexpected change and frequent bouts of anger with confusion, rejection, retaliation or other mis-attuned reactions, it aggravates the child's anxious clinging and an organismic panic that often takes the form of coercive rage and sometimes, endless temper tantrums. Even in the case of most well attuned and intuitively empathic mothers, often the child cannot be sufficiently soothed or easily satisfied. The child's persistent attempts to recreate the lost and longed for bliss of a symbiotic state that once prevailed must inevitably end in frustration, disorganizing rage, and experiencing the mother in the cast of his own projected destructive and unbearable negative affective tones. When mother's empathic attunement and reflective function makes it possible for her to sustain her libidinal availability, she can respond to this destructive upheaval with consistent holding, containing, and tolerant mirroring which leads to ameliorating repair of this challenging disruption.

Repeated episodes of such cycles of disruption and repair in the presence of mother's constancy and libidinal availability succeeds in gradual, but progressive neutralization of primitive aggression which tames and turns the destructive energy into generative fuel for ego growth and crystallization of positively cathected introjects of good self and object representations. When the mother is able to libidinize this crucially fateful interaction with her junior toddler, so that there is a surplus of libido over the quantity of aggressive energy during these battles of will, the good maternal introject can survive and the positive affective valence of these episodes will nurture and sustain self-representation, enhance self-cohesion, boost resiliency and buttress the child's feeling of vitality and confident expectation. When this proceeds optimally and the mother proves adequate to the task, the child learns about the constructive and fulfilling results of self-assertiveness. He will learn to say no and also to accept the inevitability of many negating obstacles he confronts. He will begin to experience and establish boundaries between self and object, wish and reality, internal and external, and what he can and cannot do. He can begin the process of accepting loss, tolerating ambivalence, expect and accept imperfection and vulnerability in himself and in others and relinquish omnipotence and grandiosity gradually, in tolerable increments. When the good mother survives the onslaught of rage and destructive wishes the child can develop the confident capacity to be self-assertive and succeed in forging paths toward fulfillment in the face of persistent obstacles and unyielding challenge. Ego resources as well as self-control can flourish, problem solving and mastery take hold and storms of internal affective turmoil can be better contained. Periodical upsurge in negative affective experiences of daily routines, in these cases, do not annihilate the goodness of the self, the object or the connecting links of relationships. The foundations of the road towards self and object constancy can be laid down.

Under these favorable conditions the terrible twos are not quite so terrible, the battles of will not so intense and temper tantrums are for the most part manageable and infrequent. When this child enters the third year, having resolved conflicts of rapprochement more or less optimally, he enters a period of consolidation well equipped and is therefore ready to build upon previous acquisitions, grow and expand his ego resources and cognitive capabilities in accordance with age appropriate expectations.

In the unhappy circumstances of failed rapprochement resolution however, unresolved conflicts of the anal-sadistic, power struggle, control, and omnipotence continue. The higher order challenges of the consolidation period heighten, rather than diminish in intensity. Opposition, omnipotent defiance, rage storms and sado-masochistic, coercive modes of interaction dominate. Grandiosity of the primary narcissism era along with idealized part objects persists. Ambivalence and loss cannot be tolerated. Reality and fantasy cannot be segregated and boundaries of self *vs.* object, wish *vs.* reality and internal *vs.* external cannot be identified or maintained. Ego growth and higher orders of defensive and adaptive functions, in this situation, are not reached. Self and object constancy have no grounding and triadic conflict resolution of an oedipal nature are not available. Self-reflective and empathic capacities are missing and the terrible twos never come to an end. Ego, superego and ego ideal remain in their pre-oedipal states of archaic organization.

When, as the consequence of unresolved rapprochement crisis, neutralization of aggression and the healing of the split falter, pre-oedipal modes of relatedness, defense, adaptation, and narcissistic pathology, also known as disorders of the self, pervade. In treatment of these constellations of symptomatology, successful outcome depends on the extent to which the transference manifestations of splitting, primitive defensive operations and sado-masochistic object relations, reminiscent of rapprochement crisis are worked through and reparative restoration of the sense of self thereby accomplished.

The implications of these developmental considerations of the pre-oedipal period cannot be over-emphasized with respect to oedipal resolution, achievement of self-cohesion, identity formation and the capacity to function self-sufficiently as a well-integrated member of a family, the community and circle of peers.

Triadic mode of function

The fourth, fifth, and sixth years coincide with the oedipal period, when the child is in the throes of resolving the momentous conflicts ensuing from the wish to exclusively possess the beloved parent of the opposite sex and eliminate from the scene the parent of the same sex who is also the object of his love as well as envy, rivalry and fear. A favorable outcome to this drama depends entirely on resiliency and empathic attunement of both parents, each playing their own individual as well as joint part in enabling the child to survive this universal and uniquely humane intrapsychic battle.

While questions might arise with regards to the universality *vs.* culture-specific validity of the Oedipus Complex, particularly in the light of the rapidly changing cultural norms with respect to gender roles and family constellations on a global scale, we need to distinguish the subjective/intrapsychic implications of this phenomenon from its cultural/objective features. We should bear in mind that the subjective quality of identity, or that of the sense of self, is not independent of the culture or the intersubjective field that it engages, shares, produces or is born in. In this sense there is always a dialectical dimension concerning the developmental status of the self and the qualitative aspects and circumstantial features of the object(s), along with the prevailing contextual conditions at the time. This would mean that possibilities of expression, interaction and dialectical elaboration depend on what developmental state of the self and what corresponding modes of relatedness happen to be at hand, in addition to and besides the circumstances dictated by the external reality, the environment and the cultural milieu.

The primary narcissism of the undifferentiated early oral phase of "normal autistic period" followed by a symbiotic phase, coinciding with the qualities of the emerging self, soon to become the core self, can accommodate merely to a monadic mode of relatedness. Here the object is experienced as a part of the self before it becomes no longer a part of the self, but a possession. In the later part of the first year and beginning with differentiation, the intersubjective self enters a dyadic realm of relatedness as the libidinal energies invested in the idealized symbiotic object are gradually withdrawn and reinvested in the self as secondary narcissism. This coincides with the anal-sadistic phase of the psychosexual development when the (part) object has to be controlled and overpowered and stripped of its own will, power, or intentionality. The critical upheaval and self-promoting assertive strivings of rapprochement and struggles over omnipotent control take place within this dyadic context. The triadic mode of relatedness becomes feasible once gradual relinquishment of infantile omnipotence has begun and mutuality on the basis of the appreciation of the subjectivity of the object begins to become operative.

Objects

Having elaborated upon the development of the self and its evolving capabilities we should also keep in mind the development of the object. Objects are initially experienced as part of the self. In the later stretches of the monadic mode of relatedness they are treated as a narcissistic possession of the self. The object's independent presence, when acknowledged in early dyadic mode, is stripped of its subjectivity. It is used, controlled, dominated, and subjected to destruction. As mother's libidinal constancy and concern results in the gradual achievement of the capacity for concern in her infant, the object's subjectivity separate, but similar to one's own, can be recognized. With the dawning recognition of transgressive damage inflicted upon the object and fear of the loss of the object, attempt at repair of the damage and recovering the lost object, the subjectivity of the object begins to take hold, to be recognized and accepted. The depressive position can now be a context for care and compassion towards the object and its vulnerability. In the state of healthy secondary narcissism the object's subjectivity is allowed, respected, and accommodated to, as self and object constancy can begin and a triadic relationship and triadic conflict resolution can be undertaken. This mode of resolution allows for ambivalence in a sustained relationship that ties the self to an other, as well as to a second other, while at the same time tolerates, respects, and values the relationship between those two others to the exclusion of one's self.

In a hypothetically traditional family of one man, one woman, in a marriage, parenting one child, the prototypical model of classical Oedipus Complex fits squarely. In all other variations of domestic or casual relationships of whatever gender, identity or socially sanctioned roles, essentials of triadic dynamics are relevant in accordance to each particular variation and apply to the basic tenets of psychological development, normal narcissism and character formation, across the board, in any culture and in any time frame.

The triadic drama of Oedipus Complex cannot be confined to the abstracted bare bones of a triangular state. On those bare bones we need to place the human psycho-physiology of the instinctual life of libidinal drives, aggression, sexuality and gender, activity, passivity, rivalry, envy, triumph, defeat, shame, pride, greed, anxiety, danger, guilt, redemption, resolution, disillusionment, and, ideally, contented resignation to the demands of undeniable reality. This is an interminably complex drama that never settles completely and is revisited and recapitulated in themes, sub-themes and in mundane events of the daily routine or in the critically momentous milestones of one's life cycle, regardless of variations in time and cultural context. This recapitulation also applies similarly to the resolution of rapprochement crisis, as in the first, second, third and other enumerations of subsequent "individuation." When the first renditions of individuation or the Oedipus Complex have passed favorably and uneventfully recapitulations can be vitalizing, growth promoting and enriching. Where the original conflicts have remained unresolved the foreseeable challenges of each future juncture may lead to disintegration, chaos, regression, and collapse of unstable defensive structures, at great cost to the well-being and the coping capability of the individual.

The essential question

From the foregoing elaboration of the development of the sense of self and the emergence of the core of one's identity we will now leap ahead to the identity of the analyst when he or she has experienced the life altering event of immigration. The professional identity of the analyst is made of the characteristic features of a healer. Whether a physician or not, the psychoanalyst seeks to alleviate suffering, sooth the sole and remedy mental deviation and pathology. This takes forms sometimes akin to a surgeon, other times likened to an obstetrician and many times in the transferential guise of a parent and usually with the deeply moving compassion of a fellow human being. In his therapeutic mission the analyst enters the fray, armed with his own tools of empathy, insight, and the hard won gains derived from his own experience of a long and arduous journey of introspection and transformation. A journey of soul grinding search and mind boggling immersion into the forbidden depths of depravity and unfathomable evil that humanity has uniformly despised and detested in terror and abhorrence. He has dared to seek and see the forbidden and has surmounted the most obstinate of protestations from his own innermost censors.

In his devotion, empathy, and consistency he is the guardian, the guide, the witness, the arbiter, keeper of secrets, and the ultimate confidante and refuge. He is the receptacle of love, longing, envy, admiration, exultation, rivalry, hatred, vilification, fear, and nameless commotion. He strives to be and to remain receptive, attentive, responsive, responsible, warmly engaged, intimate and neutral, focused on the therapeutic task, in the best interest of his analysand. This and much more is his task, method and analytic identity and the lion's share of his working self-concept. This is an aspect of his identity encasing and containing his prehistoric self, his childhood and adolescent self, his mature and real, as well as his ideal self. His analytic identity is formed out of the conglomeration of all the ingredients that rendered him the human he had been and the analyzed and trained specialist that he has managed to become. Yet his analytic identity only complements other components that define the more completely nuanced totality of his multifaceted identity, as a younger or perhaps older, of one or the other gender (if not ambiguous), parent, child, grandparent or grandchild, sibling, spouse, artist, golfer, diabetic patient, avid reader, and so on. Other endless attributes may be qualitative, quantitative, moral, social, financial, etc. One particular attribute we hold as salient in the present discussion is the analyst that happens to also be an immigrant. In this respect an essential question might be asked as to whether and how immigration affects the identity of a person who, as fate may have it, happens to have trained to become an analyst, and whether or how might immigration affect the analytic identity of a clinician engaged in analytic work.

Immigration and identity

Answering the question of whether and how, exactly, immigration could affect one's identity is not a simple matter. Without exact accounting for the detailed minutiae of an individual's life in specific instances of various circumstances, only certain ubiquitous aspects of the question can be considered in broadly generalized terms. In some instances immigration may be a desired objective, long wished for, anticipated, planned, undertaken eagerly, and enthusiastically welcomed. Other times it may be unexpected, unsettling, not planned for, disruptive and unwanted. It might be imposed by social, political or financial dictates of an adverse nature. It may be traumatic, debilitating, debasing or irreparably damaging and destructive. It can represent an additional hardship and a costly toll on top of the disturbing impact of other previous jolts. That would be to say that all instances of immigration do not pack the same identical punch and cannot uniformly be regarded with the same degree of impact or quality of impingement. We could also assume based on the many actual instances of such experiences, that the impact of immigration reverberates through the experience and identity formation of unborn generations that will follow.

In many ways we may find aspects of divorce, a well-studied phenomenon, and its impact on one's identity that closely resemble many instances of immigration. As disruptive and life altering as divorce is, at times it can be salutary, in that it brings to an end a situation of unrelenting distress and unbearable suffering and ushers in a new phase with hopeful promise of liberation, peace of mind, and new vitalizing and exciting options or possibilities in the future. It is usually not an isolated single event. In divorce, as in the case of immigration, the events and determining factors leading to its culmination begin long before its actual occurrence and the after effects continue to unfold and multiply into the long term future for those involved. Also, at times a divorce comes about after inordinate amounts of discord, dysfunction, antagonism, violence, and pervasive harm, much of which continue still in its aftermath and negatively influence the unfolding course of the subsequent events. In certain situations, similar to some instances of immigration, a new set of aggravating circumstances will be compiled on top of disturbances that have already been responsible for inducing intolerable pain and discord. Yet other situations of immigrations/divorces are relatively well conducted, with minimal amounts of hardship and more or less benign consequences. In some cases the arrangements are made deliberately and based on realistic and practical grounds and end up with less emotionally intense and manageably subdued after effects. Many instances of immigration fit this mold when a difficult life circumstance in one's homeland is deliberately and relatively harmlessly terminated in favor of a new start that allows for leaving difficult circumstances behind, at some cost, but launch on a new beginning with choices that are more conducive to living a more fulfilling life.

On the other hand some cases of immigration have been so eagerly desired and wishfully anticipated that their final undertaking represents the fulfillment of nearly a lifetime of dedicated pursuit and adamant persistence. This might more closely resemble the joyful culmination of a lofty romance reaching a climax by ending in a blissful marriage. Here as in the case of an actual ideal marriage, one can expect a honeymoon, often richly fulfilling, but sometimes lasting only briefly or even resulting in bitter disillusionment at the very start.

This is to note that each case of immigration is characterized by its own particular preceding conditions, unique circumstances of its occurrence, and the prevailing quality of accommodations and unforeseeable exigencies that arise subsequently. Therefore each individual situation runs its own singular course and ends in its own particular consequences that cannot be easily subjected to accurate prediction. What we might generally assume, however, is that the innate resiliency of the individuals involved plays a major role in the quality of their experience and the expected results.

The stability and integrity of an immigrant's identity vis-à-vis the challenges of acculturation and assimilation largely depend on whether the individual has the capacity to bend with pressure without breaking, gaining from novelty rather than losing their bearings, building strength from adversity rather than crumbling and adapting to change rather than shirking from its unsettling demands. Such capacity is normally acquired gradually in the early years of childhood. Constancy and consistency of maternal care from early infancy onward, bolstered by optimal or good enough environmental provisions of the later years of childhood are prerequisites for establishment of a stable and well integrated sense of self and personal identity. Narcissistic and pre-genital disorders or unresolved conflicts of rapprochement render demands of reality and accommodation to change and challenges of adaptation insurmountable. In these circumstances since self and object constancy are not possible to attain self-regulation, affect modulation, frustration tolerance and mature mentalization falter and ambivalence, loss and mourning are not tolerated. Acculturation, assimilation and tolerance of change and submission to the dictates of reality, in these cases, can activate archaic defenses of splitting, dissociation, and omnipotent, coercive, sado-masochistic modes of adjustment which can lead to increased disorganization, alienation and foreclosure or diffusion of identity.

Diffusion of identity has been well described as an aspect of failure of normal development late in adolescence, when the failure of recapitulation and reiterations of rapprochement and oedipal conflicts create disintegration and collapse rather than consolidation and progressive affirmation of adult identity. Here, because of previously unresolved oedipal and pre-genital conflicts we see de-compensation and malignant regression rather than progress along the forward path of normal development and ensuing consolidation of identity.

Identity confusion or diffusion of identity need not be confined to the later stages of adolescence. They can come about during any period of life when internal turmoil or external burdens of disorganizing impingement threaten the ego's capacity to maintain self-cohesion. These circumstances include loss, separation, interpersonal conflict, trauma, likelihood of or actual exposure to physical injury or ailment and most commonly, normal milestones of the life cycle. Common examples of such milestones vary, from entering kindergarten, enrolling in grade school to entering latency, adolescence, young adulthood, starting or finishing higher education, commitment to married life, parenthood, entry into middle age, empty nest adjustment, retirement, and old age. Identity diffusion may be repaired in some instances when the offending element has been eliminated and conditions for repair and gradual restoration can be provided. In the cases of more pervasive problems of development and unresolved conflict psychoanalytic treatment and systematic resolution of those conflicts, supplemented by restorative reparation of developmental deficits will be necessary. When conditions preceding immigration, or those that prevail subsequently, have been traumatic, usual considerations pertaining to the treatment of trauma are essential. Here, also, the question of the patient's own basic resiliency and the supportive capacity of the new environment in providing safety, compassion, and benevolent connections will be of paramount importance.

The immigrant analyst

Whether the analytic training leading to the establishment of an analytic professional identity occurs before immigration or after, one thing is certain. In either case the analyst has had the uncommon and exclusively salutary experience of his own analytic journey under his belt. Owing to his own immersion in the experience of introspective examination, in-depth reflection and in particular re-living of his past experiences, whether in the form of abreaction or revival via working through transference manifestations, he has most likely succeeded in resolving many developmental, characterological and neurotic conflicts that commonly form the bulk of the grist for the analytic mill.

To begin with, an analyst, in all likelihood, has been put through a large number of filtering and vetting rituals that ordinarily are devised to establish the suitability of the individual for undertaking the demanding rigors of the training and to meet the high standards and lofty expectations of intellectual, moral, and personal integrity required for entering the profession. For the individual to have reached such a plain of superior capability and impressive potentiality, they would have to be endowed with such innate talents and constitutional strengths that would most likely ensure a high level of resiliency, ample ego strength and sustainable will towards mastery. They would need to possess a large share of healthy curiosity and substantial tolerance for, or fascination with, the unknown and the unknowable, the novelty of the unfamiliar and the uncertainty of the ambiguous. They need to be able to tolerate frustration, be trustful and optimistic, yet realistic about what is possible, desirable and reasonably achievable. They have experienced loss, acknowledged defeat, have accommodated to failure and will be able to do so again, when called for. They are psychologically minded in elements of emotional significance, psychic determinism, and the subjective world of experience in themselves as well as in others, and this guides their search and appeals to their curiosity. Compassion, empathy, and emotional attunement are inherent aspects of their interpersonal relatedness and strategy. Their own emotional openness and ability to access deeper layers of their own inner world allows them empathic attunement, which illuminates the subjective universe of others. This can create clear understanding, deeper appreciation and sensitively respectful concern for the pain and predicaments of others who may be cut off and deprived of the soothing compassion that they need in order to regain composure and to re-establish self-cohesion.

Innately endowed and constitutionally talented, they are often among those fortunate individuals who have also been aided by good fortune and favorable acts of fate, to have enjoyed sufficient richness of life, goodness of fit, adequate care and consideration, so as to bring their native strength to mature fruition. When they choose to be a member of the healing professions and then to pursue the impossible profession of psychoanalysis they are afforded yet another serendipitous opportunity to gain and grow in their capabilities and favorable predisposition and to contend with and resolve still more obstacles on the road to self-actualization and emotional growth. A psychoanalytic journey provides a profound experience of being alone in the presence of an other, when love, passion, pain, loss, confusion, conflict as well as shame, guilt, anxiety and helplessness can be encountered, grappled with, ameliorated and integrated. In this way the internal life and emotional organization can consolidate as past conflicts are uncovered, explored and adequately resolved while innate potentials are liberated. New strengths thus gained, the sense of self and one's identity becomes more solidly grounded. The past becomes an enduring reservoir of strength, wisdom of experience and illuminating guidance for the future. Pitfalls and mistakes observed, lessons learned and illusions transcended, clarity and humility is gained together with compassion for those who are confounded and perplexed by what befalls them and the suffering that goes with frailty and the fateful vulnerability of being a human in the ironic grip of existential inevitability.

Conclusion

The sense of self and our personal identity afford us an experience of permanence, relative constancy, and continuous stability from the very beginnings of our self-consciousness throughout our life cycle. While novelty intrigues and fascinates us we are leery of change and resist it as a threat to the predictability and trust upon which we base our sense of safety and secure feeling. This in spite of the constancy of change and ceaselessly unpredictable unfolding of events that inundate us, both in longitudinal developmental, in the normal course of life, as well as in the moment to moment variations we undergo in moods, needs, wishes, and intentions. In each current moment we are also exposed to countless external impingements and many kinds of relentless pressures from urgent demands of current life.

We learn to establish a relative equilibrium that allows us to maintain sufficient control and necessary integrity to tolerate frustration, keep hope, establish confidence, enjoy our success, and learn to master many of our challenges. This gives us the capacity to maintain a reliable store of intuitive as well as working knowledge, both physically and emotionally, and to recognize our own needs as well as our obligations to others. This is our enduring identity, defining for us who we are, what we mean to others and how we are seen in the eyes of those we need, those who need us and those we value. Where and to whom and what family, group, social context, and nationality we belong, normally becomes a part of our conscious as well as unconscious identity. Depending on temporal and situational elements, all these components of our identity may be in flux or transition, but we continue to be the same person in the essential core of our identity, provided that the core has had a solid developmental grounding to maintain its flexible receptiveness in assimilating ego syntonic acquisitions as well as having acquired protective discrimination in dealing with the adverse or aversive encounters.

The fundamental mechanics and basic structures of these capabilities are formed in the context of secure attachment, optimal or good enough process of separation-individuation and consequently a normative passing of the Oedipus Complex. When this foundation has been laid intact, latency and preadolescent periods can be self-affirming and conducive to progressive accumulation of cognitive, psychological, and relational enrichment, in constructive preparation for the usual turbulence of adolescence and the radical recapitulation of infantile narratives, before the eventual consolidation of early adult identity. Resilience is founded on this fortunate turn of events, usually receiving its healthy start from the benevolence of an optimal or favorable constitutional endowment.

Characterological disorders, pre-genital pathology, unresolved neurotic conflict and trauma interfere with normative developmental advances that underlie the formation of identity and a cohesive sense of self. Such unhappy turn of events creates daunting challenges for accommodating to change, tolerating ambivalence, adjusting to loss and meeting the inalterable demands of reality. Resiliency is thus compromised and regression, de-compensation and disintegration are likely at each juncture of expected advancement, inevitable challenges to status quo or even day-to-day vicissitudes of ordinary circumstance. Immigration with its multitudes of demands, uncompromising challenges, disruptive effects and unsettling impositions can be a source of intolerable distress, bitter disillusionment, and incapacitating fragmentation.

This group of pathological formation predisposes the individual to instability and confusion of identity to begin with, along with a false sense of self and "as if" status. Challenges of adolescence can create identity foreclosure, by rigidly identifying with negative and socially unacceptable reputation of extreme outcast groups, or else leading to identity diffusion, in which a sense of self, personal values and aspirations, ego syntonic assumption of adult responsibilities, and social roles are not attained.

As I have detailed above, the transition of identity in an analyst with the life changing experience of immigration is basically no different from that in other individuals for the most part. A normatively solidified core identity traversing through later phases of childhood and preadolescence, can ordinarily recast itself in accordance with developmental tasks of adolescence, culminating in identity consolidation and more or less smooth transition into adulthood and the subsequent phases of the life cycle. Given these favorable elements, the average expectable challenges of ordinary life and its various instances of loss and unavoidable traumatic events of common living can be lived through, dealt with and in time overcome. Regardless of the hardship, pain, residual scars and irreparable damages incurred the outcome need not be uniformly destructive or stifling. Under the favorable circumstances of adequate native endowment, reasonable resiliency, a supportive environmental milieu and normal development, traumatic events including those encountered in the context of immigration, can indeed be growth promoting, result in emotional, cognitive and even material gains and character strength. Not all instances of trauma are followed by post-traumatic stress and its attendant disorders. In fact many such instances actually result in post-traumatic gain. Solutions are byproducts of problems, as strength increases in grappling with hardship, and endurance is enhanced through fighting against adversity. Where there is ego strength enough to withstand the weight of the crushing assault without being inundated and overwhelmed, with focused response, persistent striving, and support from where it can be obtained and used, the final outcome can be triumphant and vitalizing. It is hard to deny that what does not kill us will make us stronger.

In this regard immigration is no different from other life events, sometimes eagerly planned and hoped for, exhilarating, fulfilling, and immensely rewarding, other times unwelcome, imposed, bitterly resented, and devastating in impact, or various other mixtures of good and bad in between. I have explained how for the immigrant analyst and the matter of transition of identity, two major elements are decidedly salutary. For one thing, the analyst's personal background usually endows him with inherent strengths including robust intellectual advantage, psychological mindedness, a relatively privileged beginning in socioeconomic terms, as well as rigorous elite education and exacting specialty training. Their training procedure selectively hand-picks them amongst many highly qualified competitors and peers who are endowed with exceptional abilities and personal attributes. This renders them well endowed, resilient and well prepared for contending with life's contingencies, to their highly significant advantage. A second salutary element is the rare privilege of undergoing psychoanalytic treatment, which builds significant measures of strength and liberated capability on top of the exceptional resources and rich endowment they possess, to begin with.

In the present volume we are treated to a rich treasure trove of poignant personal and exquisitely detailed accounts of analytic treatment of immigrants, children, families, members of successive generations, men, women, eastern as well as western natives and of course analysts as patients in treatment as well as in their role as therapeutic specialists. This variety and expanse of the observational and narrative field is truly compelling and deeply moving. I will not be able to address the rich content of such enormous reach and magnitude. As these accounts each speak so eloquently for themselves, I will merely remark on two general impressions.

First, that the transition in the identity of these immigrant analysts sensitively depicts the human struggle of separation, loss, mourning, identification, assimilation, and acculturation, along with the triumph of human spirit over adversity, with the indispensable help and support of others, first for themselves and secondly for those who came to them for help, seeking and finding solutions that would not have been likely without their analytic treatment experience.

Second, that this rich and multifaceted text clearly shows that trauma, deprivation, developmental deficit, and unresolved conflicts of pre-genital and oedipal variety can leave in their wake insurmountable vulnerabilities that can be reached, contextually regarded in transference and analytically treated with impressive results. In all examples of clinical encounter, detailed sensitively and delicately throughout the text, we cannot help but notice that it is the clinical features of the analytic process that stand boldly in the foreground, while the issues of immigration and their various implications display their penetrating relevance as incidental accompaniments forming merely the background. The immigrant patients of these immigrant analysts had the good fortune of examining their uniqueness and individuality in the presence of an empathic witness who shared with them the reality of the alienation and otherness that was such an oppressive aspect of their immigration experience. Yet alienation and otherness are not experiences in the sole monopoly of the immigrant analyst. These are conditions of human experience that spares no one. Empathy is not in the sole possession of those who are most similar to us or have had our own brand of experience.

INDEX

abuse 53
acceptance 88
adjustment and assimilation 5
adolescent age immigration 6
Agarwal, N. K. xxix
Ainslie, R. 126
Ainslie, R. C. xxviii, 137, 145–146
Ainsworth, M. D. 38
Akhtar, S. xxviii–xxx, 3, 17, 39, 84, 90,
  125, 128, 134, 138, 140, 146
Akiyama, H. 39
Alami, O. xx
Altman, N. 63
Amati-Mehler, J. 74
Amazon River 80, 93
American Declaration of
  Independence 120
American Psychoanalytic
  Association 89
American University of Beirut (AUB)
  145

Amico, J. 37
Anderson, B. S. 145
Antokoletz, J. C. xxviii, 141
Antonucci, T. C. 39
Arab collective culture 47
Arab Nationalist Movement (ANM)
  145
Argentieri, S. 74
Aron, A. 36
assimilation/adjustment 85
attachment theory 37–40 *see also*
  clinician's attachment style

Barbanel, L. xxviii, 137, 145–146
Beas River xxxv, 79–81, 93
Bell, S. M. 38
Berry, J. W. 143
Bhabha, H. 92
Bhabha, H. K. 142, 150
Bion, W. R. 115
Bodnar, S. 63

Bollas, C. 86, 126
Bowen, M. 55
Brenner, I. 93
Bromberg, P. M. 56–57
Brown, L. L. 36
Burman, E. xxix
Bush, G. 51

Campbell, R. 39
Canadian Charter of Rights and
        Freedoms 103–104
Canestri, J. 74, 127
Caribbean nations 64
Casement, P. J. 131
case studies
    Alma *see* X-Men
    Brenda 72–75
    Carol 94
    Joy 72–75
    Juan 130–134
    Laura 91
    Lewis 128–130
    María Elena 62–63
    Sofia 75–76
    Tom 72–75
    X-Men 99–100
    Yara 54
    Yasmine 53–54
Casey, S. 140
Cassimir, G. xx
Celestial Omnibus 118
Chakraborty Spivak, G. 92
characterological disorders 173
Chodorow, N. J. 66
Chomsky, N. 140
Ciclitira, K. xxix
Citizenship Act 147
Civil Marriage Act 103
clinician's attachment style 40–42
collusion 49–50, 147–149
Columbia University 31
confluence of identities 79–81

connectedness 42
"culture" 124
custom and traditions 9

Dalrymple, T. 124
Damasio, A. 122
dance and psychoanalysis 76–77
Dewan, M. J. xx
Duchamp, M. 119
Dwairy, M. 47

Egeland, B. 38
Einstein 42
electroconvulsive therapy (ECT) 40
emotional refueling 3
empathy 12
"enactment" 151
enactments of otherness 138, 141,
        143, 149–152
England's Coming Glories 112
Erikson, E. xx–xxi
Estonian Consulate 65
Estrada, N. 59
Etezady, M. H. xxx
exclusion 137–139, 141–142

Fanon, F. 141
Ferenczi, S. 142
Fisher, H. 36–37
Fisher, H. E. 36
Flynn, D. 71
Fonagy, P. 37
Forster, E. M. 118
Foster, N. xxix
Frankel, J. 143
freedom, stolen 114–117
Freud, S. 22, 122
Fuss, D. 142

Gabbard, G. O. 17
Goldberg, J. xx
Gostin, L. O. 35

Gowrisunkur, J. xxix
Graduate Record Exam (GRE) 34
Greenson, R. 20, 131, 134, 139
Greenson, R. R. 127, 131, 134
Greisman, H. C. 115
Griffin, F. L. xxxv–xxvi, 85
Grinberg, L. 68, 140
Grinberg, R. 68, 140
Group Psychology and the Analysis of the Ego 115

Harlem, A. xxviii, 137, 145–146
Heard, H. L. 42
Hegarty, P. 152
Hertel, Richard 88
Hill, S. 134
Himalayan Mountains 79
Hine, R. 112
HIV/AIDS 100–101
holidays 10
Holmes, D. E. 138, 147, 151
Holocaust survivors 93
Homayounpour, G. 23–24
Hurstfield, J. 145
hybridity 92

Ibañez, G. 140
Identities in Transition 64
immigrant analyst 170–171
immigration 2
    age 5
    couples therapy 11
    identity 39, 167–170
    Middle Eastern 49
    zero generation 6–7
"In my old San Juan" 59
internal migrations 134
International Psychoanalytic
        Conference 87
International Psychoanalytical
        Association (IPA) 98
International Psychoanalytical

Studies Organization (IPSO)
        98
intrusion 24, 54, 141, 151
Israeli Defense Forces 147

Jacobs, T. J. 127, 134
Javier, R. A. 127, 134
Jones, C. 142, 145, 150
Jones, E. 139
Joyce, A. 61
Jurkovic, G. J. 140

Keller, H. 38–39
Kernberg, O. 26
Kestenberg, J. S. 93
Kirsner, D. 26
Klauber, J. xxviii, 81
Kohut, H. 131
Kramer, M. xx
Kreutzer, T. 38
Kring, B. xx
Kuperminc, G. 140
Kurtz, S. N. 42

Lacan, J. 142
Lacanian psychoanalysis 102
"landsman" 22
learning psychoanalysis 24–26
Lebanese citizens 147
Lebanese Civil War 139
Letter of Condolence to Dr. Robert
        Marcus 42
liminal space 92
Linehan, M. 42
listening 117–120
Lobban, G. xxviii
Lomax, J. W. xx
lost in translation 74, 105
luggage 18–20

Main, M. 38
Malcom, J. 123

Marcos, L. R. 127, 134
Marxism 83–84
Masri, L. 141, 143
meeting of waters 79–81
Meloy, J. M. 36–37
mindfulness 42
"Moonlight Sonata" 118
Montague, P. R. 37
Movahedi, S. 23
"multi-cultural" policies 147
Murphy, A. 140
Myers, M. F. xx

Nandy, A. 83
Naxalite movement 83
New York Times 31

Ogden, T. 130
Ogden, T. H. 17
Oscar award 81

"pan mojao" 67
Parens, H. 86
Parvati River xxxv, 80–81, 93
Perea, J. F. 142
Pérez Foster, R. 127, 134
Perilla, J. 140
points of departure 56–57
process of therapy 48
psyche consolidation 9
Psychoanalytic Center of
    Philadelphia 88
psychoanalytic community 107
psychoanalytic institutions 103
psychoanalytic orthodoxy xxxiii, 89,
    91, 93
psychoanalytic theories 156

Rao, N. R. xx
Ray, Satyajit 81
reflections and recollections 2–3
Reppen, J. 127

Richmond, M. B. 127, 129, 134
Rio Negro 80
Rio Solimoes 80
Rizzuto, A. 24
Ruth, R. xxviii, 137, 145–146

Saunders, R. xx
Schachter, J. 89
Second World War 65
Sheehi, L. 141, 143
Shehadeh, S. 57
Slumdog Millionaire 81
Solomon, J. 38
Sroufe, L. A. 38
Stayton, D. J. 38
Stern, D. N. 126–127
Strathearn, L. 37
Sutlej River 79
SWOT analysis 9

terrible twos 160–163
The Advanced Training Program
    and Psychoanalytic
    Psychotherapy (ATPPP) 104
The Babel of the Unconscious 74
The Impossible Profession 123
The Interpretation of Dreams 71
Thobani, S. 147
Toronto Psychoanalytic Society and
    Institute (TPS&I) 103
transference(s) 18, 76, 85–86, 117, 123,
    131, 134, 163, 170, 175
    counter- 42, 47, 70, 74, 106, 134
    multiple 39
    negative 70
    paternal themes 22
    unobjectionable positive 22
transformational object 87, 126
translation 104–105
translucent 120–122
triadic and oedipal conflicts 159
triadic mode of function 163–164

Tummala-Nara, P. xxviii–xxix, 137,
    144–146
Turner, G. 147
Twemlow, N. A. xx
Twemlow, S. W. xx–xxx

United States Department of Justice
    33
University of California 35

Volkan, V. xxii

Walker, K. xxix
Watchel, P. L. 57

*What to Expect When You Are
    Expecting* 70
Wilde, O. 115
Wille, R. S. xxv–xxvii, 81
Winnicott, D. W. 130, 132, 145
Wittig, B. A. 38
World Jewish Congress 42
wrecking effects 138, 151

youth Congress movement (India) 82

zero generation immigrants 6–7